A PLAUSIBLE GOD

MITCHELL SILVER

A Plausible God

SECULAR REFLECTIONS ON
LIBERAL JEWISH THEOLOGY

FORDHAM UNIVERSITY PRESS

New York / 2006

Library of Congress Cataloging-in-Publication Data

Silver, Mitchell.
A plausible God : secular reflections on liberal Jewish theology / Mitchell Silver.
   p. cm.
Includes bibliographical references and index.
ISBN-13: 978-0-8232-2681-8
ISBN-10: 0-8232-2681-6
ISBN-13: 978-0-8232-2682-5 (alk. paper)
ISBN-10: 0-8232-2682-4
1. God (Judaism) 2. Judaism—Doctrines. 3. Liberalism (Religion) 4. Lerner, Michael, 1943—Teachings. 5. Green, Arthur, 1941—Teachings. 6. Kaplan, Mordecai Menahem, 1881—Teachings. I. Title.
BM610.S515   2006
296.3'11—dc22   2006021331

Printed in the United States of America
08 07 06   5 4 3 2 1
First edition

FOR ORA, ISAAC, AND HADASS

CONTENTS

PART 2

ACKNOWLEDGMENTS

To ask a friend or colleague to read a manuscript even once is to request a substantial favor; an expectation that it be read twice by the same person would be downright unmannerly. That far I would not go. On one hand, the result of my minimally decent manners is that the benefactors of the book only get to read a version of it unimproved by their criticisms. On the other hand, these benefactors avoid the exasperation of re-reading a book whose author, at times, stubbornly declined to take their good advice. The comments of friends and colleagues who read earlier drafts of this book were often so penetrating and insightful that I frequently felt that they, rather than I, should have been writing it. What authors commonly say is true here, too: Much of whatever may be good in this book was inspired by others, and where a reader might find fault, it is probably due to my failure to attend to sage counsel.

Hillel Dolgenas, Joel Greifinger, Joel Marks, and Dan Willbach not only read earlier drafts, but were also extremely generous with their time and willingness to discuss the issues. The written reactions of Arthur Goldhammer, Kathleen Sands, and Toba Spitzer were invaluable in getting me to rethink basic issues. I also received helpful comments from Ora Gladstone, Ellen Grabiner, Amy Herrick, and Nelson Lande, all of whom read large parts of earlier drafts. In addition to philosophical advice, Joel Kupperman guided me toward a more reader-friendly way to order my ideas, and Larry Blum suggested ways of capturing a publisher's interest. Dan Dennett's sympathetic reading was enormously encouraging, and his readiness to read a manuscript of a colleague with whom he was only slightly acquainted bespeaks both his kindness and devotion to philosophy.

ACKNOWLEDGMENTS

The comments of anonymous readers from Fordham University Press were enormously helpful. I am very grateful for their efforts, as I am for the efforts of Toni Ellis and Ted Wagstaff and, from Fordham University Press, Helen Tartar, Katie Sweeney, Kathleen O'Brien, Loomis Mayer, and Nicholas Frankovich.

A version of chapter 8 appeared as "Secularism, Humanism and Idolatry," in *A Life of Courage: Sherwin Wine and Humanistic Judaism* (IISHJ and Milan Press, 2003).

Ora, Isaac, and Hadass provide the daily portion of domestic happiness that allows me the luxury of worrying about God.

PREFACE

I never thought that I would need to bother with God. My earliest thoughts of God were laced with skepticism, and well before leaving childhood I had concluded that belief in God was a symptom of intellectual immaturity. As an adult, my devotion to Jewish identity shunned all talk of God, and I affiliated with Jewish institutions that explicitly labeled themselves as "secular." I knew that most of the world was still enmeshed with God, but most of *my* world found no place for the divine. The stereotype that I stereotypically imagined most Americans had of educated Northeasterners was true of my friends, family, and associates: We were a godless bunch.

I had presumed that our godlessness was a function of our modernism, which in turn I thought had something to do with our attitude toward rationality and science. We secularists were the rational ones, the modern ones. God-believers were still mired in supernaturalism and magical thinking. I knew, of course, that there were many people able to function in the world, even as scientists, while maintaining belief in God. However, I thought of them as either too timid, too needy, or too intellectually sloppy to bring their modern, rational mindset to bear on their entire set of beliefs.

But a change has come to my world. Increasingly, for many years now, God has found a place in the lives of family, friends, and associates who claim to be, and appear to be, every bit as rational and modern as I am. Moreover, they are not obviously more fearful, needful, or intellectually careless than I. They would be offended to be called believers in magic. Indeed, they assert that their belief in God is wholly compatible with a naturalistic worldview. It was neither surprising nor interesting to me that there were *super*naturalists who preserved a corner of their minds for the pre-modern and were comfortable with God; but that there were thoroughgoing modernists who, by every measure of their moral, political, and metaphysical beliefs, I felt were my peers and who went about sincerely proclaiming belief in God, I found intriguing and challenging. What was going on here? How can these people, who thought and acted just like me, believe in God? It was that question that was the original impulse for this book.

Early in my inquiries and reflections, it became obvious that one thing that was going on was that the God that I had been dismissive of since my youth was *not* the God that so many of my fellow "moderns" were now embracing. I have come to call the first the "old God," and the second the "new God." The old God is hardly outmoded. He (and it is best to call the old God "He,") surely has far more contemporary adherents than has the "new" God. But the old God is literally incredible for me, and for anyone, I would argue, who is thorough and consistent in their modernism. Belief in him is simply not a live option for such modernists.[1]

But, things are otherwise with the new God. The new God has proven to have a powerful allure to modernists, and can fairly claim to be the sole competitor to atheism for the modernists' allegiance. My fundamental premise is that the modernist has only two options consistent with her modernism: new God or no God. I want to understand the differences that it makes if one chooses to believe in the new God (supposing for the moment that such belief can be a matter of choice) rather than choosing to remain godless. I seek an analysis of these options, and not just an analysis of the intrinsic truth merits of new-God versus no-God beliefs, but equally an analysis of the personal and social implications of each mode of belief.[2] I also want to attend to the implications for individual and institutional action of choosing to give one's beliefs a theistic, or atheistic, vocabulary regardless of the cognitive content of the beliefs. It seemed worth an extended reflection to figure out what it meant to reside in the no-God camp when so many I respected and felt close kinship with had opted for the new God.

It soon became clear that seeing only two options (no God or new God) over-simplifies. In truth, as we survey the descriptions of the new God, we find that we have been offered many new gods, and, for that matter, "no God" also comes in a variety of formulations. Indeed, whether there is a meaningful distinction between some of the "new-God" and some of the "no-God" conceptions is a major theme that I came to explore.

If the new-God/no-God dichotomy is too simple, so is the labeling of one branch of the dichotomy as the "new" God. Just as the "old God" is not old in all ways that a thing can be old, the newness of the new God is also restricted. This new God is mostly new only as an important element of (relatively) popular Western religion. The new God is hardly new as an idea. In fact, these "new" conceptions, or close relatives of them, have long been the gods of some traditional theological elites. If anything justifies calling them new, it is the recent attempts to make these abstract, philosophical gods the conscious objects of mass worship, and the apparent success of these attempts. Although perhaps still a small minority of humankind, there is now a sufficiently large population of science and reason devotees to create a social demand for the scientists' and philosophers' gods. More and more individuals and social groups are influenced by belief in these "new" gods. The choice between new and no God confronts modernists more than ever, and a growing number who have faced it are choosing the new God.

My concerns are nonparochial, but I will approach them mostly through the work of three twentieth-century Jewish theologians: Mordecai Kaplan, Arthur Green, and Michael Lerner. For me, their new gods are the most serious challenge to nonbelief. In part, this is due to broad social affinities. Like them, I was raised as a twentieth-century American Jew. They also declare a frank loyalty to science, making them unambiguously modern. Their liberal politics and humanistic morality are also germane; when I weigh the consequences of religious belief with these thinkers, we will be using a common scale.

My focus on these three theologians, however, is completely in the interest of the general issue: Should we moderns have any truck with God? Kaplan, Green, and Lerner's work only provides the focal point to make the issue sharp; their theologies may deserve exegesis, but this book has no exegetical ambitions. I hope that I do not distort their thought, but a balanced and well-rounded representation is not the primary goal. They give us food for thought, and I am interested in the taste, digestibility, and nutritional value, but the recipe, preparation, and chef's intentions are out of my study.

Although the issues are of nonsectarian theological import, the discussion is most often placed in a Jewish setting. Not only are three Jewish thinkers used as models of new-God theologians, but it is also the religious life of American Jews that is often this book's testing ground for the new God's implications. Still, I believe that investigations done on this testing ground yield results that are applicable on a much wider social and psychological territory. It is the new God, in all its guises, without regard to parochial dressing, that is my ultimate subject.

Although a premise of this work is that belief in the old God is not a live option for moderns, I make few claims for the most part about what is good to believe in the realm of theology, let alone about what is theologically true. Rather, my interest is *"given* certain metaphysical beliefs, what is the best way to express them and think about them?"* That is, ought moderns be new-God theists or atheists?

Because much of what I will have to say, especially initially, will reveal the hollowness of much new-God talk, I fear that at times I will come off as the grinch who stole God.[3] Alas, a degree of grinchiness is the analyst's lot. The preacher, the poet, and the visionary can soar above mundane understanding, aiming at an emotional and intuitive grasp of the essentials of their subject, but the virtue of a critical analysis is unsentimental understanding. Unsentimental should not mean unsubtle or blind to emotional nuance, but it aims at no emotional effect and must be no respecter of its subject's majesty, lineage, or friends. I do not mean to be debunking or deflationary, but I do want to understand how belief in the new God works and what it amounts to. In searching out and pressing fundamental assumptions and moral implications of the new-God theologies, some assumptions will be judged untenable, some implications undesirable. Hence, the debunking or deflationary appearance. However, regardless of the tentative results that the discussion reaches at various stages, I am conscious of grinding no axes.

As the discussion progresses, the virtues of new-God belief come increasingly to the fore, and the debunking tone turns to a tone of apologetics. But neither debunking nor apology is the intention; I try to let the chips fall where they may.

For both atheists and theists, my attempted indifference to where the chips land may at times try the reader's patience. People tend, rightly so, to be passionate about their religious beliefs. Dispassion in a discussion of religious belief and disbelief is felt to be not only unfeeling, but also, in itself, evidence of a lack of understanding. In the realm of religion, we usually want champions of our deeply held convictions; but just because these convictions are so important, I want to bring the most patient, thorough, and sympathetic interpretation that I can muster to both new- and no-God belief.

Although forswearing conscious axe-grinding, I don't pretend to unbiased neutrality. I approach these theologies as a secularist, long interested in theistic belief sensitive to the power of theistic language, but indisposed to claim belief in God or to comfortably make un-ironic use of "God." Part of my motivation for these reflections is to see whether my secularist pose compares well to a "new-God" theism.

My lack of experience with mystical states strengthens my secular bias. Nothing that I say is meant to denigrate the value of mystical experiences or to deny the phenomenological accuracy of mystics' descriptions of these experiences (see James 1902); I intend to give them full weight. Nonetheless, my personal innocence of them surely contributes to a secularist bias. Mystics seem inclined to theism.

I will now turn to some matters of method and style.

Dan Dennett likens his philosophical method to sculpture; first, he roughs out the shape of the problem, with no expectation that these efforts will result in a finished product with clean, sharp edges. He then goes over the material again, ultimately aspiring to get the "fine details just so" (1984, 3). The reader will find that I too repeatedly return to familiar ground, resurveying terrain already covered, but I do it with no expectation that I will ever get the "fine details just so." Rather than sculpting, the metaphor for this method is circling. We will keep going around the same issues in the hope that with each pass, by stopping at different points on the route, we get new perspectives and notice different details. The result is not a final picture of the problem that is "just so"—complete, accurate, definitive. My hope, rather, is that we do get a richer picture with each go-round and end up with an album of portraits that, while not identical, are consistent and mutually illuminating.

Some questions will reappear prominently in our circling of the issues: What must the new God be like to be credible to moderns? Can the new God do what the old God did? Is a particular form of the new God especially useful? Can nontheism in a given matter do as well as new-God belief does? Can pretending to believe have the same effects as actually believing? What is clear about the new God and what is mysterious, and what should our attitude be toward the mysterious elements? How much of new-God devotion is a matter of taste rather than belief? Is all religious belief a matter of taste?

Part of my motive for making these (and other) questions recurring themes is an aspiration for thoroughness. Philosophers trained in the analytic tradition can become fetishistic about crossing "t"s and dotting "i"s, even where some readers would be content to have them left uncrossed and undotted, confident that they know where the crosses and dots would go. By making certain themes motifs, I am also motivated by the belief that every new context sheds a new light and reveals possibilities that require the reopening of old questions.

As is typical in philosophy, every issue is entangled and dependent on other issues in a way that makes an orderly lineal account inevitably begin with some question begging simplistic discussions. Hence, my circling back is also meant, in part, to discharge the initial question-begging assumptions and refine the simplistic early discussions. The chapter headings would lead one to think that the definition, uses, and effects of God are separate issues, with the ones dealt with in earlier chapters laying the foundation for the issues discussed in subsequent chapters. But the discussion cannot be arranged with one question neatly resting on an answer to the other. It is more like a teepee, with all of the issues leaning on each other, although even that image is misleading, for teepees have separate poles. I *do* separate out issues, for that is the only way to advance an inquiry, but I remain conscious, and so should the reader, of the merely expository necessity of the separation. Definition, use, and effect are not quite so separable.

This is a book of reflections, not an extended argument for a specific thesis; even so, many of the reflections do take the forms of arguments. Arguments, of course, should be judged for soundness. However, since insight more than demonstration is my overall aim, I hope that should the reader find any of the arguments unsound, she finds them nonetheless of interest. Sometimes, lines of inquiry that I found interesting and compelling led to claims that were inconsistent with other lines of inquiry. Rather than suppress the inconsistencies, I noted them and then speculated on how they might be reconciled. Sometimes, I found the reconciliation less convincing than the arguments that led to the apparently incompatible claims. Even in those cases, however, I let stand the competing discussions, reluctant to let go of whatever partial truth each might contain.

I have tried to make the philosophical issues accessible to nonphilosophers, at least in the main text. I have used the notes at the end of the book for technical elaborations and caveats, as well as for nontechnical pertinent, but tangential, discussions. Putting those thoughts into endnotes is not meant to devalue or disparage them – it is simply to acknowledge that they divert from the main flow of the larger discussion.

I will refer to Green, Kaplan, and Lerner as "the theologians" or "our theologians." There are very significant differences among the three thinkers, and when I ascribe a position to them as a group, usually at least one could justifiably complain that his position is being misrepresented. So I ask the reader to bear in mind that I am using the group to stand for a theological tendency and not to take my generalizations about "the theologians" as a fair or precise interpretation of any of their individual theologies.

I rarely speak of "a possible God" or "God, should it exist," although often that is what is meant. Furthermore, I sometimes speak of "God" for brevity's sake when I think that the context makes it clear that what is meant is "belief in God." I vary the pronoun for God between "he," "she," and "it." Philosophically, the neutral "it" is always best, but 3,000 years of Western religious language makes "it" too jarring in certain contexts. The "he/she" alternations, of course, serve the ideal of equality.

"God" is always capitalized, "gods" never. The "he/she/ it" pronouns for "God" are not capitalized. I felt that a lowercase singular "god" would be, again given our legacy of religious language, distractingly impious. The uppercase "He" and "She" felt like such a false note of piety that I might be accused of irony when none was intended. There is no consistent logic to all of this, but I hope that it comes near to a consistent tone.

I have spoken of circling, but "spiraling" better captures the intent. For all the going round, progress is made. I end up in a different, and I hope in terms of understanding, a "higher" place than where I started.

The book is divided into three parts: chapters 1 through 7, chapters 8 through 10, and the three appendices. In chapter 1, I describe the general historical and sociological importance of the new God. We see that the "new God" theology, the theology that Kaplan's, Green's, and Lerner's work will be used to exemplify, is representative of an ancient, sustained, and recently growing stream of thought. Chapter 1 also argues that we who are susceptible to this new-God theology, the "moderns" I spoke of above, are also, despite some countertrends, growing in numbers and influence. Much of the remainder of part 1 deal's with Kaplan's, Green's, and Lerner's version of the new God. Chapters 2 and 3 try to get a handle on the nature of the new God(s) by carefully extracting a definition of divinity from the theology of Kaplan, Green, and Lerner. In chapter 4, I catalogue all of the things that belief in any God might be expected to accomplish, things that belief in the old God did accomplish. Chapters 5, 6, and 7 look at the functions of belief in God described in chapter 4 and explore how well the new God performs those functions.

Although basic general issues frequently take the foreground in part 1, part 2 makes those general issues its primary focus and almost fully leaves behind the detailed discussion of the theologies of Kaplan, Green, and Lerner to reflect on the wider meaning of the new-God and no-God options. Chapter 8 examines the virtues of "humanism" as an alternative both to new-God theology and to a secularism that refrains from embracing humanism. In chapters 9 and 10, the discussion more explicitly takes the form of conclusions. A mélange of metaphysical, moral, political, and aesthetic considerations underlie the claims made in these concluding chapters.

In three appendices, I deal with issues that are best described, even if paradoxically described, as fundamental digressions; their pursuit would disrupt the discussion even though they are among its central assumptions. Theologians often claim that God cannot be spoken of meaningfully at all—that language utterly fails God. The first appendix argues that if we are going to speak of God, we ought to admit that we *can* speak of God, and that our God speech can be meaningful. If you are of the belief that one shouldn't demand that talk of God be logical and coherent, it might be best to start your reading of the book with this appendix.

The second appendix is addressed to those who, after reading the book or perhaps at some point along the way, consider themselves unambivalently modern, but who are so disappointed with the new-God *and* no-God options that they want to deny that modernists must choose between the new and no God and would prefer to make straight for the bosom of the old God. I do not argue that this choice is unwise or foolish, but to strengthen the book's premise that old-God belief is *and should be* an epistemically tough sell to a fully modern person, I attach this second appendix, wherein I argue that returning to the old God does indeed involve quitting the modernist stance because, from the point of view of reason, we have no grounds for old-God belief. Personally, I do not regret this, for although he had his uses, the old God was not without his faults beyond the epistemic ones. In what follows, except for some comparative purposes, those faults of the old God do not concern me. This work is strictly an internal discussion among "moderns," a reflection on *our* religious life.

Throughout the book, the notion of "truth" is bandied about. The third appendix reviews issues regarding the nature of truth and gives an account of the concept(s) of truth that underlie my discussions in the first two parts. I hope that these reflections have some merit apart from any particular ontology, but if ontological questions seem essential to you, if you are eager to get to what a friend of mine called "metaphysical bedrock," appendix C is where the rubber meets the road.

To my surprise, in the end, I found myself much more sympathetic to the new God than I thought I would be, and although I remain disinclined to join her faithful, I am content that others are.

PART

1

THE NEW GOD'S RELEVANCE

The work of Michael Lerner, Arthur Green, and Mordecai Kaplan reveals a new God. So what? Who are the adherents of this God? These theologians are not even identified with the three major American Jewish denominations, let alone central to historical Jewish theology.[1] They have hardly made a dent on the larger, gentile world's religious traditions. Measured by its direct influence, the new God of Lerner, Green, and Kaplan is of little interest to a general reader. It is merely the God of a few, highly educated, contemporary American Jews.

Direct influence, however, is not the only measure of significance. A fine specimen of an important species is also worthy of study. The new God of Lerner, Green, and Kaplan is among a burgeoning pantheon of new gods and is also typical of a certain kind of old God. Thus, these theologians' God is of great interest for two reasons. First, the "moderns" I alluded to in the preface, the rejecters of magical thinking, increasingly includes people drawn to the new-God theology. The new-God theology is not simply the theology that "moderns" find most credible, yet not quite credible enough to have real influence on their lives; more and more the new theology does have significant influence in the lives of "moderns." The population of "moderns," despite the common interpretation of recent electoral results, is expanding. Hence, the theology is not an esoteric stance without a parallel practice or trickle-down influence on popular belief. Granted, its popular influence has surely not been exerted primarily via Kaplan, Green, or Lerner; most people have gotten the new God from other sources. However, a close investigation into Lerner's, Green's, and Kaplan's thought will be a case study in the intellectual foundations of a wider religious phenomenon. Their new God

3

stands in for many new gods, and new gods are the only gods possible for a growing number of "moderns."

Second, these theologians merit study as specific exemplars of a broad theological tendency. This broad theological tendency that is represented by our theologians has been a major trend for at least a century in Western theology, and its lineage is even longer. For millennia, throughout the world, it is has been a standard approach in elite theology and philosophical reflection on God. This alone makes the theologians' theology worth examining.

Later in this chapter, we will discuss this kind of theology's increasing influence on "moderns." First, however, we turn to examples of essentially similar theologies embedded within other traditions. When we examine the theologies of Lerner, Green, and Kaplan, we will find that they are echoing and developing religious thought of epochal length and world breadth.

Eastern Thought

In ancient Indian religious texts, God, or at least the ultimate object of worship, is often characterized as an impersonal, self-subsistent Being, a Being that encompasses all of reality. The Brahman of the Upanishads is not separate from the universe or humanity; it is their true nature. "That thou art," the Chandogya Upanishad declares, instructing the initiate to identify with all of being, for all of being is just a manifestation of Brahman (Easwaran 1987). Medieval Vedanta reinforced the Indian monistic tradition. The soul, Atman, is identical with Brahman, as are all beings. Indeed, the multiplicity of beings is illusory—maya. In truth, there is only one Being: Brahman, the one, all-encompassing reality. Brahman is commonly conceived of as the Hindu "God." Note, however, the nature of this deity. This is no creator God that transcends its creation. This is no person-like God that wills the good and frowns upon evil (it contains all good and evil). Popular Hinduism throughout the ages may have contained a pantheon of personal gods, and in the spectrum of Hindu theology, there were more or less dualistic as well as atheistic elements. Nevertheless, the uncompromising monistic Brahman of the Upanishads and Vedanta arguably represents the core of the high Indian theological tradition, and this Brahman is much closer to the theologians' God than the God of our fathers. In asking whether the theologians' metaphysics contains a deity, we come close to asking whether Brahman is rightly translated as "God."

Venerable orthodox Buddhism is nontheistic, but commentators have recognized theistic elements in Buddhist traditions that are not simply attributable to vulgar expressions of popular religion, and wonder whether "our customary distinctions of 'theistic' and 'atheistic' . . . adequately . . . represent the living, growing reality of Buddhism" (Deberry 1969, xviii). Insofar as there is theism in Buddhism, it does not resemble the old-God monotheism of Western tradition. Any Buddhist God will be the object of mystical experience, the Being in which the apparent divisions in the world of our everyday experience dissolve. It will be, in short, much more comparable to the God of the theologians than to God the father. By examining the new God's claim to divinity—the claim to divinity of the theologians' God—we, in effect, shed light on whether Buddhistic conceptions of reality properly invoke the name of God.

The Philosophers' God

There are many doctrines of ultimate reality in Western philosophy. Some characterize themselves as atheistic. Others claim to be theistic, and some of those clearly are that—concerned with providing an abstract and logically coherent account of traditional Western religious monotheism. However, a significant strand in Western thought that claims to be theistic attaches the name "God" to views that are very dissimilar to a straightforward conception of the old God. I will only mention a few exemplary cases of philosophers' gods that are nearer kin to the new rather than to the old God, but a thorough survey would find many "gods" of philosophers to be only gods on something like our theologians' reckoning.

Stoicism held various, not always consistent, doctrines in its five-hundred-year history in the ancient world, but the identification of God with the laws of nature remained pretty constant throughout. A monism, Stoicism insisted that there was nothing outside of nature, and nothing that was not ruled by nature's laws. For the Stoics, God was immanent and natural if he was anything.

Benedict (Baruch) Spinoza, the seventeenth-century Dutch-Jewish philosopher, was accused of atheism, in spite of the fact that he is forever explicating the nature of God. The accusation of atheism arose because Spinoza's God is a variant of the new God, and to some old-God loyalists, as well as philosophical verificationists, the new God is indeed tantamount to atheism. Spinoza held that there was only one thing, "one substance." The one substance constituted the entirety of being. It was nature, it was God, and we, and all that is, are a part of it (Spinoza 1677).

Not only did Spinoza deny the separateness of God and the world, but he also explicitly denied that God had personal attributes such as will, intentions, or desires. Spinoza's God is complete and wants and aims at nothing. Moreover, everything about God, which means that everything about everything, is necessary. There is no room for petitionary prayer to Spinoza's God. He can't answer, because "he," firstly, is clearly an "it," and secondly, is a fully determined it. Taken as a whole, the universe must be just as it is. Spinoza's is an extreme rejection of supernaturalism. Not only is nothing outside of nature and its exceptionless regularities, but nature is also constituted by logical truths that cannot even *coherently* be imagined as other than what they are. This is naturalism with a vengeance. To the extent that the theologian's God strays from Spinoza's, as we will see that it does at times, the wandering occurs when the theologians are lured away from their naturalism, away from their rejection of anthropomorphism, and toward the old God that they are ostensibly abandoning.

Georg Wilhelm Friedrich Hegel, the influential nineteenth-century German philosopher, claimed that his views were fully compatible with orthodox Lutheran belief, which, were it true, would make Hegel an explicator of the old God—but it is not true. Hegel, like Spinoza and our theologians, made God immanent in the world and co-extensive with the totality of being (Hegel 1807). Hegel's totality is much more dynamic than Spinoza's, which makes him closer to many of the theologians' descriptions of an evolving God. The theologians like to speak of God as a process, as more of a verb than a noun (Green 2000, 3). Moreover, the process involves apparent conflict and divisions, all of which are reconciled in God. Hegel too makes God a process wherein "contradictions" are resolved, ultimately into an all-embracing organic unity.

Hegel's emphasis on forms of consciousness as the quintessence of the divine, as the godhead in effect, is also reminiscent of aspects of the theologians' theology. For they too stress that God's clearest manifestation is in the human form, by which, of course, they refer not to our primate bodies, but to our human consciousness. Furthermore, in both Hegel and the theologians, there is the suggestion (as well as a reluctance to explicitly state it) that the totality of being achieves a self-consciousness that is immanent in the world and which also transcends individual self-consciousnesses.

The Scientists' God

Many scientists have been content to remain loyal to the old God. In some cases, they simply fail to bring their professional mode of thinking to theological questions, and in other cases, they consciously refuse to do so in the belief that religion is about matters—meaning, value, ethics, emotion—that are not amenable to rational, let alone empirical, investigation.

Yet there have also been scientists for whom belief in the old God was unsustainable. Many became frank atheists; but scientists unwilling to subscribe to the old God have not always been prepared to abjure religious language. Frequently, it is something like the new God that such scientists deify. Giordano Bruno, the sixteenth-century astronomer, was burned for describing God as immanent in nature and nature's laws. In our own day, the physicist Stephen Hawking and the chemist Charles Misner both speak of the laws of nature as the mind of God. In doing so, they follow Einstein, who remarked that in thoroughly understanding nature, we would come to know "God Himself" (Weinberg 1993, 193–94). Steven Weinberg suspects that Einstein's God was mostly metaphor (196). Perhaps so, but Einstein explicitly endorsed Spinoza's theology, and Spinoza certainly thought of himself as a theist, a prototype of one strand of new-God theology.

Spinozism is not the only new-God element that has attracted scientists dabbling in theology. Pauline Rudd, the Oxford biochemist, claims, much like Green, that religion is not about beliefs, but rather about "experiences." She couples this subjectivist understanding of religion with the Stoicist/Spinozistic account of religion as "a desire for truth and understanding, a harmony of the wholeness"[2] (Richardson 2002). The physicist Joel Primak, echoing our theologians' deification of god-seeking itself, terms scientific research, the quest for truth, into "a kind of religious practice" (Richardson 2002).

Scientists are not always, perhaps not primarily, scientists; in their other identities, they run the gamut of theological positions. If, however, any doctrine can vie with atheism as the dominant theological position of scientists, it would be a doctrine that would fit in nicely with the view of our theologians who present the God that the scientific community finds most acceptable.

Christian Thought

The "new" God has a long pedigree in Christian theology, even if that theological strand was frequently declared heretical when it made its departures from orthodoxy too evident. John Scotus Erigena, a ninth-century Irish theologian, provided a pantheistic interpretation of traditional Christian doctrine, and Jakob Boehme, the early-seventeenth-century Lutheran mystic, declared that his visions showed him that God was not an entity separate from the word (MacIntyre 1967).

Erigena and Boehme were not the sole pre-modern Christians whose thought resembled new-God theology, although it is in recent Christian thought that an immanent God becomes mainstream theology. With the exception of Karl Barth, the most influential twentieth-century Christian theologians have distanced themselves from the traditional conception of a real, transcendent God. Paul Tillich's and Rudolph Bultmann's positions have been characterized by Reinhold Niebuhr as holding that "all religious statements are mythological" or "symbolic" (Mehta 1965, 39). Niebuhr considered that sort of view pervasive by the second half of the twentieth century: "Many people have been saying that kind of thing about the New Testament for years. There are very few theologians today that believe the resurrection actually happened" (Mehta 40). Indeed, Bultmann declares that he wishes to "make religion logically independent of a supernatural being" (Mehta 34). Tillich, we are told, concedes "the substance of atheism" and merely "presents atheism in theological language" (Mehta 35).

Christian theology here raises the crux of the question that we will put in the following chapters to our Jewish theologians: *Are these "new God" religious views substantially different from atheism, and if not, what is the justification for retaining theistic language?* Tillich would *not* claim that they are *substantially* different from atheism, and Dietrich Bonhoeffer, the German theologian killed by the Nazis, whose work became a staple of post–Second World War Christian theology, also doubted that God was needed: "Man has learned to cope with all questions of importance without recourse to God as a working hypothesis . . . it has become evident [even in religious questions] that everything gets along without 'God' just as well as before" (Mehta 175).

Similar to our theologians, neither Bonhoeffer, Tillich, Bultmann, nor their epigones abandoned religion or references to the divine. The divine that they continued to refer to is very like the theologians' God. Bonhoeffer refers to God as "the beyond in the midst of our life" (Mehta 181). Bultmann, for all of his demythologizing project, still talks of using the story of Christ in reconciling man to his faith in God. Tillich, too, speaks of the object of our "ultimate concern," of the experience of "the unconditional," and of "the ground of being" (Mehta 49), all phrases that would readily find a home in our Jewish theologians' work. "God" Tillich tells us, "is not a being, but being itself" (Shermer 2000, xiv).

This Christian anti-old-God theology continued into the second half of the twentieth century. Jurgen Moltman's theology of hope could hardly sound more Kaplanesque when he speaks of "the promise or power of the future" and sees the Christian's task as working for the social transformation that will fulfill that promise (Shilling 1967, 203). Leslie Dewart, in *The Future of Belief*, denies God's personality, but finds a place for God as "an expressive force that channels [people] to go out beyond themselves" (Shilling 210).

Christian "process theologians," inspired by the work of Alfred North Whitehead and Charles Hartshorne, have emphasized how their God is unlike the old God; he is not, among other things, a male, an intentional controller, a moralist, a sanctioner of the status quo, or an unchanging, unevolving Being (Cobb 1976, 8–9). The God of process theology is a new God, who, like the theologians' new God, fosters the good rather than guarantees it.

There are Christian theologians who have been shaped by the contemporary modes of thought lumped together as "post-modernism." For them, God is often simply a way of telling a story, and is never definitive or context-free (Vanhoozer 2003, xiii,-.xv, 207). Like the new God of our theologians, the Christian, postmodern God is at least as much a creature as the creator of humans.

The motivation for the new-God theology among recent Christian thinkers is stated forthrightly by the Reverend John Robinson, the Anglican Bishop of Woolrich: "If Christianity is to survive, it must be relevant to modern secular man, . . . men can no longer credit the existence of gods or a God as a supernatural person such as religion has always posited" (Mehta 2). It is clear that the modern theological rejection of supernaturalism is not just a Jewish thing.

Of course, many modern theologians elaborate the old God. I do not wish to suggest that he is driven from the field, any more than I mean to imply that all elite theology in the West has always been about the new God. Yet just as clearly, the new God is no idiosyncratic, marginal, theological idea peculiar to a few Jewish theologians. The new God, or close look-alikes, has a long history, a history of breadth and depth, and in the last century has come to be a central theology among Western religious thinkers.

Are There Many Moderns?

However significant new-God theology has been among theologians, there are reasons to doubt that such thought has ever had any social importance. Even in Eastern religious traditions, where mainstream theological thought was fairly pantheistic, popular religion was directed at anthropomorphized incarnations of ultimate being. I have said that the old God is incredible to "moderns," but are there more moderns than just you and me (should I even count on you)? Does contemporary Western society really contain meaningful segments for whom the old God is incredible? Results of a 1996 *Wall Street Journal* survey would lead us to believe that it does not. Ninety-six percent of Americans report that they believe in God, and lest we think that it is the new God that most of them have in mind, 90 percent believe in heaven, 73 percent believe in hell, and 65 percent believe in the Devil. Of course, many of these respondents may be giving new-God metaphorical twists to these notions: hell becoming an alienating despair, and the Devil transformed into human inclinations to selfishness and cruelty. There is, as we will soon see, at least some reason to believe that that is the case—that all of this theism is not standard old God belief. Nonetheless, we have here strong prima facie evidence that the old God is alive and well, that there is no clamoring for a more credible God to fill the void, and therefore no need to assess this more credible God and contrast it with no God. The new God may be the only God that has even a ghost of a chance of being believed by "moderns," but if there are not many "moderns," why care about it? (Besides always caring about one's own idiosyncrasies.)

It is certainly true that the old God still has a strong following. The high profile and influence of "fundamentalism" among Christians, Hindus, Muslims, and Jews is indisputable evidence of the old God's staying power in the modern world. However, new-God and secular counter-tendencies are not to be dismissed as either false projections of nineteenth- and early twentieth-century social theorists or as peripheral and now diminishing aspects of modernity. Secularization may never have been, or may never become, as thoroughgoing a phenomenon as some predicted, but it was, and is, no myth. If its future career at this point appears less promising than it looked fifty years ago, nonetheless secularism is by no means a has-been without any prospects. Secularism may yet sweep the social world. The statistics cited above were for 1996 America (Shermer 2000, 21). In Europe, theism is substantially weaker. Now, in spite of America's domination of cultural commerce, Europe is arguably a more ideologically and culturally mature sphere. Its dwindling theism may foretell developments.[3] Although belief remains high in America across the board, even in America there is a noticeable decrease of theism correlated with advanced education. Seventy-five percent of Americans with a graduate degree, 20 percent less than the general population, believe in God. Seventy-five percent is high, but a 20 percent falling-off is worth noting. God-belief among American scientists drops to just *below* 50 percent. Modern education does appear to erode belief. As such education more deeply permeates a population, old-God belief may become increasingly difficult to maintain.

Phyllis Tickle, an American journalist who has reported extensively on American religious life, gives a new-God-ish interpretation to the statistical findings of pervasive American theism and apparent supernaturalistic belief. Tickle implicitly disputes Michael Shermer's claim that "at the beginning of the new millennium in the Western World, it is safe to assume that when we are discussing 'God' we all know what we mean by this term: an all powerful, all knowing, all good higher being who created the universe and us and grants everlasting life. If you believe this you are a theist. If you do not, you are not a theist" (Shermer 258).

Our theologians are not theists by Shermer's lights, but Tickle suggests that lots of Americans aren't Shermer-type theists either. Not that Tickle denies Americans' religiosity, but she describes the underlying theology as amounting to no more than an affirmation of "hope, faith, and brotherhood, which worships and expresses and is active in the name of the God we reference as Ground Zero in our daily God-talk without requiring that any one of us declare . . . either the particulars or certainty of God" (Tickle 1997, 171).

Tickle goes on to say that the specification of theological beliefs in America occurs privately, in small settings, with trusted others. One's particular beliefs are considered to be immune to rational critique. "God" is the catch-all label that we need for the public rituals where our common devotion to "hope, faith, and brotherhood" is enacted, but that public "God" has no further meaning. With all the particulars left unspecified, our public theism is probably a riot of equivocations in which there are many new-God beliefs among the rioters.

Tickle's account of America's God, if true, would make our theologians' God mainstream. In both cases, God is largely a term to describe deep feelings, fundamental values, basic attitudes, and humane hopes. The theologians try to bring some intellectual rigor and philosophical depth to this stance and thereby must produce various specific theological claims. However, it is a theology that is, as all theologies are, in the service of a faith. If Tickle is right, it is a theology that serves the *dominant public* American faith.

Even if Tickle is wrong, and the *Wall Street Journal* survey showing majority belief in angels, miracles, the Devil, and so on is properly understood as indicating that widespread *old*-God belief is America's public faith, Tickle still points us to the reality of significant new-God religiosity and theology. At a minimum, we find in America a plethora of New Age pantheisms, Unitarian-style pluralisms (wherein many different doctrines are co-equal paths of faith), Eastern-influenced mysticisms, ubiquitous theological relativisms, and unaffiliated "spiritual" groupings of many kinds. Of course, many of the groupings are not embracing new-God theology out of an inability to tolerate the dissonance between old-God belief and a modern mentality. Still, the burden of that dissonance is an important factor for some[4] and it is a crucial factor in the liberal Jewish community, a community with many members teetering between explicit atheism and the theologians' God. If they are to be won to theism, it will have to be to a theism that does no violence to their sense of themselves as rational, science-accepting, unsuperstitious people. They may allow, they may even be eager to affirm, that there are more things in heaven and earth than are dreamt of in the scientific worldview. They may endorse the notion that there are limits to rational explanation, that the deepest currents of their being are not objective phenomena that can be analyzed and understood, but their embrace of "things beyond reason" cannot come at the expense of reason. It is not simply that their daily lives and occupations immerse them in a scientific, naturalistic orientation; that is true of many old-God believers, too. It is that they also see *the source of their moral and political beliefs in Enlightenment rationalism: egalitarianism, feminism, toleration*—these can of course have religious sources. For the liberal Jews, however, these are an Enlightenment inheritance. Liberal Jews instinctively suspect that to abandon rationalism is to leave important values precariously ungrounded.

Throughout contemporary liberal synagogues in America, one finds congregants comfortable with the theistic liturgy because they are able to root it in a new-God theology. Atheist Jews have long found reasons to participate in the traditional theistic liturgy, but their self-conscious atheism usually prevented those reasons from having a spiritual dimension. They "prayed" and pronounced "God" for social and cultural reasons. There were no metaphysics, no ultimate concerns involved. Others require more "authenticity" to keep praying. Asked to advise an atheist who feels hypocritical in continuing religious practice, Rabbi Jonathan

Gerard suggests that he has "merely lost faith in an older and unacceptable notion of God" (*New York Times Magazine*, Feb. 9, 2003, p. 26). Presumably, faith can be restored with a newer, acceptable notion of God. The "new God Jews" can say the prayers *and* mean them. As a child, I would sit in synagogue with adults who mumbled the prayers as quickly as possible. They seemed to be praying to get through an obligatory recitation—important to say, in spite of the fact that there was no significance to the *meaning* of what was being said. Today, many Jews care enough about meanings to demand change in ancient prayers, or at least reinterpretation. Most of these Jews may not be very familiar with the writings of Kaplan, Green, or Lerner, but the theologians' work creates a cultural and intellectual context for liberal Jews to be modern and sincere believers.[5]

Hence the "moderns" are not a negligible group. They are admittedly, a very ill-defined group, without sharp borders. No one today fully escapes the pull of scientific, naturalistic thinking, just as no one's psyche is free of anthropomorphic projections. Yet for all the fuzziness of the "moderns" and the "pre-moderns" as categories, there are, I believe, many people, certainly many American Jews, who are reasonably put in the former group, people for whom the constraints of modern belief play enough of a role in their psychology to make old-God belief impossible. It is up to the reader to decide if he or she is one of them, a "modern," for whom old-God belief is impossible. If you are, then the usefulness of the new God, *your* only theistic option, becomes a question of some weight, a question to which we now turn.

2

A FIRST PASS AT DEFINING ''GOD'': THE ALL AND THE ONE

Ihave no quarrel with the view that the experience of God is more important than the concept of God, but as one of my primary interests is how a particular kind of God concept affects human experience and practice, definitions, descriptions, and conceptualizations seem the right places to start. There are those, including Michael Lerner and Arthur Green, who are uncomfortable with attempts to define God, holding to some version of the doctrine of "ineffability," the view that words cannot encompass God. In appendix A, I discuss why we should be dismissive of the doctrine of ineffability, a doctrine that serves to discharge theologians of the obligation to strive for clarity and consistency. So let us here say no more of the ineffable (indeed, how can we do otherwise) and examine ideas of God free from the fog of that all-purpose disclaimer.[1]

God the Organic Totality of Being

The simplest conceptualization of God, one that Green and Lerner sometimes flirt with, is that God is everything. "God is the totality of all Being and all existence that ever was, is, or will be, and more than that," writes Lerner (1994, 413). Note the "and more than that." Like Lerner's, Green's cup also overflows when he is pouring existence into God. God "embraces all of being . . . [and] contains within it all the variety and richness of life, yet is also the Oneness that transcends and surpasses all" (Green 1992, 9). Having noted them, let us for the moment leave aside the "more than that"; and the "surpasses all" additions to the deity. Lerner's all that "ever was, is, or will be," and Green's "all of being" is quite enough to deal with for now.

14

Defined simply as "all of being," it is difficult to deny that God exists. "God" is just a name for whatever is, and so long as anything is, God is. So defined, is God a useful or important concept? Is it a concept properly labeled "God"?[2]

Logically, it is useful to have a term to refer to everything. Sometimes, we want to make an unqualified generalization. Sometimes, we want to talk about everything. "Everything makes me happy," "everything stinks," "everything looks like Winston Churchill." Such generalizations are seldom true; still, we want to be able to assert them. But, we hardly need "God" to concisely make such points; "everything" does quite nicely. If anything, using "God" as a synonym for "everything" tends to mislead. "God makes me happy," "God stinks," and "God looks like Winston Churchill" are synonymous with the previous trio in almost no one's ideolect. We neither need nor want "God" as a mere name for everything.

However, if we want to imbue collective being with certain properties, associate all being with certain connotations, or foster certain attitudes toward or relationships with the totality of being, God may be just the ticket. Yet, "God" will not do any of these things if we restrict the meaning of the term to "all being" without any further characterization. Stripped down, all being is simply too neutral an entity to carry much moral, emotional, social, or intellectual freight. Granted, it is a lot of being and may be "the only Being there is" (Green 1992,14), but it is only being and that is all and it cannot make you feel the way that the theologians want it to do; it is so hard loving plain being.

Which brings us to the additions. God is not only all of being. God must be all of being *plus* because without the plus, God cannot minimally function as God.[3] What might the nature of this "plus" be? It is not, although the theologians sometimes talk as if it is, additional existence outside of "all being." It sometimes sounds that way because the theologians are drawing on a tradition where God transcends his creation and so has being outside of creation, but being outside of all *created* being is not being outside of all being. Being outside of all being is just silly. The God-making additions are rather features that Being, or all beings collectively, have. God is "all being" *rightly construed*. It is the correct construal that is meant to have all of the connotations that lets God be God. It is the correct construal of all being that earns it the divine title. The addition to all being is further description of it.

The additional features that make the universe (henceforth my neutral term for "all being") into God are usually structural or processional. The claim is that the universe deserves to be called God by virtue of its inherent structure or by virtue of its natural processes (Lerner 1994, Kaplan 1934, Green 1992). We are offered different candidates under these headings to anoint as the God-making trait. Green emphasizes the unity of all being and he is far from alone in this. It is the rejection of dualism that Green sees at the heart of Jewish monotheism.

Green's is in some ways more, in other ways less, radical than Maimonides' monotheism. Maimonides rejected any dualism within God, but he did not equate all of being with God. By extending God to all of being, Green rejects the Creator/Creation dualism that Maimonides allowed. In that way, Green is more monotheistic, or at least less dualistic, than Maimonides. For Maimonides, God had no parts. God is a homogenous whole. Maimonides believed such homogeneity was what was required of a perfect unity. Green finds divine unity more in the organic connectedness of the whole. The landscape of Being may not be uniform, but the soil is common and the mutual dependencies are ubiquitous. Insofar as Green allows differentiations within God, he is less monotheistic than Maimonides.[4]

The key structural element of Green's Being is that it is not a heap of beings; it is an organic whole. Lerner makes a similar point when he compares our relationship to God with a liver cell's relationship to the entire organism (Lerner 1994, 412–13). All of being may not be the same, but it all works together for a common end, and no part of being would be what it is without the rest of being. Therefore, another aspect of Being's oneness is that the whole is implicit in each part.

Let us call this the "organic" conception of the universe; all beings serve a function in the being of Being. The universe could not be what it is, nor do what it does, were it not for every one of us, where "us" ranges over everything from people to pebbles and mountains to molecules. Everything is connected and everything plays its part. It is important to note that by itself, this organic conception of the universe ascribes no intention or function to the universe, not even the minimal one of persisting to be. It only claims that whatever the universe is, it is by virtue of the nature and relations of its parts.

Is an organic universe sufficiently godlike to merit the title? We can approach this question by inquiring into some purported effects of believing in an organic universe; although we have yet to determine what a belief in God does in one's life, we can anticipate that analysis and tentatively ask whether a belief that the universe is essentially an organism is, in at least some ways, functionally equivalent to belief in God.

The theologians have inferred from the organic conception of the universe a host of spiritually significant implications:

1. The welfare of the whole universe depends on the welfare of each part and, pulling in another moral direction, the welfare of each part depends on and should be subservient to the well-being of the whole.
2. Each part of the universe should "identify with" every other part and with the whole.
3. The "meaning" of each part's being can only be discerned by viewing the whole universe.

These claims are closely related, but let us take them one at a time.

Strictly speaking, it is not true that the welfare of an organism always depends on the welfare of each of its parts. Indeed, the claim that a particular part's welfare should be subservient to the whole assumes that the welfare of the whole may diverge from the welfare of a part. This assumption is correct. While it is usually the case that my well-being requires the well-being of my lungs and kidneys, there may come a time when I am better off getting rid of a lung or a kidney. Sometimes, an organism's well-being requires the excision or destruction of a part. The organic universe justifies an anti-individual collectivism as easily as it justifies intrinsic concern for each of its constituents. After all, I have no concern for my individual organs independent of my general self-concern.

It is a little trickier to assess the claim that the organic universe implies that the well-being of each part depends on the well-being of the whole. That is because it is hard to decide just what constitutes the well-being of an organism's individual parts. If the well-being of the part is *defined* as making its optimal contribution to the well-being of the whole, then it is trivially true that the well-being of the part depends on the well-being of the whole. It is uninteresting to learn that what is good for the universe is good for John Doe if we stipulate that John Doe's good is whatever is good for the universe.

If, however, we allow a conception of the part's good that is not synonymous with the good of the whole, it is not clear that the organic conception implies that a part's good depends on the whole's good.[5] If it turns out that a part can have interests separable from the whole's interests, we require further argumentation to demonstrate that the part's interests should be subservient to the whole's interests. People who worry about themselves more than they worry about the universe, even if they accept the organic nature of the universe, are not rarities, nor are they obviously irrational. We will return to this point later.

Understanding the organic nature of the universe is also supposed to encourage you, if not compel you, to identify with all other beings. If "identify with" requires no more than an acknowledgment that one is connected to and affected by the rest of the universe, then identification with all being does follow from the organic conception. However, if "identify with" requires seeing oneself as the same as or very similar to the universe as a whole, it does not seem to follow that the organic universe gives one reason for such identification, no more than, to use Lerner's analogy, a human liver cell, if it could think, would have reason to consider itself (apart from its ability to think) as identical with or similar to a whole human being.

If "identifying with" means recognizing common interests or caring about the object of identification, we are returned to the question of why organic relations should produce a harmony of interests, let alone an identity of interests, or produce altruistic mutual concern. By itself, the organic universe has no such implications

Finally, we are led to meaning. By giving one a role in a larger scheme, the organic universe does offer a meaning to one's life. "What my life is about, is performing this function in the universe." Whether that meaning is superior or preferable to other possible meanings that one may assign to one's life is, however, an open question.

The organic conception of the universe by itself does very little to advance the spiritual agenda of the theologians. That agenda requires that the universe not only be organic, but also that it be good. Indeed, the goodness of the universe is more fundamental to the theologians' purposes than its organicity. The organicity is important only because it serves as a metaphysical vehicle for bringing the goodness powerfully into play.

All of the questions that we have left dangling—whether the individual's good should be subservient to the universe's good, whether the individual should identify his purposes with the universe's purposes, or whether one's function as a cog in the universe is the most meaningful description of one's life—depend upon the value of the universe. An organic universe that is good brings its goodness to each part. A morally neutral universe, organic or not, can hardly touch any of its parts' spiritual life.

The Goodness of the Organic Universe

Is there anything intrinsically good about organicity? If there is, then nothing beyond its organic quality is required of the universe for it to begin to take on a godly character. Alas, organic status alone confers no value. An organism is necessarily complex, but complexity to no purpose is not superior to purposeless simplicity. An organism also has parts that depend on each other to be what they are. In that way, an organism, as an organism, does manifest "mutuality," but this feature should not be mistaken for "helpfulness" or "solidarity" with their normative connotations. Nothing in our stripped-down, organic universe is trying to help or support anything else. No virtue is manifested in such helpfulness. Like a bunch of pick-up sticks leaning against each other in teepee fashion, the parts of the organic universe depend on each other. Take away a stick and the whole structure will collapse. If, however, there is no point or value to either their teepee-like stand or to their fallen disarray, their collapse involves no loss or gain—only a value-neutral transformation. Even if the sticks are broken and utterly changed by the collapse, no good is squandered. If the individual sticks in the teepee formation were not valuable, their transformation during the collapse is a matter of indifference. If the individual parts of an organic universe have no value, the arrangement by which they support each other also has no value.

But isn't survival the point of every organism? If nothing else, can we not attribute to every complex, interdependent organization of elements the goal of remaining what it is, the goal of perpetuating its form?

We can, but again no value falls out of this conceptualization. Darwin has certainly taught us that we should expect to find things arranged in a way that propagates those particular arrangements; indeed, "organisms" are the prime examples of those fit-for-survival arrangements (Darwin 1859). What value, then, is there in endurance apart from the value of the endurer? Neither survival nor mutual survival has any value if we don't care about the survivors, either as individuals or as a collective.

Bare-boned organicity injects no goodness into the universe. Coupled with something(s) of value, organicity may have important axiological implications; by itself, it doesn't. The universe may have a form that is a self-perpetuator or be the organized whole that permits the self-perpetuation of some of its parts, but the sheer doggedness of form has nothing of the divine about it.

Talk of Darwin, organisms, and perpetuating forms suggests that we are talking about life, and if the universe is a living being, or less grandiosely, makes possible, gives rise to, and houses life, might there not be value in that?

It is a rhetorical challenge to denigrate "life" because, when we hear the term, we quite naturally think of the particular life forms with which we are familiar. The beauty, virtue, and meaning that inhere in the life we know are perhaps the greatest repository of value that we recognize. Even so, if we confine our conception of life to beings that sustain themselves in an environment and grow and duplicate, it is not clear what is valuable about those processes. Of course, those processes have made possible forms of being that we *do* find valuable. All joy, suffering, kindness, cruelty, art, science, philosophy, poetry, love, sex, laughter, consciousness, and striving that we are aware of, not to mention the color, power, ingenuity, complexity, and drama of the biosphere, have emerged through life. It is these potentialities in life that we value, not the abstract reproductive power itself.

Organicity may be the basis of the universe's godlike qualities, but by itself it makes no God out of all being. It is insufficient as the "plus" to "all being," the plus that apotheosizes all being into divine Being. The organic universe gives *us*, the organs or the cells in the universe, no reason to care about, identify with, or find a common purpose with other cells or the whole organism. If organicity is to have the spiritual effects that the theologians claim for it, it will have to be combined with some features that give the universe and its parts nobler interests than mutually dependent persistence.

3

A SECOND PASS: GOD AS THE POTENTIAL FOR GOODNESS

The dominant doctrine common to our theologians is that God is that feature of the universe that makes good things possible. Each of the theologians offers a number of suggestions regarding which potential-realizing features are divine. The possibility of love, justice, personality, full personality, peace, contentment, autonomy, altruism, as well as the potential for conquering pain, overcoming evil, ending alienation, and realizing bliss have all been put forth as descriptions of God. We will take some of these candidates up in detail after first exploring the general idea of God as potential.

There is an ambiguity in thinking of God as potential. We might think of a God that is not yet realized, that does not exist, but might. We would then have a potential, not an actual, God, a God who might be, but is not yet. Although sometimes the theologians talk this way, this is not what they usually have in mind. Instead, God fully exists as the ground of other potential goods. God's actuality *is* certain potentialities (or, in more expansive views, God's actuality is all potentialities, but this is more Hindu than Jewish; Jews tend to want to absolve God of the bad stuff, even if they like to see God come up with excuses along the way). God is what makes, or helps to make, or more modestly, at least allows, good things to happen. Typically, God is characterized as the potential that enables us to do or be good.

God as Energy

This enabling capacity sometimes leads to the characterization of God as sheer potency, as energy that animates our angelic urges. Lerner calls God the "Force" (1994, 35), thereby echoing *Star Wars* theology. He provides images of God as a depersonalized energy that is always being transmitted and that we can choose to tap into when we will. At times, Lerner sees the divine energy at work even without us flipping the "on" switch (1994, 181–82). God is the "energizing force" behind natural history. Arthur Green is also tempted by the image of God as energy. God, he tells us, is not "'will' in our highly personalistic human sense," but rather a "striving" inherent in the universe. While Green's "striving" energy may still contain overtones of intentionality, in denying that divine energy is "will," Green is clearly toying with the notion of God as blind, amoral power (Green 1992, 127).

God as simply the ur-energy of the universe is problematic for the theologians' purposes (which is probably why this characterization is a minor tendency in their work). Pure energy, however powerful, aims at nothing. We, or other users of "the Force," direct and shape the energy. True, the energy is necessary for our good works, but it is not responsible for the goodness in them. God as energy seems a primitive notion of the divine, wherein power alone—think lightning, thunder, and earthquakes—stir humanity's religious feelings. Inert, unformed matter is as much a necessary resource of our good works as is energy, but it is seldom deified, probably because unlike energy, it does not have the ghostly property of invisibility or the frightening quality of danger. The occasional equation of God and primal energy is backsliding by the theologians. If God is the potential for good, as she must be to fulfill the most wanted divine functions, she must either be energy with tendencies toward the good, or she must be energy combined with all the other features of the universe, which, together, can shape things for the good. Amoral energy is no God for us.

God as the Potential for Self-Consciousness

The potential for self-consciousness is the good that the theologians frequently identify as God. This good is often combined with the potential to soothe troubled self-consciousness or achieve a fuller, broader, or higher self-consciousness, but at times it is the universe's mere capacity to harbor self-consciousness itself that is the godly good. As humans are the only forms of self-consciousness we know, humans, or persons, represent the divine. "God is the process by which the Universe produces persons, and persons are the process by which God is manifest in the individual" (Kaplan 1985, 74; see also Green 1992, 71). In other words, *the person-making process,* of which persons (tautologically enough) are the embodiment, is God. As Arthur Green puts it, "The person—every person—is an earthly replica or small repository of the fullness of divine energy" (1992, 28). We encounter God in ourselves and in other people.

The theologians' most frequent characterization of God is the universe's potential for *better* self-consciousness. "Better" self-consciousness takes a number of forms, some of which make the improvement a matter of who or what is self-conscious. While there are qualitative differences in self-consciousness that our individual, ordinary human selves can hope for, the really big upgrade comes when a *new self* is the object of consciousness. The entire universe is the ne plus ultra new self. A self-conscious universe is offered as the very best self-consciousness; therefore, the process that makes a self-conscious universe possible has an honored place among the theologians' descriptions of God. There is a fair amount of vagueness and ambiguity in the theologians' accounts of the relation between ordinary human self-consciousness and a self-conscious universe (Lerner 1994, 36). Sometimes, the former is seen as equivalent to the latter, and the problem is simply getting the former to realize or acknowledge it. Each one of us is the self-conscious universe, although we, mired as we are in false dualisms, are reluctant to accept this description or we are forgetful of this truth. Sometimes, human consciousness is seen as a stage in the development of a not-yet-formed, universal self-consciousness. We are part of the process whereby the universe will, or may, become self-conscious. Sometimes, human self-consciousness is a proper part of a self-conscious universe, neither separable nor equivalent to it.[1] There would be no self-conscious universe without us, since each of us is a component of the self-conscious universe, but no one of us is in any sense equivalent to it. Sometimes, the self-conscious universe is quite separate from individual human consciousness, but one with which human self-consciousness can either commune or merge (Lerner 1994, 414–15). Sometimes, universal self-consciousness is the ground from which all individual human self-consciousness has emerged (Green 1992, 65; Kaplan 1985, 75; Lerner 2000, 7).

Few of the theologians stay consistently with one of these characterizations. Yet the characterizations are clearly not interchangeable; there are differences between them that have important implications. Some characterizations have a self-conscious universe as already existing, others as only a possibility. Some have the self-conscious universe as wholly dependent on human self-consciousness, but others reverse the existential dependency (Green 1992, 32). Some emphasize the collective nature of the contribution that human self-consciousness makes to universal self-consciousness (Green 1992, 25), others make it more of a dyadic relationship between the individual and the cosmos.

The theologians can also become slippery on whether they are calling God the *processes* that make for self-consciousness or the *state* of self-consciousness itself. Is God the victory or the struggle? Our theologians would be inclined to argue against this distinction, claiming, with some justification, that self-consciousness is nothing more than an ongoing process, the achievement of self-consciousness simply the embodiment of self-conscious-making activity. Granted. Nevertheless, we can still distinguish between phases of the activity that have not yet crossed the threshold, not yet become an embodiment of self-consciousness, and mature processes that actually realize self-consciousness.[2]

God as the Possibility of All Value

Contributing to (or connecting with) the self-conscious universe is not the only valuable process that the theologians identify as God. All sorts of do-gooding, or the structural possibilities in the universe for do-gooding, are called divine. Some God-identified processes are surprisingly specific. Lerner at times appears to equate progressive social activism with God,[3] but most God-identified processes, like Kaplan's "the power that makes for salvation," are fairly amorphous.[4] A sampling of the more amorphous God descriptions would include: God as an inspirational voice driving us to "the ideal" (Lerner 1994, 36); God as the possibility of "normative man" (Kaplan 1985, 78); God as the creative and re-creative urge in man (Kaplan 1985, 81–82); and, especially, God as the possibility of transformation and transcendence (Lerner 1994, 37, 408–9).

Obviously, the movement of individual self-consciousness toward universal self-consciousness is one sort of transformation. The general transformative processes alluded to, however, are not restricted to the movement from human to universal self-consciousness. As Jewish thinkers, our theologians are attached to the deep-rooted, but flexible tradition of *tikkum olam*, repair of the world. Cabala, Jewish mysticism, describes the origins of the creation as a shattering of God's essence. It is the task of religion to gather and repair the scattered spirit of God. For the theologians, this very gathering and repairing itself, or the fact that the universe gives scope for such reparations, becomes God. What constitutes this repair work? Lerner is fond of the term "healing" to describe the process (Lerner 2000, 7). Neither Kaplan nor Green shies away from the traditional term "redemption" to describe the reparative effort. God is redeeming work (Kaplan 1934, 403; Green 1992, 174–78). More concretely for the theologians, God is the ethical, social, and political acts that make for a better world. Kaplan is somewhat hesitant to specify the nature of that better world (1934, 403). A pragmatist at heart, Kaplan believes that ideals must evolve with human needs (Kaplan 1985, 73; 1934, 310, 317), but he would doubtless be sympathetic to Green's and Lerner's vision of a good world. It is a world of human equality, human solidarity, and ecological harmony (Green 1992, 175–78; 2000, 175, 213). Racism and patriarchy are vanquished. No person is humiliated (Lerner 2000, 33). The suffering of the sick and the poor is attended to. The environment and the animal world are respected and loved rather than exploited. The conditions for the flourishing of each and every human life and for the fullest development of every person are established (Kaplan 1985, 74). All people lead lives that they experience as meaningfully connected to other people and the natural world. Such is the redeemed world, the goal of the divine transformation. The theologians' God is the principles embedded in the universe that make that transformation possible. Energy, oraganicity, heightened human self-consciousness, and even universal self-consciousness are all candidates for apotheosization because they all seem to the theologians to imply or be implied by the great transformation. God is this great overcoming.

God as a transforming power is a central doctrine of our theologians, but the precise nature and locus of that power is more up for grabs, especially the question of whether the divine transforming power is transcendent or immanent. Reluctant to come down on either side of the question, the theologians hedge. Kaplan, primarily an immanence man, still seeks to find a place for transcendence in his scheme: "god is the life of the Universe, immanent insofar as each part acts upon every part, transcendent insofar as the whole acts upon each part" (1934, 316). Here, Kaplan is terming "transcendent" the organicity of the universe as viewed from the perspective of the whole, but as Kaplan doesn't think that there is an observer that has that perspective, his use of the term "transcendent" seems more of a concession to tradition than a theological position.

Lerner also makes God both immanent and transcendent; his transcendent aspect of God, as opposed to Kaplan's, really is out of this world, an unexperienced and intangible power (Lerner 2000, 36). Lerner's version has the virtue of being an honest transcendence, but also the vice. It is not a re-description of this worldly stuff that is exalted by the title "transcendent," rather, as genuinely otherworldly, it partakes of the most hoary, ghostly, mystifying properties of the old gods. It is an object of awe without having any specifiably awesome properties.

Green's God is "largely" immanent, but the experience of the divine immanence suggests something "beyond" (1992, 8). Indeed, for all of these thinkers, a main function of transcendence is to underscore the magnitude of the transforming work that is God (Kaplan 1934, 105; Lerner 2000, 7). It is work that takes us beyond our petty selves, beyond our narrow community, beyond our constraining past and oppressive present, beyond our selfish interests and limited horizons. It is out of this world, if this world means the current realities, but it is a possibility for this world and thus fully immanent. For Kaplan, the world to come is simply this world redeemed (1934, 403).

The Theologians' Naturalism

The theologians' flirtation with "transcendence" makes their commitment to naturalism suspect. Indeed, we find among them explicit expressions of ambivalence toward naturalism, but none of the theologians can consistently turn away from naturalism, for a confession of naturalism is the ticket of admission to serious consideration in the modern world.

Of the three, Kaplan's naturalism is the most robust. For him, the rejection of naturalism is the sign of an "unphilosophical" and an "unscientific" mind (1934, 314). Kaplan's entire project can be viewed as an attempt to reconcile Judaism and naturalism. We saw how even his toying with "transcendence" did not transport him to otherworldly regions. Green and Lerner also bid for naturalistic credentials. Neither wants a theology that is the least incompatible with scientific findings. Lerner warns us not to "discard science" (2000, 64) in the quest for a spiritual life, and Green attempts to show how his understanding of creation dovetails with Darwin (1992, 54).

The naturalism of all three thinkers, however, is motivated by more than just the desire for scientific respectability. It also serves their theodicy and religious psychology. The theologians want a God who is powerless to intervene in the world and they want an activist humanity that does not wait on God. Kaplan explains supernaturalism as largely an attempt to manipulate unseen, mysterious forces into benefiting us (1985, 70). The abandonment of such magical rites is, for Kaplan, a crucial and welcome implication of naturalism. For Lerner, God is not "a Force that is going to intervene to straighten things out"; rather, God is the structure of the universe that *gives us* the possibility of straightening things out (1994, 183, 255). As for Green, "rather than messiah redeeming us," he tells us, "we redeem messiah" (1992, 187).

The practical import of this naturalism, the payoff of the immanence theology, is a God who is not separable from us, who works through us, and who depends on us. No magical invocation of God in this religion, no blaming of God, no shifting of responsibility from or passive dependence on higher powers. Furthermore, if we are going to encounter God at all, it will be in the things of this world, and especially each other, as individuals and in communities. These are the fruits of naturalism that the theologians are loath to forgo.

The extreme expression of this theology of naturalism and immanence is the depiction of God as a human attitude, or a human response, to human needs and experiences. For Kaplan, belief in God comes from "the universal need of human nature for courage, hope and self-improvement" (1985, 73). "Man has yearnings to be at one with life at its best," and this "is the divine aspect of reality" (1934, 317). God is not an "objective fact," but rather a "value," says Kaplan (1985, 83), and Lerner echoes the idea when he tells us that the healing transformation, which he has identified with God, is "not determined by 'the facts' but rather by an orientation toward the facts" (Lerner 2000, 133). Green argues that religious experiences are the data of theology, and that any of life's more intense moments may constitute a religious experience. God, Green suggests, may be more in our responses to the experience than in the object(s) of experience (1992, preface).

"Naturalism" may not be a sufficiently nontheistic term to capture this strand of the theologians' work. This is God as a social construct or personal interpretation, the same sort of account of "God" provided by classic atheists: God as projection of human need, God as wish fulfillment and power fantasy.[5] No longer an objective structural feature of the universe, this is a God that one can as truthfully deny as assert. At most, there is the claim that there is a natural inclination to label and interpret certain human experiences as God, but a natural inclination to certain labels hardly justifies the labels or any interpretations of the labeled. Much of the history of science and psychotherapy is about correcting compelling natural *mis*interpretations of human experience. Alternatively, the claim may be that the "God idea" (Kaplan's term, 1934, 330), independent of any truth value that it may have, plays an important and useful role in human life.[6] "Usefulness" as a justification for belief is on somewhat firmer ground than "natural inclination," but "usefulness" makes the God idea relative to contingent, changing human ends, which themselves will require independent justification.

God as a response and attitude and as a heuristic device or motivational fiction is the theologians at their least theistic. It is also, for a modern secularist, the theologians at their most interesting, for it raises the question, "What is the secularist quarrel with *that* God?" We will address that question in a chapter 7. First, though, I want to look at ways that the theologians appear to hedge their naturalism.

Naturalism Hedged

Lerner openly declares that he "has no intention of giving a naturalistic picture of human life, or nature," but his definition of a "naturalistic picture" makes it difficult to assess whether this is a genuine retreat from naturalism. In rejecting naturalism, he tells us that he means to deny that "the world [reduces] to that which is the case, or can be described in language, or can be reduced to a set of things that interact with each other in lawlike ways" (1994, 414–15).

Now the denial that "the world [reduces] to that which is the case" is either incoherent or means that the present state of the universe ("that which is the case") is not necessarily the future state of the universe—that is, the universe can undergo change. That the universe can undergo change strikes me as perfectly compatible with naturalism.

The denial that the world "can be described in language" is our friend "ineffability." I rail against ineffability in appendix A, but I do not charge it with being especially incompatible with naturalism. True, ineffability is an ally of mystification, and mystification an ally of supernaturalism, but I am not sure that these alliances are transitive, and there is surely no strict entailment between ineffability and supernaturalism.

The third claim that Lerner rejects does seem to touch the core of naturalism, that everything, without exception, follows the "laws" of nature. But Lerner's use of the terms "reduce" and "things" confuses the issue. "Things" has the connotation of inert passivity, but no naturalist need deny that the world, at some levels, contains active, living beings. Many a naturalist will admit that aspects of reality, although completely composed of smaller units that obey the laws of nature, may themselves, as complex wholes, obey no discoverable, exceptionless "laws." To believe that there may be no laws of psychology or history in no way vitiates one's naturalism. Physics operates as thoroughly in historical events as it does in astronomical ones, but that does not mean that it can explain the former as it does the latter. No "law" may explain Napoleon's defeat at Waterloo, but the laws of physics were not suspended during the battle. In this sense, a naturalist can agree that "the world" does not *reduce* to "things that interact in a lawlike way." So it is not at all clear that Lerner has distanced himself from any but a caricatured naturalism. In fact, in his embrace of naturalism, Kaplan is clear that naturalism can recognize levels of reality where autonomous functioning emerges, levels where mechanistic/physicalist explanations fail (1985, 69). Kaplan's non-reductionist naturalism is the most tenable form of it, and it is not clear that Lerner rejects that form of naturalism.

In determining what is to count as a retreat from naturalism, one must decide whether any sort of super-person, such as a self-conscious universe, is ipso facto a retreat from naturalism. One might well argue that the existence of such a mind, and certainly the possible evolution of such a mind, is compatible with natural processes. After all, human minds are the result of the evolution of natural forces and are constituted by the complex, dynamic organization of natural phenomena. Why could not other kinds of minds naturally emerge or indeed, why might they not already exist? Why cannot one of those other minds be constituted by the totality of nature?

I can think of no disproof of the existence, let alone disproof of the possible future emergence, of superhuman minds or a universal mind,[7] but it is certainly the case that the existence of such minds is supported by no empirical evidence and does no naturalistic theoretical work. Naturalism, as worldview, is closely allied with Occam's razor, the principle that we don't multiply metaphysical entities needlessly, especially when these entities do not link up with the phenomenal world. So whenever our theologians posit a God with intentions, desires, hopes, concerns, or any of the attributes of personality and mind, they attenuate their claim to naturalism. They are aware of this and at times reject conceptions of a person-like God,[8] but for all the metaphysical discomfort, the theologians cannot resist the pull of God the Person, however much they have dumped God the Father. Lerner urges us to "leave behind" the "patriarchal, authoritarian, judgmental" God (2000, 7–8) and to embrace a God that has intentions, a God with a voice, a God that sends us messages, makes demands, and begs us to join in the divine work. God is a transcendent consciousness and has the accompanying attributes (Lerner 1994, 36, 340). Green is also eager to abandon paternal, pastoral, and royal descriptions of God (1992, 15), and although he falls into careless talk of a personal God far less often than Lerner does, still, for Green, God is not a "blind process" but, rather, person-like enough to be conceived as a "great striving" (1992, 54).

Lerner and Green's "transcendent consciousness" and "great striving" may not have beards and sit on thrones, but they still smack of supernaturalism. There is no positive role for any cosmic personality to play in a naturalistic account of reality, and its lingering presence in the theologians' thought taints their naturalism.

The theologians' recourse to personalistic God-talk, although sometimes offered as literal description, is most often defended as useful metaphor. Even Kaplan, the least mystical and most staunchly naturalistic of the group, the explicit denier that God is a person (1985, 75), allows anthropomorphic God-talk, although he, perhaps mistakenly, thought it was losing its appeal (1934, 397–99). Green and Lerner are less ambivalent defenders of anthropomorphic language (Green 1994, xii–xiii; Lerner 2000, 32). The poetry of a personal God and the traditional God-talk are *tools* they employ eagerly and repeatedly. So we must ask: Is the God that the theologians forge God enough for divine labors? Is belief in their God a useful tool?

4

THE USES OF
BELIEF IN GOD

What use is the new God? More precisely, what use is *belief* in the new God? Is belief in the new God as useful as old God belief? If it is not, might we do just as well as atheists as we would do as new God believers?

Answers to these questions must begin with a survey of the uses of belief in the old God, the person-like God of our fathers, who was both the source of our existence and the grounds for hope, perhaps even the guarantor, of the triumph of the good. A digest of the uses of that God creates a standard whereby we can evaluate the new God.

So, what use was belief in the old God?

The usefulness of a belief in any God is largely, although not entirely, a psychological matter. If, for instance, belief in God provides hope, it does so with or without God. I want, therefore, to explore the possible uses of belief in God while putting aside the question of the existence and nature of God, that is, while putting aside the question of whether a belief in God is a true belief.[1] I also put aside, until a later chapter, a central question of this book: How well does the God—a credible God—of our theologians, Arthur Green, Michael Lerner, and Mordechai Kaplan, serve the following uses?

Social Conformity

When we find ourselves, we find ourselves already encultured. True, the institutions and practices that form our lives are subject to change. Upon reflection, we can revise or abandon them. Self and social reformation are crucial components of human freedom, but although our cultural endowment is not immutable, there is a cost whenever we change it. Society must readjust, find a new equilibrium, and invest in new lubricants to reduce the friction generated by the new social designs. Change takes time and energy, both valuable resources.

What we now designate as religious traditions have been, until very recently, structural features of most cultures. Somewhat maginalized in the modern world, their presence remains an important social reality for many and may become so again for the rest of us. An individual courts conflict and disapproval if she flouts the religious conventions of her society.[2] What qualifies as flouting depends, of course, on the society that she keeps. Some Jews flout when they violate the Kashrut laws, others when they keep them. However, if your ethnic group, community, and family retain an array of religious practices, nonobservance has a personal price. It separates you from them and invites their disapproval. "You're not lighting Sabbath candles? Not going to synagogue? Not fasting on Yom Kippur?[3] How, then, can you be with us, and what are we to make of you?"

You may continue religious practices, for the sake of fitting in or even because you find the traditions enjoyable and satisfying, without believing in God. There are many reasons to do as the Romans do when you are in Rome without necessarily believing what the Romans believe. Still, religious practice certainly becomes harder to rationalize, harder to savor, and harder to do well without the correlative religious belief. Many contemporary Jews take a certain perverse pride in their ability to observe without belief, and indeed interpret the tradition as being indifferent to dogma and concerned only with practice. Yet, surely, even in Judaism, belief has nourished observance, and it is far from clear that genuine nonbelieving observance will become enduring tradition. This is not to claim that the tradition, which is itself evolving, must keep that old-time, religious belief in order to flourish. Religious practice's creedal support can evolve, too. But it is to doubt that the traditional practices can flourish with *no* justifying beliefs. Belief in God is not the only doctrine that undergirds traditional religious practice, but such a role is one important use of that belief. The practice, in turn, is an element in social solidarity and harmony.

Even if one could happily go along with religious rites and rituals without the dogma, there is still social value to be found in dogmatic belief. Solidarity and harmony gain not only from common external practice, but they are also enhanced by like-mindedness. It may be totalitarian to compel it and illiberal to value it, but uniformity of belief smoothes the social waters. We are not only troubled when people act differently from the way that we do, we are also troubled when they believe differently from the way that we do, especially on big things with big consequences. God is a big thing, and some hold that belief (or nonbelief) in God has big consequences. In some communities, belief in God is the attribute of any respectable member. In some families, its absence is alarming and disruptive. In addition to doing as others do, believing as others believe helps to keep the peace.

Less altruistic than peace-keeping, but a use of theism not to be over-looked, is the help that it might afford in social advancement. Some social circles, some career opportunities, and some romantic prospects may be closed to the nonbeliever. The believer will have other of those same options closed to her. The specific social context will determine whether, on balance, belief or nonbelief maximizes opportunities, but potential social advancement should still be registered as a use of belief in God.

Belief in God may also be a mark of loyalty. For many groups of people, be it a nation, tribe, or family, there are few things that they value and try to pass on to others that rank higher in their concern than their belief in God. To reject that belief may be taken by them and may be experienced by the rejecter as a betrayal of what the group holds most dear. Loyalty to the God of one's fathers is akin to loyalty to one's fathers themselves. Realizing social fidelity is no small use of traditional religious belief.

Both surrounding and interspersed with what we do and what we believe is how we talk. It is the form of much practice and the main manifestation of most belief and it also has a harmonizing social use all its own. Talking as others do, regardless of what I believe or (nonverbally) do, makes me understandable. If God-talk is the talk of the town and I want to be a man about town, I had better talk the talk. However, the expressive functions of God-talk go well beyond communication.

Someone To Talk To and About

Belief in God licenses God-talk, and God-talk may be the only language adequate for the expression of certain emotions. Prominent among these emotions is gratitude. We feel lucky, we feel "blessed." We appreciate beauty and goodness—sunsets and sonatas, courage and kindness. Life itself, our's and others', is often experienced as a gift. There are turns of good fortune that come to us. We do not fully understand the origins of many welcome things and are unsure that we merit them. We want to show our appreciation. We do not want to callously seem that we take our good fortune and the wonders of the world for granted. We are, after all, well brought up. A gift elicits a "thank you," but thanks are typically addressed to someone, the gift-giver. The appearance of ingratitude, we fear, may discourage further generosity. Even without any such fears, the expression of gratitude for goods that feel like gifts is a natural urge. Thank God.

Sometimes, it is not quite gratitude that we wish to express, but sheer joy at the abundance of our bounty. We simply feel that we have so much, and it is so good, that we must give verbal vent to our happy prosperity. Part of the joy of riches is their display, and this is as true of spiritual wealth as it is of material wealth. Moreover, the fullest vessels need a way to overflow lest they burst. Can there be any greater expression of abundance than declaring one's experience of God's fullness? Hallelujah.

God, however, is not employed only in the vocabulary of happy talk. God can also serve when we give voice to our deepest desires, and the distress and fears that often underlie them. Green says that the basic fact of theology is that we find ourselves praying (1992, 16). Not all prayer is petition, but petition is certainly one of prayer's basic forms. Desire and need flow into request. Inability to straightforwardly purchase or earn our wants leads to begging. We require an address for our petitions, someone to plead with, someone to hear us rattle our beggar's cup. Please God.

Our anger at misfortune, disappointment, and injustice also seeks outlet. Human malefactors are usually satisfying objects of our scorn and wrath, but some hurts are too big to lay at the door of human criminality. Ivan Karamazov needs to believe in God to draw up his indictment (Dostoyevsky 1881). We must hurl epithets at something greater than human when our suffering and disillusionment has superhuman grandeur. Job may have resisted the advice to curse God and die, but when our anger and pain knows no bounds, our venom seeks a boundless culprit. If nothing can be more praiseworthy than God, nothing can be more blameworthy either. It feels that for some things, only God's shoulders are broad enough to bear the blame. Madonna Marrona.

Even when we are not blaming or seeking redress from God, we require God's infinite empathy to understand our infinite pain. We may not expect anything to be done about it. We may only want a sympathetic ear, an understanding soul. But who can understand some of our deepest pains? Nobody knows the trouble I've seen. Nobody knows, but

Jesus. So Jesus is really the only one with whom I can discuss it. Or *tayere Gott.*

Finally, there are experiences for which our mundane vocabulary fails. An awareness of a presence not perceived through the senses; a feeling of unlimited power; a strong identification with others; a dissolution of the self; a unique experience of beauty; a sense of invulnerability; an awe-inducing vision of the sublime; or some compound of these and other special, esteemed and uncanny emotions. Such experiences' significance and value demand that we resort to the most extreme words at our disposal. The best, the most important of experiences, call forth the best and most important of words. No word is more high and mighty than "God."

These expressive functions of belief in God fall into two categories: God as the person to whom we address our fears, desires, and hopes, and God as the name with which we label our profoundest emotions. Belief in God is not absolutely required for either function. "God" can be treated as a *façon de parler.* "God-talk is just a manner of speaking. Don't be so crude as to take us literally." The theologians, as we will see, frequently, but not always, take this stance. We will discuss it later, when these forms of expression, such as prayer, are our topic. For now, we will just note the question, "Without belief in God, how well does 'God' the trope do the expressive work that we have catalogued?"

Security, Comfort, and Solace

Belief in God not only facilitates the expression of certain emotions, it can also engender emotions, some of which are highly valued. A number of such God-grounded emotions can be grouped under the heading "someone is caring for me." These are the emotions that make "children of God" such a powerful and enduring image of the human-God relationship.

Humans, like other animals, seek anxiety reduction, and how better to reduce anxiety than to believe that a powerful agent cares for you and stands ready to assist you? Even if there is no expectation that the cause of a particular anxiety will be divinely dealt with, there is comfort in the belief that somehow, in the end, things will be all right. God guarantees a happy ending, which gives one the security to relax, enjoy the show, and not live and die with every threatening plot twist. The Director gets the final cut, and he is believed to be more of a romantic than a tragedian.

Better still, belief in God is often tantamount to the belief that there might not be any final cut. People have a range of attitudes toward death, but it is widely regarded to be a bad thing. But if there is a God, the decree might be lifted and there might be life eternal for those who believe in him. If life temporary is a troublesome emotion, belief in God is an important palliative.

In a world filled with contingency, where one's well-being and very life appear to be at the mercy of blind chance, where the realization of one's worst fears and nightmares seem possible, belief in a God that guarantees safety may be the best defense against constant panic and dread. Walking life's tightrope, doubtful of our skills and the rope's strength, subject to unpredictable, uncontrollable, and irresistible gusts of wind, we might find that we have no heart to move forward without God, the strongest, biggest, and most finely woven of safety nets.

Even if you cannot be assured that God will come to your aid, cannot be certain that God will secure your ultimate happiness, grant you life everlasting, or protect you from intolerable evils, belief in God keeps those outcomes as live options. God justifies hope. The cavalry may or may not show up in time, but it is fortifying to be able to listen for the distant trumpet. If there were no cavalry (or Calvary in some religious traditions), there would be no grounds for hope. Many feel an enormous gap between their puny powers and their enormous needs. They don't see how this world can ever satisfy the world of their desire. The empirical means at hand are hopelessly deficient for the task. Whether or not God can be relied on to take on the task, his existence gives hope that it might yet be done. God is the ever-present and last(ing) hope.

When, in spite of hopes for immediate protection and rescue, sorrows do come and threaten to overwhelm, belief in God opens avenues for solace. God can restore the loss that worldly power cannot restore. We cannot raise the dead, but God can, and there is comfort in that. God can compensate for the loss for which the human imagination cannot conceive of compensation. We are sympathetic to Ivan Karamazov's refusal to accept that anything might redeem the torture of children because we too cannot imagine the form of such a redemption. However, we can escape Ivan's anguish by having faith that God's surpassing compassion and ingenuity have devised unimaginable redemption for all losses.

Beyond making good on losses, there is consolation to be had simply by justifying them. God can give meaning to the losses that human understanding finds horribly meaningless. This final form of solace, the provision of meaning for loss, opens a vista onto a wider use for theism. For it is not just our losses to which God gives meaning; God gives meaning to our acts. By keeping hope alive and consoling us for personal losses, belief in God fends off despair. God's despair-defeating functions, however, are not confined to ensuring happy endings for one personally or even by sustaining the *hope* of personal happiness. God allows meaning even in the face of terminal personal hardship by giving that hardship significance. No personal happiness may compensate us for our suffering, but that doesn't mean that our suffering must remain unredeemed. Our travails might be the bricks and mortar used to build, or sustain, a better world. Our losses and our gains are not for naught if God has a plan and we are part of it. In playing our part, our lives are imbued with dignity and meaning. Being part of God's plan connects us to the whole universe. With that connection, we triumph over the absurdity of a pointless, isolated life. No longer separate, no longer alienated from the universe, our life story is transformed from a tale signifying nothing into a chapter in the greatest story ever told.[4] There is solace that it was not all in vain.

Viewing your life as part of God's plan not only gives it meaning, but also gives it meaning that you can be proud of, meaning to which you enthusiastically contribute. For the, or at least a, point of God's plan is the triumph of justice, the establishment of the Kingdom. Insofar as the desire to see justice prevail generally, not just in one's own case, is a personal goal, it is somewhat misleading to view service in God's project as a meaning-but-not-satisfaction-providing viewpoint. *We want* to see the wicked punished and the righteous rewarded, even if the former have done us no personal harm and the latter have done us no personal good. It is because service to God gives my life that particular meaning, makes one of *my* purposes the general good, that I can take personal satisfaction in the meaning of my life. I am helping to usher in a world of love and justice. Later, I will argue that it is not irrational to prefer your own interests to the universe's interests, but if the universe does have interests, making them your own vastly inflates the meaning of your life's work.

Many of the preceding comforting functions of belief in God derive from the alternative reality that a God-inhabited universe offers. Most of us have some dissatisfactions with the apparently godless realities of everyday life. Some others of us find the mundane world thoroughly unpleasant. It is frustrating, dangerous, hopeless, capricious, unjust, and pointless. The desire to "transcend" those realities is endemic. Transcendence becomes for some almost a psychological necessity. They need to live, at least in part, at least in the depths of their soul, in a world that is satisfying, safe, hopeful, orderly, just, and meaningful. Belief in God is not the only way of gaining access to this better world, but it is the standard, traditional mode of transcendence and it wraps all the wanted blessings into one package. Nothing comforts like a belief in God.

Giving Morality a Home

By assuring us that justice and goodness will ultimately prevail, a belief in God satisfies our moral sense, and it plays even more fundamental roles in some people's theory of moral psychology. Some believe that God creates, reveals, and motivates morality, and that if he didn't, if there were no God, moral life would be impossible. It is God, they believe, who decides what is right and wrong. This divine decision is not a judgment that, because of his infinite wisdom, God invariably gets correct. Rather, it is a fiat that creates moral standards; prior to God's decision, there is no right or wrong. In making decisions about morality, there is no conceptual room for God to err. It is God's decision that defines what is to count as a moral error. On this view, without God, there simply is no right or wrong, no morality, and if you subscribe to the view, the loss of belief in God entails a loss of belief in morality.

Less metaphysically extreme, but practically equivalent, is the view that only from God can one learn the nature of morality. God's revelations, whether through Scripture, tradition, priestly inspiration, the small voice of conscience, or a booming voice from the skies, is the sole reliable guide to morality. It would be of no use if morality existed independently of God's will, but we were hopelessly out of touch with its principles. If you believe that moral knowledge can only come from God, your belief in God allows you to believe in the possibility of moral knowledge, for without moral knowledge, without moral instruction, we would remain in such total moral ignorance that it would be as if morality did not exist for us.

Finally, there is God the motivator. It is not enough that we know right from wrong, we must also be moved to act on that knowledge. Like Dostoyevsky's Kirilov, some hold that if there is no God everything is permitted (Dostoyevsky 1871). It is human belief in the inevitability of God's justice that curbs humanity's amoral natural will. Take away heaven and hell, along with the innumerable other forms, some exceedingly subtle, that divine reward for the righteous and punishment for the wicked take, and what is to constrain our beastly urges? Believers have long condemned those who have said that there is no judge and no judgment, for they have held that if there were neither judge nor judgment, anything goes. God enforces the moral law, and without enforcement, indeed, without the belief that there will be enforcement, who would be law-abiding? None, or too few, say those who see belief in God as the main motive to morality.

God's function as motivator of morality need not depend on the rewarder/punisher conception of the role, a conception that, while it may keep us in line, does not appear to do much to promote a virtuous or noble character. Neither fear nor self-interested hedonism recommends itself as the core motivation of good character.[5] God, however, is not restricted to punishments and rewards in his influence on morality. God can also inspire. Our love or admiration for God can make us want to please or imitate him. It may be argued that without the ideal of God, not as cognitive guidance on how to be moral, but as conative empowerment enabling us to enact good deeds, our moral lives would be fatally enfeebled.

God the Theory

Aristotle claimed that human beings desire knowledge. It does seem that beyond the practical applications of knowledge, there is an intrinsic satisfaction in understanding the how and why of things. While many have a taste for mystery, it is a delicacy—not what we seek as daily fare and even as a delicacy—it appeals because it titillates the desire to understand. A central function of God has been its role as an explanation. God is a theory of origins, causes, reasons, and outcomes. God answers to the desire to have answers, to understand things. Not just any old things, but things of ultimate personal consequence, things that are profoundly perplexing, things that seem to be at the root of all knowledge. For many, God answers questions that would be disturbing, in part because it would be intellectually unsatisfying, to leave unanswered.

Belief in God is a potential workhorse. It aligns our beliefs and practices with our community and traditions. It gives us courage and hope for our endeavors, comfort and consolation for our losses, and protection and sanctuary from our worst fears. Belief in God gives us the language to speak of our most precious experiences and a being to address when expressing existential emotions. It grounds our morality and gives us a perspective from which to understand the deepest questions. It is a lot of work for one belief to do. A question for modern-minded people is whether any conception of God that is powerful enough to do this work is credible enough to sustain belief.

5

THE USEFULNESS OF
A PLAUSIBLE GOD

Not only must a God worthy of belief be credible, so too must a God worthy of disbelief. That is so because, in the modern world, only such a God is a candidate for belief.[1] It hardly pays to disbelieve in something that is not in the running to be believed. So our concern is with a credible God, and our interest in the theologians' theology is due to their God's credibility. However, as we have seen in the previous chapter, credibility of belief is not the only measure of a belief's value—usefulness is also important. A candidate for belief must be credible, but credibility is not enough. A belief's acceptance should also depend on utility. Although we often flatter ourselves that a belief's truth or falsity should be the sole criterion for its acceptance, we should also assess what we gain by adding it to our mental furniture.[2]

We now will judge the theologians' credible God's candidacy for belief by the standard of usefulness. Having described the uses of belief in the old God, we are now in a position to evaluate the usefulness of belief in the new God. My underlying concern is whether the theologians have made God plausible at the cost of making her effete.

Rather than describe a God meant to incorporate the fullest range of properties that appear in the theologians' conceptions of God, I will impose on them a minimal God that I hope is in keeping with much of what they say, and, most importantly, is the God that I, in my capacity as the representative modern person, believe is the most credible God that can be distilled from their theologies.[3] This will be the baseline God of the theologians, the God that we shall test for utility. Frequently, we will depart from the baseline to see how a different version of the new God that is found in the theologians' conceptual pantheon measures up to a particular function. However, unless a nonbaseline version of the new God is explicitly introduced, it is the baseline God that is meant when I speak of the "theologians' God," or of the "new God."

In addition to the theologians' God and its variants, we will also require a conception of a "traditional" God. When appraising the theologians' God's utility, the utility of the traditional God is a key standard to bring to bear. The appraisal of usefulness, like most things, is a relative matter. Belief, too, in a new God's usefulness is most significantly assessed relative to the usefulness of belief in, on the one hand, no gods or, on the other hand, the old God. The old God was sketched in the last chapter before describing his usefulness. It is to a fuller description of the old God that I now turn.

God of Our Fathers

For our "old" God, the God of our fathers, we need not go so far back in the tradition and make God an actual father, king, man, or even human, but we do have to make her a person. She must have the psychological qualities that we normally consider definitive of personhood. Indeed, the most straightforward way of interpreting the idea that we are made in the image of God is to say that like God, we are persons.

What are God's personal qualities? First, God is an agent. God does things in accordance with her will. She intends for things to happen. She acts. Second, God is a good agent. Her will is just, merciful, loving, kind and generous, never wicked, uncaring, hateful, cruel, or mean. Third, her will is directed toward our world. She can and, on occasion, does will things to happen in our world. This is because she cares about us and our world. She is never indifferent. Fourth, she is, at a minimum, very powerful and very wise, so that the exercise of her will is always effective. Nothing is beyond her control. God accomplishes what she wants to accomplish. Fifth, God is a comprehending and empathetic being. She can understand our prayers and feel our pain. Sixth, there is a sense in which God is the cause of the existence and nature of all of being. If there is anything that she does not control, it is because she has chosen not to control it. Finally, God is a self; she sees herself as a unified subject and is conscious of her acts as hers.

These are not all and the only things that can be said of the traditional God of Western monotheism. As a description of the old God, it is incomplete, but these are the features that made belief in her so useful. We turn now from the God of our fathers to the God of our friends.

The Baseline Theologians' God

The theologians' God is a fundamental structural feature of the world. "Structural" is not meant to connote static. God is a structural feature of the world in the same way that anatomy *and* physiology are structural features of organisms. God is the (or some) stuff of the world and their (or some of their) natural ways of operating. More specifically, God is the structural features of the world that allow good things to happen. The world has structures that allow for the emergence of life. Those structures are divine. The world has structures that permit life to become conscious and self-conscious. Those structures are divine. Beauty, knowledge, justice, virtue, creativity, and love—they all exist because the nature of the world gives them scope to exist, and this capacity of the world's nature is divine. Moreover, the world is structured so that humanity as a whole can (not necessarily *will*) become happy and good. Whatever it is about the world that makes these actual and potential goods possible is God.[4]

Hence, the baseline God of the theologians: God is whatever there is in nature that makes good things possible. Belief in God amounts to no more than the belief that there *are* things in nature that make good things possible, both the good things that are actual (e.g., friendship) and the good things that are still only potential (e.g., lasting, universal peace).

Although this conception leaves open the precise nature of God, nothing about it suggests that God is at all person-like. God has no will, intentions, or desires. We have all of those things, and insofar as God "made" us (i.e., we evolved in a universe whose structure allowed for our evolution), those things are God's handiwork and perhaps part of the divine process for realizing goods. God itself, however, for all that this conception demands, is an impersonal, indifferent, nonintentional structure. If all persons in the universe were to be destroyed, and along with them every existing conscious intention, God would remain as the potential to reconstitute intentionality and all other good things.

The merit of this conception of God is its utter credibility. Some good things exist, so the universe must have structures from which they emerged and that allow them to exist. There is no denying the corresponding reality to this part of the conception, short of denying that there is anything good in the world. Granted, it is not quite so certain that better things are possible or even that the good things that do exist can continue to exist. Nevertheless, there are no compelling reasons to doubt that some better things might yet emerge, and no irresistible evidence that rules out the possibility that some of our most cherished hopes can come to pass. That is all that this baseline God asks one to believe: that goodness is not ruled out. This conception makes theism equivalent to optimism and pessimism tantamount to atheism—the nonbeliever in this God must believe that the world is irremediably bad. Theism, under this conception, only requires that you think that the world is not hopeless.

It seems to me that belief that the universe is salvageable is at least as rational as the belief that it is doomed. Perhaps they are both matters of faith, but the hopeful faith is not epistemologically inferior to the despairing faith. After all, belief in this God does not ask us to believe that moral progress and spiritual light are very likely or even more likely than moral degradation and spiritual darkness. Belief in this view only asks us to believe that the universe does not rule out progress, that the universe does not have an inevitable evil destiny.[5] This God is credible because it only asks us not to believe the worse. It is an easy God to believe in.

Is this God worth believing in? Does it merit the high title "God"? What is this belief good for? We begin our investigation by considering the baseline God as a theoretical explanation of some persistent questions.

God as Explanation

What makes for a good explanation? Philosophers of science debate the issue, but we will not delve into that debate. Our interest is with the psychology, not the logic of explanation.[6] For our purposes, a good explanation is one that satisfies a desire to understand. Its quality depends on how thoroughly it satisfies the desire. A good explanation need not be true, need not be of assistance in navigating reality, need not be accompanied by any evidence, and, because one person's meat is another person's poison, need not make sense to all contemplators. If your desire to understand X is well satisfied (not necessarily extinguished) by explanation Y, then, for you, Y is a good explanation of X.

In this sense of explanation, the traditional God had done yeoman explanatory work for ages. First and last, things—the whence, whither, and wherefore of the universe and of humanity—all are part of a story in which the traditional God is the protagonist. The story was intellectually satisfying to most people and was felt to contain no disturbing loose ends. There were details that the story did not go into, but that did not undermine the tales' basic lessons.

Then, with the arrival of natural philosophy and science, there arose a class of carping literary critics who increasingly found faults in the traditional narrative. Those of us with even a passing familiarity with this critical literature (i.e., science and philosophy), no longer find the story starring the old God even remotely satisfying as a literal explanation. It is not simply that we think that the story is fiction or lacks evidence; even if we had photographs from the Garden of Eden documenting God as a Michelangeloesque Jehovah creating Adam with a puff of divine breath, the story, although perhaps accepted as true, would not be a satisfying explanation. We would still want to know how it is compatible with other things that we know that seem to conflict with it: fossils, entropy, Auschwitz. Worse, we have a host of questions that the story of the traditional lord of hosts doesn't even address: What accounts for her existence? What motivated her to create the world? Why this world rather than some other? Even if we moderns believed the traditional explanation's premises (which we do not), that explanation would not satisfy our desire to understand. Our desire to understand, like a gourmet's palette, has become subtle and sophisticated. We have developed special tastes and an exquisite tongue that can detect the absence of the minutest wanted ingredient or the presence of an unwanted one. All sorts of things count as explanatory deficiencies for our educated, mature sensibilities. The traditional God was a good explanation, but she no longer is. She does not explain what we want to know. Still, she should be credited with past work.

That this useful aspect of the old God is past is one of the reasons that the theologians feel quite easy about making a new God that does not seriously aspire to this divine function. The old God has lost its explanatory power, which makes the new God's lack of explanatory power less of a disability. For moderns, in the realm of cosmic explanations, religion no longer is competitive with science and secular philosophy. It is no longer something that moderns seek from God, not because science has all the answers, but because the type of answers that we now find satisfying (for this sort of thing) must take the form of science.[7]

The theologians' abandonment of God as explanatory theory is explicit and yet ambivalent. Kaplan tells us that "religion is not intended to answer ultimate questions" (1985, 86), Lerner concedes that science's "methodology and . . . discoveries are appropriate for the questions it asks" (2000, 65), and Green says that he has "no essential argument with an evolutionary approach to the tale of life's origins" (1992, 54). In fine, science and religion have different aims, operate in different arenas, and speak to different issues. Stephen Jay Gould was a recent champion of this position (Gould 2001). There are two magisteria Gould tells us, each sovereign in its realm. Science's domain is the explanation of all natural phenomena; religion gets spiritual values and ethics. The theologians want to be viewed, and view themselves, as Gouldians. They want no dust-up with science.

For all their consciousness of religion's competitive hopelessness in the kingdom of explanations, the theologians cannot help occasionally trying to give some explanatory credentials to the new God. Being bounced from the ultimate explanation and final theory role is too radical a diminution for God's fans to swallow without at least some ambivalence, and so, although they have sworn to abstain from having religion impinge on the scientific domain, we have instances of the theologians falling off the "I ain't explainin' nature" wagon. Right after endorsing an "evolutionary approach," Green denies that it is a "blind striving" (which is, of course, exactly what Darwinian evolution is). There is an underlying reality, a "universal force," that Green posits as driving the natural processes (1992, 54). Lerner declares at one point that the story that physicists tell us "seems implausible" and implies that we need to supplement it with a notion of divine energy for a more plausible account (1994, 413). Lerner also alludes to contemporary physical theory regarding observer effects on measurement in order to endorse the call for a "postmodern science that would reconnect with some elements that used to be called 'natural religion'" (2000, 66). So although they know better, there is some theologian backsliding; the theologians can't quite let go of the explanatory function of God.[8]

But, the theologians' Gouldian instincts are right. The new God really is of no explanatory use. She is a label proclaiming that there is an explanation, compatible with nature, of all the good things that are and yet might be, but she is not that explanation. To say that nature is so structured as to have allowed for the emergence of good things is simply to say that there *is* a natural explanation for them. To say that nature is so structured as to allow for the emergence of further goods is an act of faith. Such statements are introductions to explanations. The actual explanations will tell us *how* nature does it.

There are philosophers and scientists engaged in formulating the naturalistic explanations for the emergence of things that we value. Consciousness and self-consciousness, willpower and freedom, family love and social cooperation—these are only some of the goods whose evolution are the subject of recent research[9]—but "God" has no part to play in these explanations. The deity adds nothing to their explanatory power.

The thing that the theologians are most tempted to have their God explain is subjective religious experience. Usually, they sensibly settle for calling God a name for these experiences. Green is most forthcoming here. "God" is a name that "I give to the object of my wonder," and we attach the word "God" to our "search for meaning." Green also recognizes that we are free to choose other names for our experiences and desires (1992, xxiv). However, the theologians sometimes speak as if they can infer something from the experiences about the causes of the experiences. God is then not a name for the experience, but rather a causal explanation of it; God becomes the explanatory theory of religious experience. Green, when he says that "God" is used to "articulate" the experiences, waffles between "God" as naming and God as explaining such experiences. Lerner, however, is unequivocal in the belief that we need to conclude from our experience that there is "*something more*" [italics in original], be it called "soul," "spirit," or "God," needed to explain our beliefs and values, which (our beliefs and values, that is) must be understood as a manifestation of this "something more" (Green 1992, xviii; Lerner 2000, 9).

There is nothing unreasonable about positing theoretical entities to explain data. Scientists do it all of the time. It is fair to say, too, as Green does, that religious experiences are the data of theology (1992, xix), but there must be more to the posited entity than the assertion that it explains the data. It must organize the data so that their relations are ordered by some logic. It must aid in predicting new data of the same type. It must help us to manipulate, for our purposes, the relevant phenomena. At least it must do *some* of these things if it is to satisfy our desire to understand. Of course, some people may have their desire to understand the cause of religious experiences satisfied by labeling that cause "God," in much the same manner that the Molière character was satisfied that he understood the cause of opium's sleep-inducing properties by positing a soporific power in the drug. But, naming is not explaining. I do not deny that naming certain experiences as "God" may have important uses, but explanation is not one of them.[10] The theologians are on their firmest ground when they stick to the position that their God is meant to explain nothing.

God, the Maker of Morality

As the creator of morality, God has failed to satisfy the scrupulous for thousands of years. Plato analyzed the problem in the fifth century BCE

(*Euthyphro*, 390 BCE); if God creates morality, then there is no right or wrong that is logically prior to God's creation. Moral "good" and "bad" and "right" and "wrong" are simply names for God's creative preferences in certain domains; they do not explain those preferences, and they certainly do not morally justify those preferences because the preferences themselves are the standards of moral justification. If God creates moral standards, morality would become synonymous with something like "doing God's will" or "being in harmony with God's creation," but then God's will, God's creation, indeed, God herself, can no longer meaningfully be described as good. If God is the standard of morality, describing God as morally good would just be calling God godly; true, but uninformative—and not much of a compliment either (or the ultimate in meaningless compliments, I cannot decide which). If God is the creator of morality, then God stands outside of morality and is beyond good and evil.[11] The price of making God the creator of morality is that God stops being morally good. This is a heavy price; moral goodness was one of the old God's best features.

The theologians' God is better situated than the old God to create morality, for it has fewer pretensions to moral goodness. It is only a structure making good things possible, and it is quite plausible that our moral sense and moral codes evolve from this structure, which is itself pre-moral. In this area, the new God has a decided advantage over the traditional God, but the new God does not do anything that atheism does not do as well. This is the first of many occasions that I will have to make that assertion. The frequent functional equivalence of atheism and the theologians' theology is unsurprising, however, for the baseline God is so thoroughly naturalistic that a godless nature can be expected to perform about as well as a godly one—when it is the new God making it godly. In this case, the evolution of morality is explained and grounded equally well whether we call the initial structures "God" or not.

If, however, we add to those structures a *tendency* to evolve moral insight and virtue, and not merely the scope to evolve them, then that does enhance both the power of the structures to ground morality and our reasons for calling these structures God. However, attributing this virtue-making tendency to the structures is not part of the baseline conception, although it is a prominent variant (Lerner 1994, 62; Green 1992, 94). It is a variant that makes the theologians' God more useful, but it is a variant that erodes her credibility. That the universe naturally *bends* to the creation of morality and virtue is not incredible, but it is less credible than the weaker claim that the universe *allows* morality and virtue to emerge. We find here a dynamic that we will find often. As variants of the theologians' God become increasingly useful, they become decreasingly credible. The old God is the limiting case; as the theologians' variant gods approach the old God, they will be more able to carry her traditional burdens, but they will also become more unbelievable. Morality is unusual in that some variant gods of the theologians are in some respects more useful than the traditional God. For most other divine functions, the old God worked best. Still, even in the moral realm, usefulness is bought with credibility. Structures that make probable the emergence of morality are less credible than structures that merely make possible the emergence of morality.[12]

God, the Moral Instructor

The old God was in a better logical position to be the teacher of morality than she was to be the creator of morality. Whatever the principles of morality are, and wherever they came from, the old God could be counted upon to know them and tell it like it is. Not just a reliable reporter, but an infallible one; a teacher deserving of complete trust.

Difficulties arise, however, if there is uncertainty in identifying divine communications or interpreting divine lessons. Even if it is always safe to follow God's moral instructions, we remain in moral danger if we cannot be sure which instructions are God's or what constitutes following them. This danger has always been around, but becomes increasingly acute as diversity of respectable religious opinions proliferate in a society. When there is both consensus that a text is the word of God and an unchallenged understanding of the morality that that text enjoins, God's homiletic function proceeds smoothly. However, in the presence of competing scriptures or interpretations, although God remains reliable, access to her instructions does not. There are too many false maps about to have confidence in any map. In the old God's heyday, most societies kept heterodoxy at bay, and belief in God provided fairly clear moral guidance. Now that we are offered a wide choice of gods, the relationship is reversed; instead of shaping our morality according to God's teachings, we identify God's teachings according to their fit with our morality. We recognize the true map because we already know the lay of the land, but in knowing the lay of the land, we don't need the map to learn it.

The theologians' God has a lovely suppleness as moral teacher. An impersonal structure seems ill-suited to serve as an active instructor, and therefore we can read nature through our moral lenses and find what lessons there we will. As befits the pluralistic times, the theologians' morality is prior to, and helps to identify, the theologians' God. They know what they believe the good to be, and armed with this knowledge, the theologians find God. They admit that other moral values will identify a somewhat different God.

The theologians, however, need not completely relinquish God's moral guide functions. They might argue that the structures in nature that make us and the things we nonmorally value (i.e., the structures that are God) are structures that imply a morality that indeed teaches, albeit nonintentionally, right from wrong. Mostly, it is suggested, we can infer these lessons from nature's organicity and unity. Those are the structures that teach morality. Morality is conceived of as the counter to narrow self-centeredness. We are callous toward others' suffering, or worse, cruel to others, because their pain is not ours. We are greedy and gluttonous because our own pleasures are given unparalleled weight. We are fearful and cowardly because our own hurts and losses are judged uniquely catastrophic. Hence selfishness and immorality. The theologians say these behaviors and judgments are a result of misunderstanding the universe's true character. It is a unity. The boundaries between "oneself" and the rest of the universe are artificial, fictitious, or illusory. If the ordinary concept of the self is ill-founded, then selfishness too becomes senseless. Insight into the flimsiness of the self leads to the dissipation of selfishness, and so God does teach morality.

Organicity works similarly, but here the self is not so much dissolved as it is rewired; it is not strictly identical with the rest of the universe, but it is intimately connected to the rest of the universe and reflective of it. Although they work slightly differently, the result for morality that the theologians derive from unity and organicity is the same. Whatever you do to others, especially other humans, but really to any part of creation, you are actually doing to yourself. Either because you are the other (as in the unity, i.e., the antidualistic, monistic view) or because, as part of an integrated whole, your interests are identical with the other's (organicity). The universe is a book in which, once we know how to read it, we see written the Golden Rule.

Before discussing whether unity or organicity does teach the Golden Rule, we must note that the unified and/or organic universe is a variant of the baseline God and see how much credibility we have paid for it. The baseline conception tells us that God is a natural structure that makes good things possible, but it does not require that all being be part of this structure or that this structure connects every part of being to every other part in a way that makes their interests common. This is asking us to swallow more than the possibility of goodness and it demands a bigger gulp to get it down.[13]

However, neither an organic nor a monistic view of the universe is too fantastic a position to dismiss out of hand. The "facts" may not make them inescapable beliefs, but if they afford sufficient benefits, the facts are loose enough to permit an embrace of monism and organicity. Therefore, what are the uses in moral education of belief in an organic and monistic universe? Assuming that such beliefs are true, what do they teach us about right and wrong? We have seen that the theologians think that they teach us that we should not be selfish because, at bottom, at the deepest level, there is no self with separable interests. But, other than giving us a general orientation away from narrow egoism, what moral guidance does non-selfishness provide? It spells out no rights of individuals (there are no individuals), it provides no conflict-resolving principles (there are no conflicts), and it constrains nothing and enjoins nothing except the very general maxim that all action should be aimed at the good of the whole. By itself, however, it does not define the good of the whole. Organicity and unity may cast doubt on the status of narrow self-interests, but by themselves they do not recommend alternative interests. "When I am selfish I serve a chimera. Fine, I will not waste my time. What is real then, what shall I serve? The one universe, indivisible? What are its interests?" Until more is said about the organic, monistic universe, we cannot attribute any interests to it at all. To seek moral guidance from it, we have to understand its purposes, its natural ends, its health, or at least some comparable term that can reasonably stand for its good. By giving the universe purposes, ends, health, and so forth, we increase its moral legibility. Again, though, we pay with credibility. People have interests and ends, plants and animals have health and interests. Are the theologians taking these metaphors literally to reap moral instruction from God?

God as Motive for Morality

Finally, we come to God as the motivator of morality. Morality requires more than that there be standards of right and wrong and that we know of them. We also must be moved to enact them. "Why care about morality" is among the hoariest of ethical questions. God is the hoariest answer.

The most common form of the old God's motivational power is direct, clear, and understandable enough for a child to appreciate. In fact, it is similar to that other great motivator of childhood morality, Santa Claus. Like Santa, God "knows if you are sleeping, he knows if you're awake, he knows if you've been bad or good."[14] So, like Santa, there is no deceiving God's moral judgment. God is also Santa-like in dispensing rewards and punishments according to her moral assessments, but eternal bliss replaces Play Station Three as the boon upon her approval, and eternal torment substitutes for an empty stocking as the wages of sin. In addition, God is never coming to town, she is always in town.

Commentators have pointed out that such heavy-handed rewards and punishments (and heaven and hell are, by definition, as heavy handed as one can get on the reward-punishment continuum) do not seem to be the sort of motives that we want for morality. While the promise of heaven and the threat of hell may exact conformity to moral standards, we can wonder if they build good character, which in our post-Kantian consciousness, we think of as desiring the good solely for goodness' sake. The objection, however, is unsound. The old God could build character, for she sees into our hearts. To please the old God, it was not enough to do the right thing, you were also judged by the spirit with which it was done. Therefore, seekers of heaven aspired to cultivate righteous feelings as well as perform righteous acts. God wants the moral acts and the moral feelings. Admission to heaven wanted a good record on standardized external acts and good responses when God interviewed your soul. That one's moral motives were ultimately grounded in a vision of one's highest, long-range interests may have formally classified such a God-fearing morality as egoistic, but it is an egoism that effectively motivated the full panoply of moral action and sentiments. Only the strictest of Kantians would deny the usefulness of belief in the old Santa-God as a moral motivator. Of course, for some of us, that God is no easier to believe in than Santa.

Can belief in the more credible theologians' God also motivate morality? She is no judge and therefore awards no prizes and passes no sentences. Sometimes, of course, we speak of impersonal entities as being rewarding or punishing. Some mountains, unconscious though they may be, are punishing to climb and offer a rewarding vista at the peak. The climb and the vista have properties that, when engaged, return pleasure and pain. Perhaps the structure of the universe rewards virtue in deed and thought and punishes vicious thoughts and deeds. Maybe that is just the way that the universe, unintentionally, operates. Karma, in Eastern religious thought, seems to function along these general lines, and if the karmic laws are as pervasive as Santa's judgmental observations, it seems that they should motivate as effectively as any Santa-God. Natural laws operate without judge or judgment, and if the natural law returns good for good and evil for evil, the new God, a natural law herself, may motivate morality.

Such karmic qualities, however, go beyond the baseline God, which tells us only that the universe permits the good, not that it rewards it. Is there evidence that justifies supplementing the baseline God with karmic tendencies? Is there reason to believe that, morally speaking, what goes around comes around? Efforts to marshal such evidence is voluminous, but quite indecisive. Ingenious attempts to show how human nature and nonhuman nature make the righteous prosper and the wicked fail do not defeat common observation to the contrary. Goodness neither protects from suffering nor leads to ultimate happiness. At least the evidence does not drive us, or even incline us, to conclude that it does. Too many innocents and good people have come to ruin for even the most myopic of Pollyannas to overlook.

Perhaps there is some reason to think that the psychology of wickedness precludes happiness, that bad people can't be truly happy. Even here, though, the evidence is at best delicately balanced.[15] Philosophers have found no arguments linking immorality to unhappiness as vivid and compelling as the link made by the image of an angry God consigning the wicked to hellfire, and, insofar as a link between one's morality and one's well-being can be forged through the theologians' God, the same link would bind morality and well-being in a godless world. In fact, the whole project of showing that there are natural, structural ties between goodness and happiness is motivated by a desire to maintain that connection in a world without God. New God defenders of the morality/happiness connection deploy arguments developed by nontheistic apologists for morality, apologists determined to show that the collapse of faith was not a moral collapse. If the arguments work at all, they have to work without resort to God. The usefulness of these arguments is unchanged by giving them divine connotations, and their usefulness has always been limited. The morality/ happiness nexus remains abstruse, whether or not the naturalistic bonding mechanism is made sacred. A subtle, complex, highly theorized passage from immorality to unhappiness might do as a philosophical justification for good behavior, but it will not do as quotidian motivation to lead a good life. Belief in the theologians' God can neither bribe nor scare us into more righteous lives.

Perhaps, however, it can inspire us. God, old or new, is more than a benefactor to impress or a scourge to be mollified (also more than an impersonal dynamic to exploit). To see her as such is to relate to her in the crudest way. Rather, she is an ideal to admire, a force to love, a principle to embody, a model of perfection to imitate. We want to imitate God because we perceive it is good to be God. We want to please God because we love her. It is our love and admiration for God that motivates morality and that thereby makes our belief in her morally useful.

I leave aside the details of how this may have worked under the old God's regime. It is easy enough to see how one might have considered a perfect person an ideal worth imitating, even though most depictions of the traditional God made him hard to love (whether as angry, boastful Jehovah or passive, earnest Jesus).[16] At least the old God was the right sort of thing to love, to admire. How, though, precisely, can the theologians' God inspire our better selves? I am hard-pressed to see how any impersonal structure becomes either an ideal to imitate or a beloved to please. To arrive at a God that can be a moral inspiration seems to demand traveling a substantial distance from the baseline God. The structure must become, if not flesh, then at least spirit.

The argument for God's motivational use in morality may be most strongly made by enumerating cases. Many of our greatest moral heroes and the noblest human actions were rooted in faith. Mohandas Gandhi, Martin Luther King Jr., St. Francis of Assisi, Bartolemé de las Casas, the Ba'al Shem Tov, Nachman of Bratslav, the Chaim Chofetz, and other moral heroes were explicitly religious; all tied their moral being to God. Others, such as Lincoln and Schweitzer, clearly found guidance from faith for their great moral acts. Besides the famous, we all know that some of our morally best neighbors and fellow humans find their moral strength in their belief, understanding , and experience of God. Of course, there are moral heroes from the ranks of the not explicitly religious and even from among declared atheists, but I suspect that the list might not be as long or impressive as the religious exemplars.[17]

However, as much as God has been a muse to moral heroes, she has also been a diabolical siren, tempting some believers into great villainy: Crusaders, inquisitors, al-Qaeda terrorists, Zealots, Kahanists, BJP Hindu fanatics, to name but some. Who could confidently say whether religious motivation is a net gain or loss for morality? It should probably just be declared a wash. Without religious exhortation and inspiration, we would likely lose some (not all) of the extremes of moral motivation. Fewer saints, but fewer fanatical villains, too.

If you are of moderate tastes, you will think it a good deal. On the down side, by dropping the transcendent and ultimate importance of divine demands and aspirations and by removing the image of moral perfection as the model of the best Being, fewer human beings will approach their best. Atheists, of course, can have inspiring ideals, but in general, they are less all-encompassing and less compelling than God. Also, less imitable. Kindness, generosity, and love, as abstractions, do not draw us as powerfully as the desire to imitate a kind, generous, and loving Being. Concrete human models embodying moral virtues can be inspirations, but their virtue is always partial, compromised, and limited; their appeal is rarely universal. The reduced power of these mundane inspirations inspire less than the concrete, super-human ideal, and so sole reliance on these worldly models may well result in the loss of some Mother Teresas and Judah Magneses.

Secular inspirations are also generally less dangerous than holy visions. True, history's most destructive ideals have included the megalomania of Stalin and the racial obsession of Hitler, both nontheistic visions. Indeed, it does seem that the sort of totalistic, uncompromising, *weltanschauung* that leads to horrors can more easily find a home in atheism than the totalistic view that leads to moral beauty. Still, the natural home of both extreme morality and extreme immorality, of godly goodness and satanic evil, is religion. Every once in a while, a secular vision can be proposed that is as all-embracing and as certain of itself as religious faith, and secular saints and (more likely) secular devils will be moved by it. Belief in God, however, is the homeland of all-embracing certainty, and theism can be expected regularly to generate saints and devils. I would welcome a world with fewer moral extremes and moral color—if the price of a world without Christian-identity racists is a world without Lamed Vovniks, I would pay it—but this may just be a personal preference. I do not like rollercoasters either.[18]

The baseline God is no spur to fanaticism. She is hardly less abstract than modest atheistic ideals. Indeed, all of the versions of the theologians' new God, so long as they remain impersonal structures, as ideals are functionally equivalent to nontheistic ideals. The structural features of the universe that made Janusz Korshak possible do not become inspirational by being called "God," and Korshak himself remains inspirational regardless of the label attached to the impersonal forces that helped to form him.[19] There is no more moral-inspiration mileage to be gotten out of belief in the new God than there is to be had from belief in no God, not without making the new God a person-like Being hardly distinguishable from the old God. You cannot want to be like a structure, no matter how much good the structure effects.

Belief in the theologians' God, baseline version, serves no moral function not served as well by an atheism with a modicum of psychological and social machinery that ties good behavior to well-being. Both beliefs lay the same obscure foundations for morality, give us the same dim insights into moral truth, and provide the same resistible motives to be good. The theologians' God only does better as she transforms into the shape of the old God, wherein she once again can be a beacon and magnet, guiding and drawing us to morality. These qualities are counted among her *personal* powers, and if we deny her personality, she is divested of them.

Keeping the Peace by Keeping the Faith

In spite of his reputation for atheism, Thomas Hobbes advocated uniformity of religion throughout the state (1651). Hobbes had seen religious dissension lead to civil strife, political instability, and bloody wars. He thought that religious uniformity would help, for a common religion is one less occasion for social conflict. Following Hobbes, it might be argued that belief in God, although a minimal religious commonality, might yet be sufficient in some circumstances to avoid social rancor.

Regardless of whether religious uniformity ever has or can contribute to social harmony, providing social harmony is a function of religion that is no longer needed or possible. It is not possible because in order to act as a social tranquilizer, religious uniformity must arise naturally and not feel imposed in the face of contrary religious sentiments. The generations immediately following Hobbes came to realize this and settled on toleration as preferable to imposed uniformity as a peacekeeping policy. However, imposed uniformity is the only uniformity that might arise today. We have come to live largely in a world of choices, and we would have to overturn too much history, technology, and ideology to remove religious belief from that world of choice. There is now a market of sorts in religious beliefs, and that market will not naturally produce only a single product. If we want only a single religious product, we would have to close down the market and have the religious equivalent of a command economy. With a strong enough hand, we could perhaps create a uniform religion in the modern world, but the cost of the imposition would be a net loss in social harmony. Today, it is not possible for religious uniformity to increase civil peace.

Nor is it needed. Religious toleration has become so ingrained that differences of belief seldom cause civil disorder. This claim may seem belied by the recent and ongoing horrendous violence between religious groups: In Ireland we see Protestants versus Catholics; in former Yugoslavia, Muslims, Catholics, and Orthodox clashed; in Sri Lanka, Buddhists and Hindus; in Israel/Palestine, Jews and Muslims; in Sudan, Christians and Muslims; in India, Muslims and Hindus. But these apparently religious wars are not wars over belief. The factions are not incensed that others have different metaphysical views on the nature of the Supreme Being. For the most part, even the most reactionary religious fanatics allow that people are entitled to their own religious beliefs (even if only in private). Religious affiliations in these conflicts have become the markings of different ethnic, national, or social groupings. The Israeli government and the Palestinian Authority are indifferent to the religious beliefs of the land's inhabitants; my guess is that Menachem Begin and Yasser Arafat were closer to each other in spiritual beliefs than either of them was to the Chief Rabbi or Grand Mufti of Jerusalem. Surely, there were atheist "Muslim" Bosnians who were being slaughtered by atheist "Catholic" Croats and atheist "Orthodox" Serbians. Hindus and Muslims who burn each other in Gujurat might leave a Christian in their midst unmolested because belief difference is not really what their rage is about. The Belfast Protestant who stones Irish Catholic schoolgirls has no beef with Vietnamese Catholics, and an IRA bomber would not have considered blowing up a Berlin *Kneipe* filled with Prussian Lutherans. The origins of many of these disputes may have lain in disagreements of belief, but those disagreements no longer provide their energy. There is a great need for advancing social harmony and overcoming historical hatreds and ethnic, national, and "racial" conflicts. Nowadays, however, aligning religious beliefs would be of little help.

In any event, belief in the theologians' God is a poor candidate for a world-harmonizing faith. Professing the baseline God would hardly make one religiously acceptable to the overwhelming majority of the world's faithful.[20] Moreover, the chances of worldwide conversion to the new theology, of a baseline God becoming the center of a universal religion, are no better (perhaps worse) than the universal triumph of atheism.

Oxymoronically, there is a sort of "intrapersonal social harmony" that belief in God may serve. Even if others are indifferent to your faith, you may feel that you are being faithless to others if you fail to believe what they believe. Nation, tribe, and clan may be so strongly identified with faith that departure from it can feel like betrayal. So, if belief in the baseline God felt as if it acquitted one's creedal obligations to nation and family, even though it is not quite the God of the nation or family, it might ease a troubled social conscience.

In a Jewish context, creedal loyalty caries relatively little weight. What the nation and your parents traditionally demanded was ritual observance, not orthodox faith. The ancestral *way of life* was the mark of loyalty, regardless of the accompanying beliefs.

Although the emphasis on practice is pronounced in traditional Judaism, it is hardly unique to it. Most social groups, families included, judge faithfulness on what is done rather than what is believed, but that is in part because there is an assumption that belief grounds practice and practice manifests belief. The assumption is sometimes false; habit and fear of nonconformity can sustain non-believers' orthodox practice indefinitely. Surely, though, the practice of nonbelievers is liable to be unsatisfactory. It may feel hypocritical, duplicitous, or simply empty. It may lack the energy that vitalizes the practice. Religious practice usually does need religious belief, and so, if social loyalty requires traditional practice, a belief in God may be a prerequisite to social loyalty. The relationship between religious practice and theistic belief gets more attention later. For now, we suppose that there is a relationship of mutual support and ask whether the baseline God holds up her end of things.

Since she is not a commander, a desirer, or an appreciator, it is difficult to see how belief in the theologians' God can motivate practice. This is not to say that religious practice cannot be motivated without the old God, just that it is unclear how belief in the baseline God would provide the motivation. Structural possibilities for the emergence of the good might motivate efforts to realize the good, but why would it motivate traditional ritual?

In sum, where nothing more than the word "God" is wanted to make you at one with a social group, the baseline God suffices. However, in those cases, it is seldom necessary. Where a belief with a certain content is needed, neither the baseline God nor any of its close kin tend to provide the needed content.

6

SOMEONE TO WATCH OVER ME

Emotional Succor

In chapter 4, we catalogued the ways that belief in God could deliver one from the fears and sorrows that accompany the mundane human condition. God could guarantee a good personal ending: an ultimately happy life; a good general ending, universal peace and justice; and, if you don't like endings, no ending at all—life everlasting. Even without guarantees, God keeps hope alive. Indeed, long after the race is run and the losses are suffered, hope stays alive because God can reverse any loss and compensate for any injury. Furthermore, all losses are justified and given meaning by contributing to God's plan. Belief in God transports us from the absurd and wicked world of injustice, disappointment, and pointless pain to a transcendent realm of goodness and meaning. At least, that is what belief in the old God could do. What solace is to be had from the new God?

The Divine Safety Net

Alas, the security that comes with guarantees is not to be had from belief in the baseline God. A structural possibility of goodness is quite compatible with unending and unremitting evil. There is no inevitability with the baseline God. It tells us that goodness may come, not that it must. The theologians' God is nothing that should alleviate the anxious awareness that all that we value may suddenly and irretrievably be destroyed. The universe is not compelled to preserve our lives or the lives of our loved ones nor does it lock in the fortune of our most cherished projects.

The success of all of our goals is entirely contingent. Believers in the theologians' God must live knowing not only that their happiness is uncertain, but also that their worst nightmares are possible. Much of the calm that faith famously bestows on the faithful is based on the companion conviction that "everything is going to be all right." As that conviction finds no grounding in the baseline God, it is hard to see how faith in her brings the peace of God. Belief in her is no cause to relax. Everything that you care about is still in play. Your ultimate worries are not neurotic, they are an accurate emotional reflection of the metaphysical situation.

Taking God's Perspective

Do other forms of the theologians' new God undermine the basis for metaphysical fear? Let us start with the organic universe variant. Nothing about the unity of such a universe, the interconnectedness of its constituent parts, guarantees the present or future well-being of any of its components. I may be a cog in the world machine, a cell in the cosmic body, and still come to a bad end.

Of course, from the perspective of the whole, the well-being of the part *per se* is not of much importance. In an organic universe, I supposedly have good reason to abandon my narrow, individual, *partial* perspective and adopt the universal viewpoint, for I, and my real purposes, are inseparable from the universe. Having taken the universe's perspective, I am freed from the concerns of my former, narrow perspective.

There are a number of problems with this analysis. First, why should organicity make me consider my individual interests subordinate to the universe's interests? Typically, we think it rational for a team player to make the team's success his highest priority because we assume that his individual success is best served by the team's success. When this assumption is false, the rationale for team spirit is shaken. Well, it is not clear that the analogous assumption *is* true in the organic universe. If my purposes, my deepest and ultimate concerns, are the well-being of Mitchell Silver (MS), his family and friends, the Jewish people, and the Chicago Cubs, how am I consoled by the knowledge that they all will fare poorly, but in doing so, they will serve the good of the universe of which they are members? The universal good was not what I was worried about. Rather than feeling consoled, I feel exploited. The universe is treating me as a means, not as an end. Am I to be comforted by such un-Kantian treatment at the hands of the universe?

It may be replied that I am misunderstanding how organicity comforts. By showing me my role in the universe, the organic conception of God allows me to make the universe's perspective my own. It changes my ultimate concerns. Instead of identifying with that social construct, MS, and his parochial concerns, I identify with the universe, that self-standing, natural reality of which I am an integral part. MS is not mollified, but in an important sense, I am no longer MS. His interests have disappeared, replaced by a broader—indeed, the broadest—set of interests.

We momentarily put aside the question of what is the referent of the preceding "I" that has foolishly identified with MS, but can wisely identify with the universe. Let us suppose that we can make good sense of such an identity switch. Still, what motivates the switch? True, I am liberated from the pain of hitching my welfare to the welfares of a doomed group of mortals and a cursed ball club, but the organic universe, although unified, is also not guaranteed to succeed. Its projects, for all that is entailed by organicity, may also fail. The universe's goals may have the advantage, unlike an individual's goals, of not being fated to fail,[1] but the anxiety we were trying to allay was the anxiety that came from contingency, from being un-guaranteed. Organicity does not ensure any of the universe's goals beyond persistent being, which is equally well ensured by a universe of any nature, so long as that universe cannot magically disappear.[2] By identifying with the universe's goals and disaffiliating with more self-centered aims, we have traded the gnawing fear that our petty personal desires will be thwarted, for the horror that God's purposes may fail. Little comfort there. In sum, the distress that stems from possible failure is unrelieved by belief in the baseline God or her organic universe variant, for such gods do not secure us from ultimate failure.

A second problem with employing belief in the baseline God to underwrite a warranted happiness is that it attributes a *perspective* to God, something that the baseline, even loaded with the organicity option, lacks. I cannot trade my perspective for the universe's if the universe does not have a perspective. What, then, would give the universe a perspective?

A perspective requires a location from which to observe and an observer to do the observing. The observer, in this case, must not only be able to register information, but also generate intentions. For I am being asked, when I am asked to take the God's-eye view, not only to see things as God sees them, but also to desire the things that God finds desirable and act as God would act. Presumably, the three are connected: God's perception and knowledge create God's desires and intentions. The perspective switch asks of me to see, want, and do as would God. A seeing, wanting, acting God is no longer simply an impersonal structure, organic or not. It is a belief/desire/intention system, the essence of personhood. If I am to take God's perspective, the universe must be a person, a large leap from the baseline God. Alternatively, I can provide the personality, and the universe can be a location that I can inhabit, a spot from which to view and judge things. Of course, it could not just be *a* spot, it would have to be all spots. The view from everywhere.[3]

How might the current I, MS, become the I who sees from the universe's point of view? This returns us to the question of the referent of these various "I"s. Either the referent of "I" when I am MS and when "I" am God remains the same or it doesn't. Suppose that it remains the same, that is, suppose that the "I" that is MS can give up MS's beliefs, extinguish MS's desires, abandon MS's goals, and substitute for all of these the universe's beliefs, desires, and goals and yet persist as the same I throughout. Clearly, there had to be more to the I than the beliefs, desires, and goals (and like psychological entities) if the wholesale substitution of one set of such things does not result in a new I. The traditional term for this something more is a soul. If I am a soul that *has* MS's psychology, but is not constituted by it, I might remain the soul that I am while outfitting myself with a new, simply divine, psychology. There are deep and subtle conceptual difficulties here,[4] but the surface logic is comprehensible: I used to think like MS, now I think like God. As to what I am, I am just a thinking thing that can remain who I am through drastic changes of what I think.

However, while the surface logic of massive psychological change in this Cartesian self is easy to accept, the metaphysics underlying it is not. To accept the existence of a soul that is not a congeries of physical and psychological phenomena we must accept, in Gilbert Ryle's famous phrase, a "ghost in the machine."[5] Loose talk about spirits and souls when they can be interpreted as stand-ins for psychological states, structures, and propensities is, perhaps, innocent enough. If, though, becoming God makes sense only if we are dis-embodiable, de-psychologized souls, we must note the high epistemological price that we are paying. We must believe ourselves pure spirit to become God. It is a belief that stretches modern credulity.

Perhaps the referents of the "I"s are different. Instead of the I that is MS becoming God, that I is extinguished and in its place a new I appears, with some interesting similarities to the old I (e.g., connections to MS's body, access to MS's memories), but without the belief/desire/intention system that made it MS.[6] MS can commit psychological suicide, and the living processes that sustained MS's psychology can be redeployed to instantiate God's mind.

It is murky how this process serves MS, let alone comforts him, except insofar as suicide can be said to serve and comfort those who suffer. However, the comfort that we seek from religious belief is something other, at least in the Western religious traditions, than escape from the wheel of existence. Indeed, one of the particular anxieties under discussion is the anxiety of contingency: fear of nonexistence, fear of death. That fear is not well addressed by a belief that my death will be followed by the birth of a happier being if that being is not me. Overall, it may be a very good thing that MS die so that a divine incarnation can live where MS once did. I just do not see what is in it for MS. Of course, if MS is a utilitarian, unselfishly seeking to maximize happiness, he may so love the world that he altruistically gives his, MS's, only life, so that (more of) God may live.

Perhaps it is misleadingly crude to assume that the MS-perspective I, and the God's perspective I, must be either the same or different. The literature on personal identity, indeed, the literature on object identity over time, should make us sensitive to the dynamic and vague criteria that we use to identify things, especially selves. Maybe MS can grow into God, in the same way that MS the child grew into MS the adult. At four years old, I had a considerably different belief/desire/intention system than I do now. In some sense, I am a different self with different interests. In the continuity, however, we recognize an ongoing self, too, and we don't think that the four-year-old MS, in maturing, altruistically traded in his interests for the interests of a middle-aged teacher. Rather, he became that teacher. Who did? Who is the "he"? We are inclined to say, rightly I think, that a diachronic social construct is built from synchronic ones. We tell the story of MS's life and make a temporally extended agent the hero. It is our narrative, though, that provides the temporal extension, the ongoing identity. Cannot we stretch the narrative further so that the adult MS becomes God, the identity maintained as it has hitherto been maintained by a narrative incorporation?

Creating a story wherein a mundane person takes the universe's perspective does give the theologians' God personality. Maybe we can comfort ourselves with the thought that when we become God, we will no longer care about our current sorrows. Our failed ambitions and lost loves will be matters of indifference. If we could be certain of this, we would have a guarantee of sorts, but it is an odd one, and its capacity to comfort is limited. Anyone who has tried to comfort a four-year-old with the thought that when he is older he will no longer care about his lost stuffed animal or bruised shin will be doubtful of the comfort that we will get from the belief that someday, if we are lucky enough to mature, we will no longer care about our chronic back pain or dead sister. Hence, there are high obstacles that a God must surmount before she can honestly make you fully secure. The baseline God seems ill-equipped to make the climb.

Helping Us Hope

What about the anxiety that is caused not by the precariousness of our situation, but its hopelessness? The universe may not achieve its desires, but, unlike us individuals, with our little goals, the universe is not fated for failure. It has a chance of success, and if we make its goals our goals, we can continue to hope. This is a hope that even a God bereft of any organicity offers, so long as it retains the baseline God's property of possible goodness.

Of course, any talk of making the universe's goals our goals leaves us with the aforementioned problem of attributing goals to the universe and thereby turning the universe into a person. However, the baseline God may offer ways to burnish hope that involves no anthropomorphizing, for faith in the structural possibility of goodness does seem a justification to continue to hope for goodness. Hope requires no guarantees, and perhaps not even very good odds. Hope is not expectation. The only rational demand made of hope is possibility. Certainly, hope that directs action to possible but improbable goals might be irrational if the action could have been more productively aimed at somewhat less desirable but more probably attainable goals. If a decent retirement income is acceptable, you should put savings into a 401(k) rather than spend them on possibly winning lottery tickets. When hope inspires action where the only alternative is resigned apathy or when hope is an attitude, an emotion that colors the spirit, but has no action-guiding role, then even the slimmest of hopes can be a valuable and rationally held possession.

The baseline God certainly offers that slim hope. That hope is the very definition of the baseline God; to believe in it is to believe that the universe contains the possibility of goodness, and goodness includes one's own happiness and vision of justice. But is it necessary to frame that hope as theism? Would not an atheism with a minimal dose of skepticism do as well? The hope we speak of is no more than the denial of the proposition that the universe has an inescapably evil destiny. Only an incorrigibly evil universe rules out rational hope, but skepticism regarding structural evil is quite compatible with atheism. An atheism can even remain uncompromised while going beyond mere skepticism concerning evil's ultimate victory; it can assert some evidence that the world is malleable and capable of taking on the shape of the good. This poses a question: Does labeling the grounds for our deepest hopes "God" enhance our hopes? The question is a particular instance of what, in different forms and contexts, is one of this book's overarching questions.

God has a distinguished record as a hope-enhancer. When there appeared nothing else to pin hopes on, people found hope through their faith in God, but that record as a hope-helper was built by the old God, the God of unlimited power, broad awareness, and interventionist capabilities (however uncertain her inclinations). It is a stretch of the baseline God to attribute power or awareness to it, but without personifying the universe one could perhaps claim that, since the universe contains the totality of being and its properties, all power and all awareness, at least in a distributed fashion, are attributes of the universe.

Alas, the power and awareness contained in the universe are not attributes at the disposal of the universe for interventionist purposes. The baseline God cannot be stretched to cover purposefulness nor can any of its nonpersonified versions. The baseline God's power is blind and uncaring. We can hope that its unintended surges come to our aid, but no more than the atheist can hope for luck in the unpredictable play of energy and matter. The baseline God offers the same hope that any rejection of metaphysical pessimism does.

One form of the theologians' new God makes humans the bearers of God's personality. We have intentions and purpose. We can be caring. We can deploy power for noble ends. Faith in God is faith that we have the possibility of creating goodness. This faith requires no supernaturalistic stretching of the baseline conception, for our personality and capacity for goodness are familiar natural phenomena. This approach, though, reduces hope in God to hope in ourselves, or at least hope in our collective selves. The theologians might not balk or be embarrassed at this formulation, but it does not seem a very different basis for hope than the most uncompromising secular humanism. All of its normative eggs are in the human basket. True, the baseline God underscores humanity's emergence from the universe, and variants of the baseline stress humanity's connection to and dependence on the universe. Now while any sane, scientifically informed, humanistic secularism would do the same, there is something to be gained by the explicit emphasis that human embeddedness in the world receives in the theologians' theology. It is only the rhetorical form of the belief, however, rather than its cognitive content, that makes this variant of the theologians' God superior to humanism as a staff of hope.

Justification

Nothing about the theologians' God, in any of its forms, directly compensates or restores a loss, and so belief in her holds no hope of this kind. No reunions in heaven with the dearly departed, no new families, à la Job, to replace the old family, no rewards granted for injuries suffered. God neither makes things come out right nor fixes them when they go wrong. Still, there is a subtle yet potent form of compensation for which the theologians' God may hold promise—justification.

There is a kind of compensation for suffering when suffering is understood as just. On some views, one form of just suffering is deserved punishment. If the sufferer merits the suffering as a criminal or sinner, the suffering is arguably a good thing. Many have consoled themselves with the thought that the sufferers of the world had it coming, and not a few may have been consoled by the belief that their own trials were merited. I find the (psycho)logic of retribution opaque, but there is no denying its intuitive appeal to many people.[7] "Because of our sins," "fallen man," and "paying off karmic debt" are all thoughts that have given sufferers some measure of solace by explaining and justifying their troubles.

The baseline God is no dispenser of justice nor is its organic variant, unless we add to the latter a karmic principle whereby mutual dependency causes what goes around to come around with a sure moral compass. However, as noted earlier, belief in such nice moral accountancy is not based on the evidence of nature, and any God that provides it is at a considerable remove from the theologians' naturalistic core conceptions. One must overlook a lot to believe that suffering is justly distributed in this world.

The more interesting form of just suffering is suffering that is a necessary means to a good end.[8] If you believe that your suffering serves some valuable purpose and if you think that it is a tool used to forge freedom, equality, justice, kindness, love, or beauty, then, although the pain may be very great, the added sting of its being pointless is removed. You might even be glad of the pain, proud of the contribution you make to the good, and happy to see the cause advanced by the only means that can advance it.

Meaning is closely related to justification. Meaningful suffering is comprehensibly connected to events beyond itself and points us to them. In its full sense, meaningful suffering, like justifiable suffering, serves some purpose. However, unlike justifiable suffering, meaningful suffering's purposes may not be good, or not good enough to make the suffering worthwhile. All justifiable suffering is meaningful, but not all meaningful suffering is justifiable. Still, I think that there is some consolation in believing that one's suffering is merely meaningful if the alternative is thinking it absurd and arbitrary.[9]

The old God was a great justifier of suffering, for the old God had a plan, and human suffering had a role in God's plan. If being in God's service had a price, at least the price helped to purchase a great prize. The realization of God's plan, the furthering of God's will, diminishes, perhaps even eradicates, the sorrows attendant on its pursuit. It certainly redeems them. Yet, once again, the theologians' God's lack of intentionality prevents her from functioning as the old God did. The baseline God is no planner. An organic God may embody blind Darwinian design, but it writes no script nor exerts any will. The theologians' God has no purposes, and therefore no purposes worth suffering for.

Might there be justification, or at least meaning, without purposes? Let us take justification first. To justify something involves showing that it meets some appropriate standard, typically a standard of moral rightness, but as the phrase "justify in terms of" shows, we can choose the standard that we are trying to meet in any particular justification. The justification of suffering involves meeting either the standard of deserved punishment or the standard of qualifying as necessary means to a worthy end. A standard of deserved punishment needs no God of any kind and, in any event, seems to be far from met by a large portion of the suffering that concerns us.

The "necessary means" standard does require ends, that is, goals and purposes, but they do not have to be those of the universe. The greatness of the universe's goals might justify great suffering, but the theologians' God does not give us a universe with goals. Humans, or other subsets of the universe, can be the agents whose ends justify some suffering. If our ends are good, they may redeem the hardship endured in their pursuit, but how does any God, baseline or otherwise, strengthen this human-goal-grounded sort of justification? Resort to our purposes and values is as humanistic in the field of justification as the reliance on our capacities was humanistic in the field of hope. Yet human goals are about all we have. We can plausibly attribute ends to animals and thereby modestly expand the possible justifications for suffering, but beyond that, any attribution of ends becomes either unfounded speculation, pure fantasy, or ignorant, empty hope: "The universe does have purposes, but they are far beyond our capacities to imagine them." This contentless ascription of intentions to the universe is a near-cousin of ineffability, and about as intellectually respectable.

There is, perhaps, one goal that we can impute to the universe and all of its elements: continued existence. It is a sort of default goal that we tend to attribute to everything. Although we know that rocks do not try to stay rocks or "try" anything at all, insofar as rocks have an interest, it most plausibly is the interest to keep on being (keep on rocking). Can this posited end, the continued existence of the universe, be the good that justifies suffering and consoles us for our losses? Only if existence, divorced from any qualitative description, strikes you as better than nothing. For myself, I do not see the difference. Being qua being, as an end, is not worth a dime. Not conscious being, not joyful being, not knowing being, not acting being, not loving, hating, laughing, creating, believing, or caring being, not beautiful or strong being. Just being. It's a great place to start, but as a destination, it justifies no journey, certainly not the one that we humans have been on.

Bare Meaningfulness

What about meaning without purposes? It is arguable that there can be no such thing, that all meaning, all semantics, is a species of knowledge, and that knowledge has an ineliminable pragmatic element; meanings are relationships between mind and the world, relationships that orient the organism toward action.

If some such argument were sound, then there would be no meanings without purposes. Let us suppose, however, that the argument is unsound and grant the possibility of nonpragmatic meaning, a meaning that is more retrospective than prospective, and even when prospective, the meaning we are considering treats the future with the passive contemplation that we normally reserve for the past. We understand why yesterday was what it was and why tomorrow will be what it will be. Here, meaning relates and contextualizes events. Things are tied together. They are given explanations. We see cause and effect, sign and signified, symbol and symbolized. Nothing mysterious, inexplicable, unconnected, disjoint, or absurd. These are not scientific explanations of how, rather, they are semantic accounts of why. No normative judgments are made, no goals are pursued. Instead, we only get a story that "makes sense."[10]

Might we take solace in understanding the ground of our suffering, not its rationale, but its explanation?[11] Is *un*mysterious, although still pointless, suffering more bearable than inexplicable sorrows? Let us test the consoling power of bare explanation with explanation at its most powerful, where the suffering to be explained comes to be understood as necessary, not to any end or purpose, or even within some particular natural scheme, but necessary in the most unrelative, absolute sense conceivable—metaphysically necessary, so to speak.[12]

I believe that such explicable suffering *is* drained of the resentment that intensifies much suffering.[13] We cannot coherently desire such metaphysically necessary suffering gone, and what cannot be coherently desired cannot be easily regretted. If acceptance of suffering, reconciliation to suffering, is a form of solace, there is consolation in understanding, for understanding is intellectual acceptance. Of course, none of our suffering, as far as we can see, flows from the absolute necessity that can induce complete understanding. Perhaps, though, insight into the local web that supports our woes pushes regret back to a distance where its weight is less felt. The suffering is diminished to the degree that it is understood. We are conditionally reconciled. "*Given the circumstances*, I can see how this had to be." We can still resent the circumstances.

So there is some solace in understanding how our suffering fits in with the ways of the world, but does the baseline God provide that understanding? No. As we concluded in chapter 5, the baseline God plays no explanatory role, at least not in any naturalistic or scientific sense, and because it is an intentionless deity, the baseline God is ill-suited as a dramatic articulation of natural events and also ill-suited to give some symbolic coherence to our tribulations. The old God, as a personification of natural processes, can become a satisfying *metaphorical* account of their workings. The new God, however, is no more than a label of the natural processes and leaves us no more satisfied or comprehending than did a direct grasp of the processes. Understanding may console, but the theologians' God does not provide understanding.

Nonrational Consolation

The discussion to this point suggests that it is difficult logically to derive comfort from a belief in the baseline God or a close variant. The logic of consolation requires the old, less credible, God. What if the belief's consoling power does not depend on intellectual content? What if the comfort comes not as a valid inference from the belief, but rather as a feeling that the belief produces noncognitively, or even fallaciously, but effectively, creates? Maybe, in logic, the baseline God should not comfort us, but if in fact it does, is its comforting effect any less valuable? There is an old joke about a man who plays the number forty-one in a lottery, wins, and becomes a millionaire. Asked why he played forty-one, he replies that he dreamt of seven number sixes dancing and decided to play the product of seven and six. Somehow, criticism of his computational abilities seems out of place.

Yet, we do not want to say that the hero of the anecdote's wealth is evidence of his mathematical prowess nor do we want to say that his computational abilities had no causal connection to the riches, for the fact that, in this instance, he was a bad (but not too bad) mathematician was a key to his success. In our joke, of course, we assume that it is just a coincidence that any dream, well calculated or not, provides a winning lottery number, and we therefore have little interest in exploring causal connections that we believe unlikely to be repeated. However, if belief in the theologians' God repeatedly consoles its believers, in spite of the fact that no consoling thoughts are implied by the belief, we must ask how this regular consolation is achieved. Whence the comforting power of this powerless God?

We can only speculate. One prominent possibility is ambiguity.[14] When asked to articulate a theology, "God" names the theologians' natural, eminently credible God, but, when propagating him as an object of daily faith, "God" becomes the name of the old lord of hosts, or at least something a lot nearer to him than the theologians' for-the-record God. There is no mystery in how comfort may be derived from a comfortless God if we equivocate in the derivation.

There are a number of possible forms that this equivocation can take. There may be an outright substitution of one concept for another. I have seen theological primers used in Mordecai Kaplan–inspired Reconstructionist religious schools that frankly employ the anthropomorphic "argument from design" to describe a God who makes the world as a weaver makes a cloak (Gevirtz 1995, 8–9). I suspect that throughout the religious world inspired by the theologians' work are people won over to "God" by the modern theology who promptly reconceptualize the "God" that won them over into the traditional comforter.

A pervasive vagueness may do equivocating work without resort to a sharp equivocation. If the image and description of God is not too precise, if it is very broad and none too specific, it will contain regions and border areas that can be worked into shape for the particular need at hand. Do we want an intellectual defense of our belief? We plow the naturalistic fields of the concept. Do we need to invoke God's name to buck up our courage in dangerous times? We trim back the foliage revealing the theurgic regions in the concept. If the concept is kept generally unfocused, we can hide inconvenient features in its blurred geography, but still have them available when the need arises.

There is also sloppiness aided by inertia and past associations. If we do not look too closely or carefully, we may simply fail to notice that there is nothing comforting in the new God. Shouldn't the new God always comfort, as did the old God? Indeed, tradition has conditioned us to be comforted by the word "God." As Pavlov's dogs salivated to the bell associated with food well after the correlation was broken, so we might for a while be comforted by "God" long after "God" is used to denote any comforting power.

Equivocations and conditioned responses are not fraudulently perpetuated misdirections. We know of religious fraud. Dostoyevsky's Grand Inquisitor argues that he uses religion to bedazzle the faithful for their own happiness, but we suspect that his own power might be the deeper motive. Although "noble lies" might be sincerely motivated, and falsehoods consciously spread in a truly benevolent spirit, there would still be moral questions of honesty, paternalism, and elitism. The equivocations that concern us are not such tricks, good or bad, but at worst illusions innocently and communally created.

A Helpful Image

I say "at worst" because, although not representative of the "literal" content of the theologians' theology, the comforting God may not be an illusion at all. Perhaps it should be thought of as a useful image, rather than as any sort of mistake, let alone fraud. Many performances are enhanced with images that are not, and known not to be, literally true. Swimmers are sometimes taught to imagine with each crawl stroke that their hands enter the water through the hole of a large donut. No one wants or expects the swimming student to believe that there actually is such a donut floating on the water forever two feet beyond her head, but it helps her swim well to imagine it. Emotions may also be conjured with images. Actors may imagine monsters in order to feel fear, the better to play fear. They do not believe that the monsters are really there. I've heard nervous public speakers advised to imagine their audience naked so as to steady their nerves.[15] The public-speaking tutors do not want their pupils to actually believe that the audience is naked. Maybe the theologians' God borrows the old God's characteristics as heuristic image. It miscategorizes such images to judge them as true or false. They should be judged as effective or ineffective.[16] It misunderstands their action to think that they work through a chain of inferences. Their mechanisms are more visceral.

The theologians often write as though the primary justification for the term "God" is its use as a linguistic image meant to do something for us, rather than to reveal the truth to us. God language is not the language of metaphysical speculation, it is the language of inspired human action and profound human emotion. Its job is to produce effects and affects, not beliefs. Or, if productive of belief, the belief itself is a kind of pragmatic device, a useful orientation toward the world, rather than an attempt at objective description of the world. One of the belief's greatest uses is that it enables us to "speak God's name" (Green 1992).

7

TALKING TO AND ABOUT GOD

Self-expression is widely held to be a good thing. Although some ideas are better kept hidden and some emotions are better suppressed, we think that there generally is value in manifesting our thoughts and feelings. Why do we think this is so? First, because until given expressive form, thoughts and feelings are not fully realized or fully experienced. If they are valuable thoughts and feelings, they merit such full realization. Second, it is often good to let others know of your thoughts and feelings, and their communication requires that they take a communicable form. Third, the expression of our thoughts and feelings may give them effects—effects beyond those of fully realizing them and communicating them to others, effects that unexpressed they may lack.

The theologians frequently defend their use of the word "God" not as representative of a belief, but as expressive of attitudes and as a shaper of attitudes. Saying "God" describes how one feels and how one wants to feel. It is also an act meant to spur certain other acts. It is not important what, if anything, it refers to; what is important is what it achieves (Kaplan 1936, 397).

Gratitude

Gratitude is an important moral emotion. It is right to acknowledge benefits conferred and to be appreciative of life's goods. However, many of life's most valuable goods are not attributable to friends, family, neighbors, or any human institution. Even when a good is attributable to the generosity of a friend, the friend and her generosity themselves are unaccounted for. If we feel ourselves fortunate, especially undeservedly fortunate, the urge to give thanks seems a laudable disposition. Should not this disposition have an outlet? To whom can we offer thanks for all of our undeserved, unattributable good fortune? We need an addressee for our thank-you notes, lest we get out of the habit of sending them. God is the addressee. Giving thanks to God allows us both to show that we are thankful and reminds us that we should be thankful. The habit of gratitude deepens.

Why is gratitude a laudable attitude? First, it keeps us humble. It is an implicit acknowledgment that much of our good fortune is unearned. This acknowledgment strengthens egalitarianism. While we thank others for all sorts of things, the paradigmatic ground for thanks is receipt of a gift. Gifts are not given in payment of services. We do not intentionally cause their coming to us. They just come. There is no moral reason that they should not have come to others. We are grateful that they came to us and mindful that others are no less worthy of them, which is a good thing to be mindful of.

Gratitude also involves a sense of obligation. Indeed, a typical expression of gratitude is, "I am indebted to you." When we are in debt, we must repay, so the feeling of gratitude inclines us to "give something back." If we are grateful for our fortunate status in the world, it is only natural that we should want to make the world a more fortunate place. A grateful attitude presages a giving attitude. If we need God to give thanks, and giving thanks fosters gratitude, and gratitude fosters egalitarianism and a sense of social obligation, then "God" has justified its place in our lexicon.

Do we need God to give thanks? Only if the expression of gratitude requires that *someone* be thanked and that we believe that no *human* agency is due ultimate thanks for our fortune.[1] *If someone* must be thanked, then we must be thankful to God, for God is all that is left.[2] There is no need, however, to turn to God if gratitude is not transitive or if it can take impersonal forces as its object. Can we be thankful, and express our thankfulness without being thankful to anyone or anything, not even to a posited anonymous benefactor?

I think not. At the heart of gratitude is the sense of indebtedness and that requires a creditor. For similar reasons, I do not think that impersonal forces are fit objects of gratitude. One cannot feel that one owes something to a benefactor whose beneficence was unintentional and who, moreover, has no goals, no concerns, and no desires and is completely indifferent to repayment.

This last point, of course, rules out the baseline God as an object of gratitude. Still, if the baseline God can intellectually establish "God's place" in our vocabulary, belief in it may be justified because perhaps "God" can then be used as an image to animate our feelings and expressions of gratitude. *Of course, the God of our verbal image is the old God,* intentionally gracious and bounteous; the image just helps us to have the right, grateful attitude toward the world by providing an auditor for our thanksgivings. When asked to reflect on the actual nature of reality, we drop the image and replace it with the respectable baseline God.

Cannot the frank atheist also enlist God as helpful image and useful metaphor? If the theologian can recommend a gracious and intentionally bountiful God as an effective image, an image *not* to be understood as an accurate representation of reality, why cannot an atheist do the same? Cannot the atheist say, "Let us speak of our good fortune *as though* it were bestowed by God in order to cultivate a useful attitude of gratitude, knowing of course, that there is no God"?

The atheist is as well positioned logically as our theologians to introduce, *as a heuristic,* an old God image, but psychologically, or rhetorically if you will, our theologians are better placed. The atheist and the believer in the baseline God have the same logical distance to leap over to get to a God that they can thank, but by getting the word "God" in the cognitive mix, the theologian makes the psychological jump easier. It may be a bait and switch, but bait and switches can work. The atheist's use of "God," even as an image or metaphor, is psychologically dissonant. It feels like a blatant contradiction. The theologians' use of an anthropomorphic gratitude-receiving "God" is equally contradictory to their beliefs, but it feels like a much subtler contradiction, less noticeable, less bothersome, and therefore more effective.

Hence, the baseline God may help in the expression of gratitude and all of the goods that flow from its expression. We have noted the value of gratitude as a reinforcer of egalitarian sentiments and social responsibility, to which we may add the value of fostering appreciation. We better realize how good something is when we thank others for it. Having a God to thank helps us to transform our blind luck into an appreciated gift.

If there is a downside to cultivating gratitude for the beneficial accidents of nature, it is one that might particularly trouble the theologians. Gratitude for good fortune reinforces the sense of a separate self. There is something unseemly about the sole survivor of a plane crash thanking God for his survival. Why should he not, with as much justice and more morality, condemn God for leaving his dead fellow passengers unrescued? Why should I thank God for my children's health rather than curse

God for the millions of children suffering from terrible diseases? Why even feel blessed for my peaceful, free life while others are tortured, enslaved, and warred upon? This grateful attitude rests on a vision of myself as significantly separate from others. I am me and they are not. A reasonable enough proposition for most of us, but the theologians' "organic universe" leanings should make them frown on such an attitude. If I am truly at one with all of being, I should be no more thankful for MS's happiness than anyone else in the universe is, for they are as much, or as little, MS as I am. Indeed, taken to the mystical extreme, it is even hard to make sense of individual good fortune, for individuality itself is an illusion.[3] Insofar as "God" is a heuristic to express gratitude, it is in tension with one of its other major expressive functions—a means of expressing connectedness.

"God" Brings Us Together

The fundamental religious experience that the theologians wish most to express is the mystical sense that "all is one" (Green 1992, 43; Lerner 2000, 74). It is an experience of overwhelming value to them and fraught with significance. The urge to give it voice is irresistible (Green 1992, xxi). "God" is the name that they give to this experience of an all-encompassing unity. They argue that it is the only word with a history nearly adequate (although still quite inadequate) to suggest the nature of the experience.[4]

This experience of cosmic unity is elusive. Few are steadily in its grips. Some never get a clear sense of it. The theologians, however, believe that everyone is dimly aware of it, and all have the potential to generate, deepen, and sharpen the feeling of universal oneness. It is an experience that can be cultivated. Speaking of it, speaking *to* it, is a central mode of its cultivation. "God" labels the experience, and by that labeling, not only are we enabled to refer to the experience, but we are also given the means to contemplate and propagate it. The name helps us recall the experience. The name helps us stimulate it for others. The theologians think that this is all to the good, for they believe that the experience mirrors a profound truth and produces the greatest happiness and highest morality. Whether this judgment of the experience is sound is not the question at hand. Let us grant the value of the experience. We still can wonder about the value of calling the experience "God."

We must be careful here. We want to examine "God" as the name of an experience, not as the name for the cause of the experience or for whatever the experience may be an experience of. We are asking about "God" as a term for the experience of oneness, not as a term for the reality, should there be any reality, to the oneness itself. Such care is often missing; and there is frequently a good deal of equivocation in religious language between mystical experience and the reality that it purports to reveal. (Although, I must concede, if all is one, the charge of equivocation does not make much sense.[5])

"God," if it is meant to refer to the baseline God, is a poor term for the mystical experience of unity. The structure of reality that makes goodness possible *may* be just an experience, but we have been given no reason to adopt this narrow interpretation. The attractiveness of the baseline God is its breadth; whatever makes goodness possible is God. To restrict God to the experiential components of reality is to implausibly declare that all good things emerge from experiences and only experiences, indeed, from one particular type of experience, the experience of oneness. It may not be implausible to say that only experiences are good or even that the experience of oneness is the highest good, but that is different from saying that these goods are created and made possible solely in the experiential realm. Nothing about the baseline God, the structural ground of goodness, suggests that it is wise to conflate it with the experience of oneness. Why make the structural grounds of goodness and the experience of oneness co-referents of "God"?

A better case can be made for naming the mystical experience after the theologians' organic God, not the baseline God. That God, which is the totality of beings integrated into a single Being—the universe as an organism—is presumably the cause or object of the mystical experience, but it is still not the experience itself, and in this case it remains a bad mistake to confuse an experience with its cause or object. It leads to self-validating certainty, good for our confidence, but bad as a guide to action.[6] Infallibility is best left to other religious traditions. If we want to speak of the experience of oneness, let us not speak of the One. The world may be One, and the experience of oneness may be sufficient evidence for the world's oneness, but let us allow for the possibility that the experience may not precisely reveal reality. That possibility can only be kept open if we have separate terms for the experience and its object.

We want, then, to judge "God" as a name for the *experience* of universal unity. Although the baseline God and the organic variant, not to mention the traditional God of our fathers, are conceived of as much more than experiences and therefore should not be asked to share their name with the subjective mystical condition, "God" does have a long history as the name of something very experience-like. God as "the still, small voice," God as a kingdom "inside you," God as Brahma that is identical with Atman, ultimate reality that is the true self—all such characterizations make God the traditional name for the mystical experience. Even in this strain, "God" is usually the name for the experience *and* its cause/object. Religion is not psychology, and like most non-psychologically oriented areas of life, it seldom needs to clearly distinguish subject and object. As pragmatic theologians, however, we ought to discern which meanings of "God" do which work. The discernment demands some linguistic housekeeping.

Most of our commonly used names for experiences describe emotions: anger, fear, hatred, pride, joy, love. By themselves, the terms convey very little content. The terms suggest evaluative attitudes, feels, intensities, perhaps some sensations, but no objective substances. Our experiences do not typically tell us what they are experiences of. For that, we need the more circuitous phrase "an experience of." Love is always an experience, and so love of a cat is an experience. The cat, however, is not an experience. If we want to speak of the experience of a cat without giving that experience a specific emotional coloration, we must speak of "the experience of a cat."

Now we can settle on "the experience of God" as the name of the mystical experience, and if God is the organic God, the phrase has reasonable motivation. However, might we not be better off with a word that directly describes the content and connotes the emotive features claimed for the mystical experience? If it is an experience of connectedness or oneness with all of being, why not call it that? Better yet, why not employ terms that are already suggestive of subjectivity and descriptive of unity: "universal empathy, solidarity, identification," "cosmic awareness," even the Whitmanesque "Self," or "world soul?" Such terms point more directly at subjectivity and more precisely at connectedness than does "God." True, they may lose the richness of the term "God," a richness that the mystical experience may seem to merit. The price, though, of that richness is vagueness and misdirection, which sully the clarity and purity of the experience, even as they laden it with precious associations.

Perhaps the *effectiveness* of a heuristic God needs the precious associations more than it needs clarity and rigor. If we want to bring people together with a name, we want it to name what we have in common, not the feeling that we have something in common. A helpful image's effectiveness depends on its being treated as real, at least in the same sense that good acting treats the dramatic situation as real. If we want God to help us feel connected, we should speak and think of him as more than that feeling, we should speak and think of him as the objective justification of the feeling, the real ground of our connectedness. Here is the rub. If God is to remain a helpful *heuristic* and not become an illusion, we must speak and think of him as real without actually believing that he is real. Here we come to the main problem with God the heuristic. Most heuristics are treated as real in limited contexts. The swimmer knows when and where to act as though there is a donut floating on the water, the actor knows when to fear the stage ghost and when not to. Disbelief in the reality of an image is manifested by the ability to drop it in contexts when it no longer serves. An image that is supposed to guide behavior in all contexts, that is always appropriate and should never be dropped, is indistinguishable from a fully held belief. The feelings and effects that we want "God" to engender are not for limited contexts. We want them to be dispositions that shape our character and pervade every area of our lives. "Belief" can only be a heuristic if it is limited belief, that is, "make-believe," but "make-believe" would rob "God" of all of its most powerful effects. Few who only conjure God when in need of consolation, thanksgiving, communion, solidarity, or existential exultation, *fully aware* that he is a spirit of their own fancy and subject to dismissal when no longer needed, will be well served by the device. They are like the rare patients who find placebos effective in full knowledge that they are taking placebos. Such patients exist, but to pull off such a trick, they must be either among the most refined and subtle of self-reflective sophisticates or fools. Our theologians, when recommending this course, are clearly among the former group. Most people cannot bring it off, but they are not fools either. For most people, placebos unmasked simply don't work. For most people, God, as a heuristic device, simply does not work.

The theologians could argue that this is a heuristic with a difference. It is not conjuring as imagination, but conjuring as creation. God begins as an image, the image creates attitudes and behaviors, which in turn makes God real. We start with an image of oneness, the image stimulates the feeling of oneness, the feeling gets us to treat each other as part of a single being, and such behavior creates the unity. The charges of equivocation, the theologians can argue, stem from a static logicism, when a dynamic dialectic is called for to understand this God-making process. "God" is the name of an image at one stage of the process, an experience at a second stage, and an objective reality at yet another stage.[7] These stages are not necessarily temporally sequential. In the life of the religious, God is at all of these stages simultaneously, and so "God" should be multi-referential, or better yet, should refer to the complex, ongoing process. "God" is the unique name that ontologically precedes its referent. In the beginning is the word.[8]

There is a sort of idealism to this bootstrapped God, where the idea of divinity gives birth to the reality of divinity. If the process can be credited, we have found a role for "God" of surpassing utility: "God" creates God, not just as a belief in the mind of the speaker of the name (although that individual belief-formation may be a stage of God in the making), but as a real property attributable to all of being. This is an extreme version of Green's claim that "the Shekinah, the divine presence in our world, does not dwell where she is not wanted" (1992, 37). It is the stronger claim that God only exists where she is imagined and named.[9]

It is not surprising to find religious thought that is at bottom idealistic, but, as is the case with many idealisms, it feels that we have pulled a rabbit from a hat. The rabbit looks real enough, and we saw with our own eyes that the hat was empty of rabbits. It is, however, hard to shake the feeling that some undetected sleight of hand, some fraud, was involved. We are disinclined to go into the rabbit-breeding business by buying a case of top hats and disinclined to make gods out of a universe that is initially empty of divinity.

Prayers are the top hats from which we are (sometimes) asked to pull the theologians' God. Prayer, employing "God" as its central ingredient, is the primary vehicle used to express and create our fundamental religious experiences, whether of gratitude, appreciation, vulnerability, abundance, or connectedness. How does prayer function? In particular, what gears in the prayer wheel does "God" engage?

Prayer

Arthur Green writes that "religion begins . . . with the need to pray," a need that precedes theology (1992, xxiii). "We find ourselves praying," Green tells us, "that is an incontrovertible fact, an essential datum of our theology" (1992, 16). Kaplan (1985, 213–17) and Lerner (2000, 274–76) treat prayer more as a religious tool than a religious given, but all three theologians agree that a fundamental justification for belief in God is the great value of saying "God" in worship. We need a belief in God because we need to say "God," and we need to say "God" because we need to pray. If prayer is not a natural part of human life, at the very least it is a crucial part of the *good* human life. Something essentially human and highly valuable is expressed in prayer, is achieved by prayer. God earns her keep by enabling our prayers.

Why should we want our prayers enabled? It is not enough to say that prayer is a natural human activity, even supposing that that is so. Not all natural actions are to be encouraged. Sexual aggression and fearful flight are natural in many situations. We find ourselves lusting, we find ourselves frightened, and we could easily find ourselves criminally raping or cowardly fleeing if we sought cultural enablers for all of our natural inclinations, rather than cultural inhibitors for some of them. Some natural inclinations are bad, and some of these bad natural inclinations are resistible. Praying, if it is a natural inclination, is demonstrably a resistible one; many people do not pray. So the issue of whether to encourage prayer turns on its value; if we want to enable our prayers, it must be because we conclude that praying is good.

There are prayers of thanksgiving, and we have already explored the value of expressing gratitude for life's unmerited "blessings." We have also discussed the ability of "God" to name and thereby strengthen the experience of oneness with the universe (an experience whose value we examined earlier in chapter 5). That naming of the mystical experience often occurs in prayer, and those prayers are valuable to the extent that the naming is. Are, however, prayers in general—expressions to and about God—valuable?

Most of the value of prayer, if value there is, will be found in its ability to realize whatever values accrue to belief in God or accrue to holding a *behavior-guiding image* of God, for prayer reinforces the belief or image and is a major vehicle for bringing the beliefs and images into play; indeed, in some cases, it is the only way to bring them into play. Is belief in God good because such belief consoles? It is through prayer that we effectuate this consolation. Is belief in God good because it makes us conscious of the beauty, joy, and sheer abundance of being? It is prayer that brings these peak experiences to consciousness. Is the image of "all humanity united in God" a prompt to empathy? That image is given life and power through prayer. Does the very idea of God stimulate ecological responsibility? The idea is made vivid and present through prayer. So say the promoters of prayer.

The attentive reader may have noticed an apparent circularity. I have said that the theologians' views suggest that we need a belief in God because we need the word "God," but I now appear to be saying that the value they find in the word "God" is grounded in the value of belief in God. Which is it? Is the base value the belief in or at least the idea of God, and is the value of verbal expression of that belief or idea, that is, prayer, a derivative value? Or is speaking to and about God the fundamental good here, and theistic belief and imagery merely useful psychological tools for supporting prayer?

I suspect that the theologians would object to the analytical separation. The idea of God, belief in God, and praying to and about God comprise a mutually supporting complex whose value to humans is bestowed by the whole. There may be insights to be had from focusing on prayer or belief or imagery as the primary bearer of religious value, but those insights should not be mistaken for a synoptic vision of the ground of religious value.

I agree, but human understanding is built by exploring one perspective at a time. Our knowledge that there are other perspectives enjoins us eventually to take those perspectives into account in our quest for a fuller understanding. It does not, however, prohibit concentrated observation from each perspective in its turn. Since the theologians suggest that prayer is prior, in some sense, to theistic belief or conceptualization, the perspective that makes prayer the fundamental value of religious life is worth taking.

What sort of verbal expressions count as prayers? Certainly not all text and talk that speak of God. Theology is not prayer nor is religious fiction that happens to refer to God in the narrative. At times, however, speaking about God is prayer. Praise is a type of prayer that can be done in the grammatical third person, adoration is another. Contemplation of God, involving talk about God, can also be prayer. We repeat descriptions of God, chant his name, and review his aliases, not necessarily to get his attention, but to direct our attention.

Hence, talk about God may or may not be prayer. Surely, that particular bits of talk about God count as prayer is partly a result of tradition shaped by historical contingencies. Some literature about God gets into the prayer book and some do not. Inclusion may have nothing to do with an intrinsic property of the writing. The politics or piety of one poet may have helped his meditations on God secure a spot in the liturgy when qualitatively similar poems of another, less powerful or respected poet fail to become enshrined. Historical circumstances, though, are only part of the story. To even be a candidate for prayer status, talk about God must be of a certain type. We put off for now what that type is, merely noting that some types of prayer are talk *about* God.

Mostly, however, we think of prayer as addressed *to* God, and we think of all addresses to God as prayer.[10] Prayer typology depends on *what* is being said to God. Praise and adoration can be directed to God as well as about him. "God, you are great" and "God, I love you" are as common as "God is great" and "I love God," but most types of prayer must take an exclusively second-person form: thanksgiving, petition, intercession, confession. We thank and plead and confess *to* someone.[11] Herein lies the key to what kinds of third-person God-talk have prayer-status potential; it is third-person God-talk that is necessarily transformable to second-person talk. We imagine God overhearing our third-person prayers, which are really formal, perhaps deferential, devices for a dialogue with God. Only praise of *a person*, only adoration of *a person*, only contemplation of *a person* become prayers. We may substitute impersonal terms that disguise the personality that our prayers address, praising the source of being, adoring the light of the world, and meditating on eternity. However, if the source of being were understood as unintelligent matter, if the light of the world were conceived of as uncomprehending photons, and if eternity were judged to be an atemporal, ever-present, mindless reality, our praise, adoration, and contemplation would not become prayer. Prayer demands a personal God.

There are a number of different forms that the person-like object of prayer can take. We can, of course, address the traditional God, a transcendent, powerful, benevolent, intelligent being, but the person-object of our prayers can be realized through alternative conceptions: An organic and conscious universe may be person enough to receive prayers, and an unconscious universe treated *as if* it were conscious may also serve (see Kaplan 1985, 216). "God" as a symbol for other human beings is a possibility, as is "God" as a stand-in for oneself or one's ideal self. All these provide person-like entities to whom we can offer prayers. The last three formations, unlike the first two (old-style monotheism and an actually conscious universe), have the advantage of not relying on doubtful metaphysical speculation. Treating the universe as if it were conscious can be done whether or not it is conscious.[12] Belief in the personality of oneself, actual or idealized, and of other human beings is commonsense metaphysics, and any symbol for them can unproblematically be given the personal treatment.

None of these is, in itself, the baseline God or the organic variant. Treating the universe as if it were a person, however, is merely applying a technique to the organic variant, and if we view our own or others' personality as part of the structure of reality that makes goodness possible, then worshipping "God" as a symbol of human personality is consonant with theological baselining. Hence, "God" can become a symbol that makes metaphysically modest conceptions fitting objects of prayer.

Reverential and Contemplative Prayer

What do we get out of verbally praising, adoring or loving the universe, others, or ourselves dressed as "God"? What are the effects of saying to ourselves, or publicly in the hearing of others, that "God" is altogether excellent and our heart's highest desire? One possible effect of repeated recitation is to persuade us of the truth of what is being recited, that is, to engender belief in the prayer's claims. If God is the universe, constant praise of God helps to convince us that the universe is good, and believing that the universe is good goes a long way toward reconciling ourselves to it.

Terms of praise and songs of love also can heighten our appreciation of the object of our devotions. As this is the universe that we are stuck with, why not learn better to appreciate it; as this is the universe that we are going to get, why not convince ourselves that it is the one that we most want? "If you can't be with the one you love. . . ." While this may smack of quietist resignation and is put to that use by some clerics, our theologians reject the quietist tendency of prayer. If anything, our theologians wish, through reverential prayer, to enlist us in the struggle to realize ideals by repeatedly declaring our recognition of their worth. If human personality is our ideal, the ritual expression of love of "God" can attach us ever more firmly to the value of human personality.

Appreciation can be more than resigned reconciliation or even loyal devotion to ideals. It can be deep enjoyment. By rehearsing the virtues and value of "God," we increase the pleasure that the universe provides us. Just as art criticism, music criticism, and literary criticism multiply our pleasure by reflecting on the aesthetic value embodied in works of art, so reverential worship adds to the delight that we take in describing the universe and/or our highest ideals.

However, most of these positive effects of reverential prayer can happen only if "God" the symbol is correctly understood by the worshiper. Loving the flag does not attach you to civil liberties if you understand the flag as a symbol of military might, and loving God does not foster loving one's neighbor if the former is not understood as a representative of the latter. Likewise, just as our pleasure in Shakespeare cannot be deepened by bardolatry wholly unrelated to his plays and poems, praising

"God's" wisdom does not enhance true appreciation of the universe if it causes us to picture an infinitely sage human rather than reflect on the creative power of vast, enduring processes unguided by any overarching master intelligence.

When the word "God" is misunderstood, most of the value of praying to God is lost.[13] Given their values, it should be important for the theologians that the "God" of reverential prayer be a symbol that illuminates the symbolized rather than obscures it; the value of devotion to the theologians' ideals and the value of enjoyment of reality's true features cannot be achieved by worshipping a misleading misrepresentation.

Although not reverential prayer, contemplative prayer that focuses on "God" makes similar demands of the word. If the contemplation is meant to have us better understand, or feel closer to, a reality, the symbol that we contemplate needs to be meaningfully connected to the reality that we hope to better understand and to which we feel closer. If meditating on "God" does not make us think of the theologians' God—a structural possibility of goodness or an organic universe—it is either misleading or empty. Now suppose that this word does have this effect, that is, contemplating "God" gives rise to knowledge of the universe's potential for goodness and its interconnectedness. What profit is there in this mediated contemplation? Why not directly contemplate the features that we want "God" to symbolize? If we say it is because we do not know what features that it should symbolize, we render "God" useless as a symbol. If we say that it symbolizes meanings and realities that are too deep, or too awesome, or too complex to contemplate directly, we merely fill the symbol's emptiness with obscurity.

Of course, there are infinitely rich associations with "God," reverberations and connotations that no other label or description can encompass (Kaplan 1936, 399). It is true that if we want to contemplate that rich legacy, only "God" will do, but, in their theology, the theologians are not claiming that whole legacy. They are dropping the King, Father, and Lord stuff. Indeed, they want to get those terms out of the prayers. So if "God" is kept in the prayers as the central symbol of contemplation, it is no longer the God of the whole legacy. We are picking and choosing from "God"'s past. Why not simply contemplate the chosen features? Is it because we want the whole unfathomable past without a few objectionable fathomable features? Fair enough. However, we should acknowledge that such prayer is in some tension with demystifying theology and may, probably does, incorporate remaining objectionable features within this unfathomable legacy that we blindly make the objects of our prayers.

We can attempt to justify contemplative prayer to "God" by completely severing the link to theology. "God" is a prayer heuristic. It is not a symbol embodying meaning, it is an image that has effects. We do not contemplate propositions with truth value when contemplating "God," rather, we contemplate images that create experiential value. We do not have to believe in centaurs or Pegasus to get pleasure from thinking about mythological beings that are horsey. We are free to use any fantastic horse image, if it works for us, in our meditations. If speaking to "God" in prayer makes one feel good, who cares what the imagery is to which you pretend to speak? Fantasy can be productively indulged without illusions. There are beautiful and uplifting fantasies. These are not Plato's noble lies. They are not lies at all, for they are not believed and not created to deceive. If incanting "God" in prayer induces desirable experiences, is not such an incantation rational? Would it not be absurd to advise someone against counting sheep as a means to sleep because, really, there are no sheep there?

To all these questions, I think that we must answer yes. Let "God" be whatever you need it to be if it makes your prayers do good things. Our endorsement, though, of such contemplative prayer comes with three further skeptical questions: Do, indeed can, most prayerful contemplatives hold God to be no more than a heuristic image?[14] If they can and do, does their contemplation have the promised effects? Can those effects be had without resort to "God"? We will find these questions usefully put to the next three forms of prayer that we discuss: confessional prayer, petitional prayer, and the overarching category of transformative prayer.

Confessional Prayer

Confession, it is widely acknowledged, is good for the soul. We think of unexpressed guilt as a festering sore that fresh air and sunlight help to heal. Do real psychological dynamics conform to this metaphor? Does verbalization diminish, remove the sting, and make a sense of guilt easier to bear? We can leave these questions to psychologists. Certainly, however, it is socially useful to have people *believe* that confession serves self-interested, psychological well-being. We want people owning up to their crimes, admitting their mistakes, and accepting responsibility for their errors. Confessions in the complete absence of fear of discovery may be rare, but the establishment of common belief that confession is good for the soul, just as widespread adoption of the view that honesty is the best policy, must lighten society's policing duties. Whether or not confession is good for the soul, it is good to have people believe that it is good for the soul. Moreover, with the widespread successful inculcation of that belief, we can expect significant emotional gains from all acts of confession, for they may lessen the original guilt and they will erase whatever guilt is associated with the additional sin of not confessing.

For the individual, *prayed* confessions have the added benefit of not necessarily leading to material consequences—good for the soul without being bad for the body. Religious doctrines usually try to undo this socially dysfunctional aspect of confessional prayer by devaluing, or by outright dismissing, confessional prayer's value when unaccompanied by social confession or social amends. Jewish tradition requires that you apologize to those that you have offended before your Yom Kippur confession to God.

There are practical social and individual benefits of confessional prayer even when unaccompanied by a more public coming clean. Acknowledgment of error is the beginning of correction. (It is always an early step in a twelve-step program.) The words of the prayed confession, even if they remain silent, give concrete form to fault. The Hebrew term often used to describe confessional prayer is *heshbon nefesh*, auditing of the soul. Without a proper auditing, there is no chance of putting the books in order. The confession, an honest, explicit look at how things stand, can initiate self-improvement. Better selves are a social and individual interest.

Confession also prepares forgiveness. The link is not logical, for one can be forgiven for what one does not admit—even for what one does not realize needs forgiveness. As an empirical matter, though confession almost always precedes forgiveness. It is reasonably supposed that this empirical link forges a mental association. "To receive forgiveness, I must first confess." Furthermore, because confession is sometimes sufficient, a good amount of guilt is probably assuaged by confessional prayer alone. It will not always work; there is too much experience of confession not followed by forgiveness for a constant and ubiquitous association. Still, many a soul surely has felt forgiven following confessional prayer.

Confession requires a comprehending recipient, but does it gain if "God" is the recipient? Yes, if "God" refers to the all-knowing judge who does not need your confession to discover your crime and who is going to punish you if you don't fess up. Yes, if "God" refers to an infinitely merciful Being who always does respond with forgiveness and has the power, in a forgiving mood, to lift the punishing decree. *Ex hypothese*, however, this is not what the theologians' "God" symbolizes.

It is an uncomprehending auditor that had no punishing plans nor any power to divert the material consequences of the sin. Why is confessing to *that* God any more beneficial than confessing directly and *literally* to oneself? Why make a symbol of oneself to confess to when the thing itself, that is, oneself, is so ready at hand? Is there something about the logic of confession that requires that an "other" be the recipient? Perhaps. Maybe a symbol of other people, a symbol of "your better self," or even a consciously pretended personification of an impersonal universe, upon hearing our confessions, does a better job of helping us to acknowledge our shortcomings, take responsibility for them, and move to correct them. Maybe confession to such "listeners" lessens guilt as no self-confession can, but it is not clear why, and it is hard to shake the lurking suspicion that confession to the new God is powerful because of connotations that "God" has with the old God.

Petitional Prayer

In spite of Jim Morrison's admonition, most people do petition the lord with prayer and think of prayer as mostly petitionary. They ask God to *do* something, for themselves, their family, their friends, humanity, the world. By now, the reader knows the analytical drill: The theologians' God does not intervene, and so the petitioner's prayer to "God," if the word is taken in the spirit of the theologians, must seek a nontheurgic effect. What might we get out of making requests of a being incapable of fulfilling them?

To begin with, all petitions are expressions of desire, and by articulating our desires we may, through our own resources, be able better to satisfy them. We see the goal more clearly, and announce, and perhaps thereby reinforce, the power of our motivation, and in naming our will, we may strengthen our commitment to its pursuit. Petitionary prayer may set a course and give us energy to move in that direction.

Paradoxically, petitionary prayer can help to extinguish desire. Articulation may reveal a desire as superficial, wrongheaded, or simply not genuine. Philosophers are fond of the quote, "How do I know what I mean till I see what I say?" but with equal insight we might quip "How do I know what I *don't* mean till I hear it said?" Petitionary prayer can help us to learn what we really do and really do not want, or less dramatically, how we prioritize our desires.

87

Prayer Shaping the Pray-er

Most modern advocates of prayer explain that they pray not to change God, but to change themselves. The theologians, as opponents of magic, must necessarily take this line, for their theology contains no God that can be changed, except insofar as God is identifiable with the one who prays. There is no changing God, unless it is by human self-transformation. We have discussed some of the valuable, human self-transformations that prayer might effect: Prayer might teach us to appreciate sheer being; it might reinforce our appreciation of the wonders of personality; it might firm our resolve to do better; it might deepen introspection and self-knowledge; it might increase identification with other humans or with the entire universe itself; and it might help to create extraordinary experiences of calm, bliss, relief, ecstasy, or self-transcendence. Finally, prayer can function as an outlet for emotions seeking an outlet. Prayer allows us to get it off our chest, whatever *it* is: an anguished cry of pain, an unburdening confession of guilt, a quivering admission of fear, or a joyous shout—a poetic, existential *Yabba Dabba Doo!* As strength would be discharged, so would love and joy. Prayer makes one's suffering, one's joy, and one's love part of the world. In a sense, it *realizes* one's deepest emotional life. All of these self-transformations are achieved by talking to God, by praying.[15]

Individuals' transformations are only part of the value of prayer. There is also community (trans)formation. I have been discussing prayer as though it is a private talk to God, and the image of the solitary pray-er is a standard one. But most commonly, and certainly in the Jewish tradition, prayer is public and communal. We talk to God together and within each other's hearing. One cannot help but wonder whether addressing God is primarily a vehicle for talking to each other or saying things that we might otherwise find embarrassing, awkward, compromising, or pretentious. It might, for example, do my heart good to express dependency or feelings of insignificance or failures of integrity, yet I am reluctant to directly and specifically report them to my fellow humans. By simultaneously, and in a standardized format, expressing these "embarrassments" to "God" within each other's hearing, we make the feelings public without being shamed. We can also praise human attributes and aspirations through God without feeling vain or pompous.

Prayer might also be a vehicle for talking with each other in a way that is unusually affirming, coordinated, hopeful, and unifying (Kaplan 1985, 218). For instance, some prayers may amount to joint declarations of intent, declarations that are given special solemnity and bindingness because they are done through and before "God," the most esteemed possible auditor and witness, the eternal witness. Moreover, we can declare our fondest hopes without feeling corny or naively optimistic. We reassure, console, and inspire each other through simultaneous, coordinated speech acts directed toward "God."

Furthermore, we strengthen, through public prayer, ties to our community's past by praying as they did and provide an anchor that can tether future generations to our community, for they can model their prayers on ours. Of course, public, ritual pronouncements need not be prayer, but speaking to "God" is particularly suited to be the core activity of lasting public ritual, which must be traditional and adaptable. "God" remains the stable, because protean, icon in our prayers.

Are these welcome changes to self and community achievable without prayer? I think we cannot discard the dialogical aspect of prayer and retain its benefits. We must talk to someone about these matters if we are to get these goods. However, will talking to oneself, or others, or some combination of self and others do as well as talking to God? We have seen how the answer often depends on which God we are praying to: It is harder to fill the shoes of the old God with human stand-ins than it is to substitute humans for the new God, but does the new God still, in general, have advantages as a listener over human auditors?

If it does, that is, if it is better to pray to the new God than to talk to oneself and other humans, it is mostly because such prayer camouflages the true nature of the auditor. By praying to "God," we disguise the absurdity of talking to an uncomprehending process, the social difficulties and imperfect communication of talking to other humans, and the solitude of talking to oneself. These advantages are real, the real advantages of softening our focus. If we spoke to each other directly, with no symbolic go-betweens, prayed cries of fear and shouts of glory would be more awkward. If we knowingly confessed to ourselves, without renaming our auditor, our postconfessional sense of forgiveness would feel less profound, and if we made humans, in the guise of our individual selves or other humans, the object of our "prayers,"[16] we would lose all connotations that the new God, by sharing her name with the old God, brings to the ritual: no ultimate power, no complete understanding, no guaranteed acceptance, no transcendent glory, no comfort from mystery. Praying to humans has none of these.

There are, however, advantages to praying to humans. No crises of faith; humans may not be all that we want them to be, but they are indubitably there. Furthermore, although humans may not respond, sometimes direct address to those from whom we seek a response is more effective than symbolic circumlocution. It may come down to matters of taste and personal inclinations. Some prefer to socialize at masked balls, others with well-identified friends. Some value oblique communication, others, sharp frontal declarations. Some are more moved by suggestive poetry than by well-defined manifestos. Some find a bit of obfuscation a helpful, tolerable, emotional and social lubricant; others, an unacceptable betrayal of a bedrock value.

Up to this point, our comparison of "praying" to humans and praying to God (understood as the new God) has brought out no decisive reason to prefer either mode, independent of personal inclination. Dispensing with God's name in favor of addressing humans goes beyond naturalism, beyond atheism and raises the specter, for it is a specter in some quarters of humanism.

Secularism and humanism are now so frequently linked that many treat them as a single doctrine, but a rejection or indifference to religion and God does not entail an elevation of human worth or significance. No human hubris need be involved in atheism. In trying to find a secular equivalent for prayer, I have proposed humans, in one form or another, as the God substitute and this does look very much like the apotheosis of our kind. Jewish tradition in particular is wary of this approach, for the struggle against idolatry, the worship of false gods, has been as definitive of Jewish tradition as any other single doctrine.

PART

2

8

AVOIDING IDOLATRY

The theologians' turning from supernaturalism is simultaneously a turning from metaphysical transcendence. Although they toy with transcendent themes (see chapter 3), the theologians' most prevalent descriptions of the divine are of an immanent God. God is not outside of nature. We are not to look for God in a ghostly, otherworldly realm. God is in nature. Although God is usually viewed as in all of nature, typically this pantheistic tendency is given a more or less humanistic emphasis. For the theologians, insofar as God can be said to be more in one aspect of nature than another, God is most in human nature. It is in human nature that we most clearly see God manifested. It is in the realization of human potential that God becomes fully realized, and it is in human well-being that God finds his contentment.[1] The old God was a transcendent, human-like being. The new God is immanent in real human beings.

Why, then, if the new God is essentially human, should we not dispense with it and speak directly of humans? In one form or another, it is a question that we have repeatedly posed. Perhaps it can most straightforwardly be put as follows: If the theologians' theology is so humanistic, why not dump it for a non-theistic humanism? Why not, as was suggested in the last chapter, pray to and about humans? Why not find the meaning of life directly in human purposes, rather than finding meaning in God's purposes, which are then identified with the noblest human purposes? What is gained by a theism so barely distinguishable from humanism?

One answer, albeit one with a paradoxical flavor, might be that the new theism, whose plausibility is grounded in its essential humanism, is valuable just because it *avoids* full-blown humanism. The theism is justified not by its humanism, but rather by its suggestion that humanism may not be all there is to value and meaning. Although God is immanent and most found in humans, God's separate name allows us to avoid a too quick identification between the divine and the human. We need God to avoid humanism. Secularism, that is, nontheism, it is feared, leads to humanism, and so belief in God is a bulwark against humanism.

There is something to this "secularism leads to humanism" claim, but first let us see what is not to it. Humanism does not lead to secularism by being identical or inseparable from it. Admittedly, humanism is easily conflated with secularism.[2] Friends of one are often friends of the other, and the enemies of each use "Secular Humanist" as a single epithet. Indeed, there are natural connections between the two, but they are logically distinct. Secularism, as I use the term, is naturalism plus atheism. It is the claim that this world, the phenomenal, natural world revealed by experience and investigated by science and *devoid of gods*, is the only world we have reason to believe exists, and that claim implies nothing about the value or role of humans nor about the proper way a human ought to live his or her life. A secularist can consistently hold that humans are worthless beings, and that one ought to get as much selfish pleasure as one can without a thought about the needs of humanity. Such a doctrine would hardly qualify as humanism, in spite of the absence of God.

However, though there is no *strict logical* link, there is a natural connection between secularism and humanism. If there is no God to ground one's values, no God to guide one's life, no God to serve, then "humanity" becomes a plausible candidate to perform those functions. Divine values are replaced by human values, divine commands by human needs, divine service by service to humanity. Something, the argument goes, must perform God's functions, for those functions serve universal human needs. If God does not, then humanity will. Therefore, if we have reason to fear rushing in where God has formerly trodden, we are well advised to keep God in place, even if the only God that we can keep in place is the new, very human-centered God of the theologians. For although immanent in humans, the new God, with its own name, has enough of the semblance of theism about it and extra-human connotations to save us from humanism. God's value is that it gives us something to worship that is *not* human. Theism saves us from humanism. We put off for now how the rescue is purportedly effected to examine why anyone, independently of any attitude toward theism, might want to be saved from humanism. Is there anything in humanism that should be worrisome to the secularist? If humanism, except for theistic scruples, is comfortable, we need not fear that rejecting God makes us humanists. Are there potential secularist worries about humanism? Let us begin by examining the theists' anxiety over humanism and see if secularists might share those worries or analogous ones.

Although the religious may rail against secular humanism's dethroning of God (the secularist part of secular humanism), their objections are equally motivated by the coronation of humanity. This is an objection that a secularist can share; one does not have to value or believe in God to question the wisdom of making human well-being one's supreme or sole value. For theists, humanism is simple idolatry. Humanism in effect makes humanity the supreme being. Granted, no sane humanist thinks of humanity as having all the properties associated with the traditional Western God, but by elevating human welfare and human taste to the measuring stick of all value, humanism gives humanity the highest rank in the order of beings, makes humanity the "supreme" being. By self-consciously embracing this measuring stick, by advocating its adoption, by ritualizing our devotion to it, we in effect worship humanity, worship ourselves.[3]

Secularists, of course, do not mind that God is not worshipped, but nontheists may still mind that humanity *is* worshipped. Perhaps worshipping as an activity is objectionable, regardless of the object of worship. Perhaps worshipping is, ipso facto, idolatry. Why might this be so? In their survey of Jewish conceptions of idolatry, Moshe Halberthal and Avishai Margalit catalogue the ideas and actions that have been labeled as idolatrous (1992). They find that idolatry is variously likened to marital infidelity, political rebellion, intellectual confusion, misrepresentation, ritual error, and lawlessness and conclude that the master notion that seems to unify these sundry ideas is that idolatry consists of worshipping that which is unworthy of worship.

What if nothing is worthy of worship? In that case, any act of worship is bound to amount to idolatry, regardless of the reality, goodness, power, or relative metaphysical ranking of the object of worship. The best, the most valuable of beings, might still not merit worship, and so any worshipping is bound to turn us into idolaters. Is humanism therefore idolatrous?[4]

To the charge of idolatry there are two possible humanist replies. The first simply denies that humanism entails worshipping humanity.

Does humanism worship humanity? It depends on the form and content of the humanism. A humanism that merely claimed human well-being was an important and appropriate human concern and purpose does not thereby worship humanity.[5] A humanism that encouraged the celebration of human accomplishments is not necessarily praying to humankind. A pedagogy that included praise and pride in human potential is not automatically a humanistic catechism. If, however, the theologians are correct in their belief that the functions of religion are essential human functions,[6] then, if humanity is to replace God in the performance of those functions, it is unlikely that it can do so in the context of such a restrained humanism; rather, it will be a humanism that structures our lives and provides us with meaning and standards. It will be a humanism that is both a communal philosophy and a form of social life. But insofar as humanism is made into an organized sect that has ritual celebrations of the value of humanity, makes communal declarations of devotion to human welfare, and proclaims the highest aim in life to be the achievement of a human good, it is hard to see how we can deny that such a humanism worships humanity (unless we stipulate that, by definition, only a supernatural God can be worshipped).[7]

The second humanist reply to the charge that humanism is idolatrous argues that humanity is indeed worthy of worship, and therefore there is nothing idolatrous about worshipping it. An organized humanism, one that engaged in such ritual activities, escapes the charge of idolatry if its devotions are directed at a human attribute that is truly worthy of worship. What does humanism find to worship in humanity?

There have been various identifications of the glorious element in humanity—the capacity for reason, or self-consciousness, or creativity, or dignity, or morality, or autonomy, or love—these are among the more common candidates. Within their variety, however, we find strong family resemblances among the candidates. They are all applications of human intelligence to a purpose that is an end in itself, a purposeful goal that moves beyond, or at least is other than, mere survival or animal satisfaction. These "nonbiological" intrinsic ends are the hallmarks of what humanists worship in humanity.[8] Humanists, in general, honor our natural capacity to transcend the rest of nature's mere biological purposes. Even if those transcendent human ends can be explained as having arisen on biological scaffolding and still continue to serve original, lower-level evolutionary purposes, the humanist values them for what they have become, not where they came from.

We will let human freedom stand in for all of the ideals and ends that have defined humanist values. Freedom—evolutionary-designed flexibility that can now choose to question its designer, that can question the "goals" of evolution itself—is the humanist value par excellence, the value more than any value that has animated humanistic visions and movements. What danger could a nontheist find in worshipping human freedom? Almost every nonreligiously based moral, political, and aesthetic tradition has put freedom or its near kin at the center of its values. Kantian autonomy, Enlightenment liberty, existentialist radical individual choice, socialist and nationalist revolution, unfettered artistic creation— all either define some form of freedom as the *highest good* or associate freedom as an integral part of the highest good. Sherwin Wine, the founder of Secular Humanistic Judaism, a communally organized, institutionalized, explicitly Jewish humanism, also puts human freedom at the center of his worldview (Wine 1995).

I have no quarrel with the choice. If I had to decide on *the* best, most valuable, most precious form of being, I too would choose human freedom. Should I make such a choice? Should I settle on a good that trumps other goods in all situations? Might there not be times that a little less human freedom is worth a lot more human pleasure? Might there not be sound judgments that include some curtailment of human autonomy as a price that should be paid to reduce the suffering of nonhuman animals? Might there not even be value in a nonsentient being whose realization may justify some sacrifice of human freedom? If a small addition of human freedom could be had by the destruction of vast and distant galaxies, however devoid of consciousness, is that destruction justified?

These are not rhetorical questions that are readily answered. On the one hand, when values conflict, how can we make rational ethical decisions if there is no highest value—to serve either as a common denominator to which we can convert other values for the purpose of comparing value quantities or to serve as the value with the highest rank and therefore highest priority in cases of value conflict?[9] It seems that a thoroughgoing rational ethics demands a supreme value, and human freedom, or human well-being, seems a reasonable choice. On the other hand, our experience and intuitions rebel at having to always defer to a single goal. Ethical life is experienced as more complex, involving many *fundamental* values, values that are incommensurable, that is, a genuine pluralism of values.[10] Such a pluralism, which neither ranks the values hierarchically nor reduces the manifold to some measurable common value, prevents us from solving many puzzles, for they will have no correct solution. There will be genuine moral dilemmas, where no matter what one does, one is doing wrong. There will be no polestar to guide one on the true path through life's thickets, no cause that can command unquestioning loyalty, no vision that elicits unshakable devotion. Humanism, though, *sufficiently specified*, does give us direction and purpose. Like religion, it tells us what is ultimately good. Having identified this ultimate good, humanism clears the path to worship, for it provides an object of worship.

The problem that a secularist can have with such a humanism is that it too readily decides the value puzzle. It worships an answer. It makes a difficult and profound question a dogma, although not, to be sure, in a censorious, illiberal way. Humanists are always ready to hear you out. However, humanists come to the discussion with their fundamental convictions and commitments settled—settled enough *to ritually celebrate them, to teach their children to worship them*. It is all well and good for humanists to deny any dogmatic attitude toward these convictions, but if humanism fulfills the functions that religion fulfills, if it becomes an organized, ritualized form of social life, then, for a humanist to reject humanist values, he must become an apostate.[11] There are good, nontheistic reasons to believe that we ought to remain more intellectually unencumbered.

It is not simply discomfort with dogma that is of concern, it is the particular dogma of humanism that worries, for it makes us, or something unique to us, the be all and end all. This evil is not unconnected to the viciousness of dogmatism. The core problem is a lack of modesty. The epistemological confidence that enables dogmatism is mirrored by a metaphysical/axiological pride that makes ourselves the objects of our highest esteem, and pride often does goeth before a fall, most especially a moral fall.[12] Humanism as a philosophy of life seems to combine two dangerous immodesties: The humanist is immodest in his claim to *know* what is the final good, and the humanist is immodest in his claim that *his kind* is the final good. The claim of certain knowledge closes us off to other possibilities, other perspectives. Options are lost, vision is narrowed, both increasing our practical and moral risk. The species-self-directedness feature of humanism reinforces this narrowness. Not only are we closed off to other understandings, but also within our dogma we have a specified, and one might add because it is so self-serving, suspect, goal: the human good. Alternative, non-humanistic ends are not available. This is not to argue against the claim that human freedom is the highest good. It is to question whether belief in that claim justifies worshipping humanity, whether belief in the claim justifies a devotional attitude toward its content.

In addition, even if there was something worthy of worship, and even if we could be certain that we have correctly identified it, still such worship might be objectionable not because it was idolatrous worship, but because it was worship. Perhaps there are harmful effects inherent in the activity of worship, in particular the diminishment of the worshipper. Feuerbach described this dynamic as the essence of religion (1841). The more we idealize God, the more we empower and praise God, the more we rely on God (all central activities of worship), the less good, the less powerful, the less praiseworthy, the less self-reliant we become. Perhaps even a being worthy of worship, if such there be, ought not to be worshipped because the *activity* of worship, regardless of its object, harms the worshipper. The claim is that humanism makes a religion of humanity, worships humanity, and that in doing so, it, like other religions, will generate dogmatism and alienation.

If humanism does carry those burdens, then maybe the humanistic theism of the theologians should be welcomed. Like humanism, it plausibly grounds our value and goals close to home, in humanity. Moreover, it is no more dogmatic than humanism and considerably more modest, and its new, vaguely pantheistic God, not sharply removed from humans, is far less alienating than the old God. If it is to be either humanism or some sort of nonhuman God, maybe the new God is the wisest choice; God enough not to be totally human, human enough not to be totally other. Close enough to be a comforting presence, distant enough to prevent egoism and egotism.

Is the theist claim that there are no secularist alternatives to humanism correct?[13] What about a simple refusal to put anything in God's former role? If there is no worship, there is no idolatry. If there is nothing exalted to Supreme Being, none can illegitimately reign supreme. Would this lack of devotion to a leading value, a highest ideal, leave us lost and impotent, knowing not where to go and indeed devoid of the will to go anywhere? I think not. We need no faith, humanistic or theistic, for there still to be strongly held values that guide our lives. Indeed, a single value can become for a time, perhaps a lifetime, or many lifetimes, the central value. As long as no value gets enshrined, no value is made immune to change, no value is *worshipped*, secularism can escape the idolatry and the Feuerbachian alienation that appear endemic to worshipful behavior, even nontheistic worshipful behavior.

If secularism takes this essentially nondogmatic approach, if it refuses to enshrine its values, if it refuses to worship its vision of the good, can it escape the theologians' charge that secularism leaves an essential human need unmet? Does the baby of human fulfillment *necessarily* swim in the bathwater of dogma-inducing worship? If it does, we are confronted with a choice: We can be fulfilled dogmatists or unfulfilled fallibilists.

We can be satisfied believers—pious Jews, Christians, Muslims, Hindus, Buddhists, or humanists—or dissatisfied infidels.

Of course, a humanist might object to being listed along with the other believers. To begin with, the humanist might argue, humanistic belief and worship is not an alienating worship. It has not the harmful consequences of God worship; if we worship ourselves, there is no self-abnegation, no self-debasement. We do not project our own qualities onto some external being, thereby impoverishing our self-esteem to enhance some fantasy figure. In worshipping humanity, we do not inflate an alien-other by self-deflation. On the contrary, we rehearse our essential human strengths and capacities. Nor must our self-worship involve deceptive self-aggrandizement. We can hold ourselves to be the supreme being without believing ourselves perfect or attributing to ourselves powers or wisdom that we do not actually possess. Saying that we are the best does not require that we think of ourselves as very good, only that we think there is nothing better. Moreover, worship of humanity may have positive effects, such as helping us to recognize our powers and responsibilities, the better to shoulder them, and filling us with joyful pride that comes not at the expense of anyone else's sense of self-worth. Humanistic worship, the humanist can plausibly argue, is not alienating worship.

The charge of dogmatism is less easy for a full-blown humanism—a humanistic attitude to humanity that was tantamount to worship—to escape. Perhaps a secularism with merely a humanistic orientation is more defensible. Humanistic beliefs without humanism can shape our values and guide our action and even be strongly held. The only alternative to narrow dogmatism is not an absence of strong commitments and convictions, an absence of values that we are willing to protect and defend, perhaps at times to the death. It does probably mean, however, that even when defending things to the death, one should be aware of human fallibility, one should have whispering in the back of one's mind Oliver Cromwell's voice "beseeching" us "in the bowels of Christ, that Ye might be wrong." But it is hard to be genuinely open to the possibility that your answer is wrong if you have been worshipping that answer. Intellectual humility should make us hesitate in apotheosizing human freedom or perhaps deifying anything. Maybe we should never be confident enough of something's value to worship it. So humanism, as *a matter of faith*, is to be avoided, and God, old or new, does avoid the worship of humanity. The old God, though, is a poor avoidance mechanism. The old God, for "moderns," is clearly as idolatrous and alienating as any humanism possibly could be. The new God does better on both counts, for it is too vague, amorphous, and slippery to securely pin on the idolatrous or alienating label. An object of worship cannot be unworthy of worship if we cannot say with any precision what it is.[14] If our worship is not directed toward an unworthy object, it is not idolatrous. Nor can we be alienated through worshipping the new God, for it is not distinctly other, and its elevation is not even relatively degrading to us. Worshipping the new God might even be a form of worship that is free of dogmatism, since it is unclear that you must believe anything in order to worship it. The new theism, in a nutshell, is useful obfuscation. Its use is that it offers the benefits of worship without the usual distasteful accompaniments. The nonworshipping secularism avoids the distasteful accompaniments, but at the costs of the benefits—or so the theologians could argue.

I think that the argument for the superiority of the new God over humanism has substantial force, but I doubt whether it is superior to a nonworshipping, humanistically inclined secularism. In the previous paragraph, it was claimed that the new theism still procures the benefits of worship, But does it? Does worship without a vivid image of God fulfill the purported need to worship? Perhaps better than does nonworshipping secularism, but, as the discussion in the last chapter suggests, maybe not much better. If new-God worship does meet the need to worship, that benefit comes at the price of engaging in intellectually fuzzy activity. A nonworshipping, humanistically inclined secularism may be epistemologically uncertain and incomplete, but it is clear and honest. Its embrace of human being and human value is unambiguous, even if it is a looser embrace than humanism gives humanity. Its uncertainties are acknowledged as ignorance, not glorified as mysteries.

Once more: The comparative assessment of the new theism and nonworshipping secularism may finally be a matter of taste. Does the value of heartfelt, if somewhat vitiated, prayer outweigh the disvalue of the intellectual fuzziness that grounds the praying? For some it surely does. They are those for whom all of the benefits of prayer described in the last chapter are spiritual necessities, not luxuries. They are those who cannot live without prayer, or at least they cannot live happily or well without prayer. Keeping faith with their deepest instincts demands prayer, and the least idolatrous object of prayer that they can find is the new God. However, there are others for whom even a hint of idolatry is abhorrent. They cannot pray to anything that might be unworthy of prayer, and their uncertainty prevents them from declaring anything worthy of prayer. So they will not pray, fearful that any prayer is liable to be idolatrous.

9

A MATTER OF TASTE

Religion Becomes Aesthetics in Marx and Nietzsche

The nineteenth century's two most influential adversaries of theism were Karl Marx and Friedrich Nietzsche. Neither would have called himself a humanist, so neither should be called on to defend himself against the accusation that humanism is idolatrous. However, each of these critics of religion had at the heart of his critique the claim that theism is antihuman, or more precisely, "anti" the most fully, the most truly, the most healthy, the most beautiful, the freest, the "highest" form of the human. Do their humanistically flavored critiques weigh as heavily against the new God of the theologians as they do against the old God of traditional religion? Do either of their understandings of the source of religious belief—for they were theorists of the genealogy of religion as well as critics of it—shed light on the social or psychological sources of the new God?

We turn first to Marx and start by addressing the common misunderstanding of his view of religion, a misunderstanding as widespread among his nominal followers as it is among his critics. This popular "Marxist" take on religion suffers from not paying close enough attention to its namesake's works. It is based on a careless and incomplete reading of Marx's basic metaphysical stance: his materialism. Popular Marxist materialism is cruder than the materialism of Marx. The popular version regards humans as puppets whose strings are pulled by impersonal, mechanistic, productive forces. Marx himself, however, emphasized the human subject as an active feature of reality (1847). Although completely from and of nature (hence the materialism), human beings are able (within the limits of the given historical circumstances) to shape nature, including human nature, not merely to contemplate it. Indeed, Marx famously upbraided philosophers for merely interpreting reality, when the point was to change it (1845). The advocacy of human power, rather than its denial, is at the heart of Marx's thought.[1] Marx's vision of human salvation/liberation pictures the full realization of this subjective/active side of reality—humans coming into their own as creative beings, conscious of and in control of their enormous creative powers—as fully emerging with the elimination of class societies and their alienating modes of production.

Marx's critique of religion begins with the work of Ludwig Feuerbach (1841). Like Feuerbach, he felt that religious belief was an obstacle to the realization of human creative freedom. For both thinkers, God was a projection of human powers onto an idealized and distant being. These powers, given to God, were lost to humanity. The all-powerful God becomes the conceptual embodiment and ideological perpetuator of the human sense of powerlessness.

Marx, more thoroughgoing (and more Hegelian) in his materialism than Feuerbach, wanted a materialistic explanation for the creation of God; how do active material beings come to develop the idea of an immaterial being that denies and thwarts their own genius? Marx's answer is that God is an outcome of production in hierarchical, class-ridden society. In a society where human labor is commanded at the behest and in the interests of a separate power (the ruling class), labor is necessarily alienating. Its products are alien to those whose labor fashions them—separate from, rather than an extension and expression of, the producer. The working classes in all class societies were alienated, but in capitalist society, the proletariat, especially prior to the development of any class consciousness (i.e., an understanding of its actual class situation), achieves the acme of alienation.[2] We can expect such a proletariat to cling to the old gods.

Does it follow from Marx's approach that a "truly emancipated society"[3] would be godless? I think not. If we were really free in Marxist terms, we would not believe in the old God, but we might, as a creative choice, care to conceive of ourselves and nature in any of various guises that acknowledge the reality of human power.

How does this Marxist analysis apply to the new God of the theologians? We do not have to think that our society is free or unalienated to realize that elements of it anticipate a freer human condition. The theologians' religion may be a glimpse of that emancipated condition.

This is not to say that the new theology is *the* religion of a liberated future nor that its adherents are the wholly novel heralds of emancipation. As we saw in chapter 1, the new God and new-God believers have been around a long time and they were and are to be found in all strata of most societies. Still, they are rare among the most alienated working classes. For slaves, peasants, and the proletariat, it is that old-time religion that prevails. Supernaturalism and magic, saviors and protectors, are the religion of the alienated powerless. Mysticism and theistic naturalism are for those more comfortable, less antagonistic, to social reality.[4] Hence the broadening appeal of the new theologies among the elite of advanced Western societies.

Although advanced Western societies are rife with old and new forms of alienation and their elites manifest some extreme and exotic signs of estrangement from human nature, contemporary Western societies contain larger groups of relatively free humans than most historical societies. The new-God believers are prominent among the (relatively) unalienated. Many of them control the conditions of their labor far more than have most traditional working classes. In some important respects, they are more like medieval artisans than the industrial proletariat—not members of the ruling class, but valued and well treated by the ruling class in virtue of their skill and individual productivity. Further reducing their alienation are the actual conditions of their lives: Abundant food, good health care, political participation, and meaningful jobs are commonplace among the congregants of the new theology synagogues. Their clothing, home decor, CD collections, even family structures are understood as chosen expressions of their sense of self, and so is their God. It is not an imposed deity. It is a custom-designed deity. The old God, if Feuerbach and Marx were right, is an expression of alienation. Believers of the new God, however, have less alienation (at least less of the kind generated by alienated labor) to express. Their lives do not require a lordly God to reflect their powerlessness. They want a God to directly express feelings of power; the mysticism and the humanism of the new theology do that. One appeal of a God that is attained by losing one's ego through its absorption into the universe (the mystic's God) is that it is simultaneously a God that is an extension of one's ego into the universe. The appeal of a God wholly dependent on the realization of human potentiality (the humanist's God) is that it glorifies human potentiality. An emancipated society would be free of gods unconsciously produced and experienced as external powers. This, however, is not the new God. The theologians have given us a God that is *explicitly not* other than us, not an alien force.

If human personality is not the Godhead of the new God (and in some accounts it is), then it is at least a crucial manifestation of the deity. If an individual human does not possess all of the power attributed to the new God (and in some accounts she does), then at least the new God's power to do good lies almost wholly in the collective human will. Rather than being evidence of alienation and powerlessness, the new-God theologies, like the humanisms and mysticisms that they resemble, can be expressions of power and belonging. We do not tremble before this new God or even confront it; we are it. Moreover, the new theology allows that we are free not to be it; we need not accept it. The new God is a choice; belief in God is a free choice. It is an *aesthetic* choice, a creation of my *unalienated* labor. Like the creation of all unalienated labor, it is not forced.

However, new-God theology is not the sole possible worldview of the unalienated. Equally unalienated is the choice not to believe.[5] Atheism, too, is compatible with the recognition that humanity is both an integral part of nature and the free, creative aspect of nature. Between an array of new gods and no God, freedom forces no choices. It is the very free—but yet not arbitrary—nature of the beliefs that most characterizes them as aesthetic choices. When the messiah arrives (or after the revolution), there will be those singing God's praises and others whistling a secular song, and neither need be out of tune. Marx leaves aesthetic choices open to a free people's taste.

We need no interpretive work to characterize Nietzsche's view on religion as relegating God to a question of taste, for Nietzsche frankly recognizes religious belief, indeed all metaphysical beliefs, as a kind of aesthetic choice. His objection to theism is not so much that it is false as that it is ugly—rooted in the psychology typical of the mass of humanity—weak, vengeful, fearful, cowardly, dishonest, and dishonorable. God, at least the God of the Christians and Jews, in Nietzsche's account, is the unattractive metaphysics of the herd and their antilife, priestly manipulators. This God is in part psychic revenge against the powerful natural elite of strength, courage, health, and pride and in part an ingenious weapon to undermine the confidence and rule of the strong, natural elite by replacing their values with values beneficial to the herd of weakling commoners. Hence, we get a God who favors the poor, the meek, the nonthreatening, the humble—a God who empowers the life-denying people who would make sins of the love of food, the love of contests and battles, the love of sex, and the love of self. In its most extreme form, we get the Christian God—part of which is a tortured, milquetoast, meekly suffering so that the guilt-ridden, self-hating, cowardly herd need not suffer and part of which is an omnipotent judge who will damn and punish forever the powerful who are envied and feared by the herd. Nietzsche does not like this God of resentment. He is repulsed by it. Nietzsche finds the Greek pantheon more to his taste than the Christian trinity and would rather keep company with Zeus than with Yahweh.

Granting the insight of the Nietzschean critique, we should question whether the new God is subject to Nietzsche's objections to traditional Western monotheism, for as we have seen above, the new God is not easily viewed as a reflection of powerlessness. It is more a Whitmanesque celebration of self and life than a Pauline denial of this world. Nor is this hell-less, judgment-less new-God theology useful for revenge fantasies. Although Nietzsche can make charges of escapism stick a bit against some versions of the new God (for he levels those charges against Buddhism, and lots of new-God mysticism is similar to Buddhism) as preached by the theologians, the new God implies an *embrace and acceptance of this world*. This is very much in the spirit of Nietzsche's saying "yes" to life. In some versions of the new God theology, the world may have its illusory qualities, but even those versions tend to hold humans responsible for taking care of and cherishing the phenomenal world. The new God theology is neither life- nor world-denying, which is not to say that it would appeal to Nietzsche; it is only to say that it avoids the central thrust of his critique of religion. What does appeal to Nietzsche is the ideal of a more advanced human, a superman, conscious that he creates his own values and conscious that he is a product of the earth imbued by nature with a drive to creatively assert himself.

For all its inegalitarianism, Nietzsche's ultimate ideal is surprisingly similar to Marx's—both philosophers wish for empowered human beings, conscious that they are free to shape choices and are self-determined because, in part, they understand how they are determined by their material, earthly, animal origins. Marx, the sociologist, thinks that getting there requires a historical process that transforms society and is optimistic that all people can enter this realm of freedom. Nietzsche, the psychologist, believes possible only the relatively rare individual achievement of human freedom, of a heroic elite that attains superhuman status.[6] However, in spite of this difference, Nietzsche, like Marx, categorizes the religious belief of genuinely free people as a conscious aesthetic choice that should be judged by aesthetic rather than epistemological criteria. So we now ask: By what aesthetic criteria shall we judge the comparative value of new- and no-God belief?

The Taste for God

Before examining religious belief as a matter of aesthetic choice, we must be clear that it is usually *not* that. The divide between the old-God loyalists and the new-God/no-God camp is more epistemological than it is aesthetic.[7] The latter group, which I have been calling "moderns," looks to science and mechanistic, empirically oriented common sense to ground knowledge claims. The old God, with its internal incoherencies; its promise of individual immortality; its claim that the world is ruled by a just, powerful, and far-sighted being; and the lingering odor of its pre-scientific, magical-thought beginnings is *epistemically* unacceptable to "moderns."[8]

However, in its most careful, least expansive articulation, new-God belief stands on the same epistemological and metaphysical ground as modern secularisms. In the theologian's theology, the "facts" of the universe are pretty much what secular science tells us they are, and any additional unknown facts alluded to by the theologians are posited, if at all, as uncertain hopes.

Hence, the new-God/no-God divide is best understood as an aesthetic one and so should be examined as a division of tastes. While it may be wrongheaded to dispute the correctness or relative rank of aesthetic preferences, it is illuminating to analyze the values and associations of a given aesthetic disposition. Which casts of mind, which emotional make-ups, and which moral leanings lead one to belief in the new God, and which minds, make-ups, and leanings incline to atheism? Is there a liberal, religious aesthetic that can be distinguished from determinedly secular tastes? If God, as is commonly said, is in the eye of the beholder, let us think of divinity as being more like beauty than truth.[9]

The new God is found not in the facts, but in the *meaning* of the facts, the deeper "truth" that they represent, or can be made to represent. The connections and continuities found throughout reality are viewed as creating a moral and metaphysical unity, a unity that redeems us all, for we can view the sad fate of the world's individual, temporary entities with equanimity, considering their fate of no independent significance. In the final analysis, it is the whole that counts, and if the whole's "end" is not assuredly good, it also can never be certified as irremediably bad. Whatever happens in our spatial and temporal neighborhood of the universe, Being goes on, and the hope for goodness triumphant in Being can never be defeated. The insistence on retaining God is a refusal to read our existence as ultimately tragic. Faith in the new God is the commitment to look at the world as a single moral entity: one for all and all for one;[10] it is to look at it with indefeasible hope. There can be no tragic ending for the "all."

I think most new-God theologians of every tradition share this anti-tragic aesthetic, but it is most salient in a Jewish context, for tragedy is the most natural reading of Jewish history, and resistance to the tragic view of existence is a prominent feature of traditional Jewish religion. The messiah may tarry, but still we believe, in perfect faith, that he will come. The lion will lie down with the lamb, and we will all, no matter how tumultuous and horrific the journey, come to rest in peace.

There is a nobility in this stance, a beauty in indomitable spirit, spirit that is confident that the final end is good. Some of the best stories have happy endings, and despair and cynicism impose severe aesthetic limitations. Moreover, if we allow that aesthetic judgments may admit practical effects, the effect of action-spurring hope is enhanced beauty.[11]

As dramatic genre, the theologians' theology—its account of the significance of human life and human history—is romance. There are confusion, sadness, and terrible events along the way, but something is learned, enemies are reconciled, and at curtain's fall, order, justice, and happiness reign.[12] A variant Romanticism, however—one that blossoms in eighteenth-century Europe and fully flowers there in the nineteenth century, and one whose spirit is present to some degree in every civilization—is more revealing of the new-God aesthetic than is romance drama by itself. Thinking of the new God as a product of this broad, romantic spirit explains many of its characteristics:

> the Romantic temperament . . . resisted the very impulse of definition, favoring the indefinite and the boundless . . . [in Romance] . . . wonder, and emotional self-expression [triumph over] . . . objectivity . . . [and] desires and dreams prevail over everyday reality. (Drabble 1998, 838)

The theologians do not want to dispute scientific facts, but the wonder and the mystery that religion provides are dear to them. Subordinating their subjective experiences to objective knowledge is distasteful, and having lived-experience's truth-value depend on objectively validated findings is disheartening. The theologians find contemplating the boundless liberating, they want to be exuberant, and a God of limitless goodness is cause for exuberance, indeed, ecstasy. New-God believers like the whiff of mystery, and an ill-defined because undefinable God is fortified against complete clarity. To hang their hopes and visions on an assessment of objective trends is unpalatable; that thread is too fragile to support such treasures.

This is a powerful brew. Hope and faith, intense emotionality, and total commitment, mystery, and infinity; the romantic sense of beauty is a compelling aesthetic, and romance can be of surpassing beauty. It is not the only form, though, of beautiful stories ("Stories" is the relevant category here. For all of theology's aesthetic modes,[13] it is dramatic narrative that is dominant.) Besides tragedy itself, there might be aesthetic and moral value in looking at human existence as farce, gothic tale, naturalistic drama, or alienating absurdity. Each is a form that can accommodate the facts of human being.

Mystery

The mysterious element in the new theology is achieved by a number of factors. Although I argue in appendix A that ineffability largely functions as a theological dodge, it also contributes to the sense of mystery. What cannot be said may still be known, but it is certainly not easily known. What cannot be said suggests a secret, and secrets are close associates of mysteries.

The vague, unspecified description of the new God adds to its mystery. The structure inherent in the universe that makes salvation possible, the theologians' baseline conception of God, leaves it entirely open as to what that structure might be. On the one hand, there are too many candidates (e.g., something about human nature, or the logic of evolution, or a propensity in being itself); on the other, it is difficult to imagine with precise detail just what sort of structure could make salvation possible because salvation as a realized condition is conceptually elusive. We think that we know what heaven *will not* be like—our world of pain, frustration, and alienation—but a positive depiction is difficult to draw. (Dystopias have always been more convincing than utopias.) It is true that mystics have told us that they experience an unshakable conviction of immortality, an immense joy, freedom from fear, and a love of all being. But, this only reports the results of their experience; it does not convey the experience. The contents of the experience remain a mystery for the uninitiated—and even for the initiated when they are not in the throes of it.

Infinity has appeal beyond its mystifying properties; there are those who delight in openness, big horizons, the sublime, and the awesome. They have less taste for the bounded, the encompassed, the contained. Infinity is catnip for these lovers of great vistas. Beyond its thrilling grandeur, the infinite also contributes to mystery. Infinity suggests that there will always be unexplored regions, further realms that are foreign to us, things that our finite selves can never encompass, and are therefore a vast unknown territory—the essence of mystery.

What is the appeal of mystery? Nietzsche notes the link between murkiness and pseudo-profundity. "The crowd thinks all water deep whenever it cannot see the bottom" (1882, ¶173). Dostoyevsky describes its appeal in terms of its power to release us from responsibility; what cannot be understood must be accepted on authority (Dostoyevsky 1881)—or on faith. Allied with the miraculous, mystery keeps the masses in awe and frees them of the responsibility of figuring out the truth for themselves.

There is also mystery's entertainment value. Mysteries leave us with puzzles, and puzzle-solving is fun, even if we cannot find a definitive solution. So long as we know that there is a solution to be found, the endless speculation is intriguing. An unknowable God is the most challenging of puzzles, a source of undying fascination.

Any sane secularism must acknowledge that much remains unknown, and much will forever remain unknown. The secularist, however, takes no joy in the mysteries of existence and she bridles at the notion that anything is in principle unknowable. Secularism is of a classicist aesthetic temperament. Clarity and sharp, explicit demonstration are marks of the beautiful, not mystery and ambiguous, subtle suggestion. The satisfaction of understanding outweighs the titillation of the cryptic. The satisfaction that a secularist finds when confronting mystery derives from solving it, and God is not solvable.

There is a moral benefit of mystery. It keeps us humble. If we do not know the whole story—the entire context of our lives—we cannot be dogmatically certain of what we ought to do. We act trembling, knowing that we act in relative blindness. We must feel our way slowly, carefully. A cocksure denier of mystery is liable to think that he knows more than he does and is liable to act with an unjustified confidence that he can foresee all of the consequence of his action. A false sense of complete understanding has led to many an atrocity. Consciousness of our own ignorance, which an awareness of mystery affords, can defend against arrogant certainty. Of course, secularists can be epistemologically modest, aware of their fallibility. Yet unlike those who interpret the world as an ultimate mystery, the secularist has no principled bulwark against the belief that she has got the fundamentals all figured out. Nonbelievers are more liable to dogmatism than new-God believers.

This is a surprising result. We normally think of religious types as the ones with absolute confidence that they understand the fundamentals, and as the ones who cannot abide uncertainty. That may be the case. Remember, though, we are contrasting the aesthetic inclinations not of the religious and the secular, groups that do not agree on "the facts"; rather, we are contrasting a subgroup of the religious, the new-God believers, with the secular. These are two groups of "moderns" who accept the same literal description of reality. They agree on what is known. It is a question of their attitude to the unknown. I am claiming that the religious have more of a *taste* for the unknown.

Emotionality

David Hume, hardly a Romantic, claimed that reason is and ought to be the slave of passion (1739). Other figures of a decidedly non-Romantic and secular theoretical bent, such as Jeremy Bentham (1789), A. J. Ayer (1936), and Bertrand Russell (1946) also believed that only emotions, of one sort or another, provide us with goals and values. If we construe emotions to encompass all feelings, sensations, desires—all of psychic life that is not purely cognitive—no one can be said to value emotions less than anyone else, for clearly emotion plays a role in any plausible analysis of value (Kupperman 1999). So any claim that new-God believers prize emotions more than secularists requires qualification.

New-God believers have a taste for *extreme* emotions: ecstasy, exaltation, bliss, rapture. The modern religious are also sensitive to the negative emotional extremes—despair, agony, anomie, and wretchedness. It seems that God, even the new God, is occasion for the former emotions and protection from the latter ones.

Secularists have less of a thirst for heavenly joy and feel less threatened by psychological hell. They are content with the more moderate emotions, the quieter joys that are most compatible with sober cognition, and their sorrows, however painful, are experienced as mundane suffering, rather than cosmic torture. Even mortality is not quite a mortal peril. "Yes, one dies," the secularists says, "so what?" The religious find nonexistence a more horrifying prospect. If the facts point to personal nonexistence, there is need to interpret them so that some form of non-personal existence mitigates the horror of dying. Secularists, being less disheartened by death, have less of a need to cast it in a consoling light.

In contrast to the claim that religion caters to emotional extremism, it might be noted that the emotional state perhaps most associated with religious feeling is the near-total *absence*, or at least total control, of emotions—the peace that passeth understanding, a supernatural calm, an imperturbability. This, too, can be understood as a kind of emotional extremism. An affective tone is part of the normal condition of human being—its *elimination* is an extreme condition—and the desire for its elimination indicates great concern with emotionality. The person who is truly indifferent to wealth feels no need to take a vow of poverty. The person of temperate emotions will be little tempted to wipe them out. Some people are less plagued by emotional volatility than are others. Since their range of typical emotions is narrower than that of others, they find the natural emotional swings less disconcerting than do others. Going from pleasant to irritating is less harrowing than the journey from the ecstasy to the agony. A harrowing trek along extreme grades can make one yearn for completely flat land, and the sensitivity to emotional extremes can make one a seeker of inner peace.

But, steeply graded mountain paths are also exhilarating. Going from irritated to pleased is not nearly as thrilling as the trip from the agony to the ecstasy. If the emotional extremists have more reason to dread their emotionality than do the emotional moderates, they also have more reason to value and indulge it. It hurts them more, but they also get more out of it. Belief in God can protect us from emotionality *and* encourage its cultivation, both of which will be most appealing to those with strong, emotional sensitivities.

I have been explaining the selection of no God or new God as an aesthetic choice, with romantics inclined toward divinity and classicists more open to secularism. Secularism, though, may also be appealing to those who refuse to aestheticize metaphysics. Theirs is a refusal to find meaning or value in the basic facts of reality. They think of beauty as a human projection that, at a metaphysical level, is inappropriately foisted on reality. This is scientism with a vengeance, but it is a kind of taste, too, this Jack Webb attitude toward metaphysics. It shares with the classicist aesthetic the distaste for sentimentality, but unlike classicism, it carries no torch for balance, symmetry, clarity, simplicity, or restraint. It claims not to be carrying torches at all.

Although those of this persuasion may think of this non-aestheticized approach to metaphysics as a demand of rationality, it is not. Rather, it is just another aesthetic choice. Reality no more tells us not to aestheticize it than it tells us how to aestheticize it. It leaves us free to choose, and the choice whether to aestheticize or not is itself an aesthetic choice. It seems to me that, in general, new-God believers are aestheticizers, and Romanticism best describes their aesthetics.[14]

10

TRUTH AND BEAUTY

Religious Truth, Relativism, and Pluralism

The Talmud reproaches those who would inquire into what is above and below, what is before and after (Cohen 1973, 27). Classical Buddhism is also dismissive of metaphysical speculation. But, such ontological abstemiousness in religious thought is exceptional and goes against the dominant religious grain. Concern with first things and last things is central to most religion, and ultimate reality is religion's special province.[1] Religion is about "the Truth," especially when that word is capitalized.[2] Hence, to "reduce" religion to judgments of taste, if religion is not to be robbed of its essence, would seem to turn judgments of the Truth to a matter of taste. If religion is about ultimate things and religion is *also* a matter of taste, then it would appear that there is no correct religious view, and therefore no final Truth. Are we offered here an ultimate relativism, a view that claims that, as far as the most important things are concerned, in the final reckoning, one judgment is as good as another?

As one of my wiser teachers would often reply to philosophical questions, yes and no. A central premise of this work is that there is no disagreement regarding "the facts" between new-God believers and believers in no God.[3] If metaphysical reality is understood as captured by the final, most accurate possible *scientific* description of the world, the picture that matches the way that the universe would be described by an omniscient observer that had no values, goals, or intentions, then the equal acceptability of new- and no-God beliefs is no relativism, for their differing Truths have nothing to do with this value-neutral, descriptive *t*ruth of reality.[4] Religious Truth, conceived properly as an aesthetic claim, does not speak to the "factual" nature of reality.[5]

Furthermore, even as religious Truth, we do not have a relativism of the anything-goes variety. That there are many stances toward God that are compatible with freedom, the facts, and goodness—many of which can also be judged beautiful—does not mean that all stances toward God are so compatible. There may be an infinite number of religious Truths, but that does not mean that any religious vision is True. There are an infinite variety of (potentially) beautiful works of art, but plenty are still rightly judged ugly—and some are ugly because of their intellectual or moral failings. Religion as aesthetics is no relativism.[6] Nor is it an absolute monism of Truth. What we have here is best called a pluralism. One religious outlook may not be as good as any other, but there will be more than one good religious outlook. Moreover, among the best ones, some may be equally good and will remain equally good when all is said and done. That is the major implication of seeing religion as a matter of taste. Religious Truth, of which I take atheism to be a species, is plural.

Dostoyevsky's Grand Inquisitor claimed that humankind hopes for the unity and harmony that will be achieved by a common object of worship (1881). If the Grand Inquisitor is right, and humanity does yearn to be united in one True religion, then that yearning is misguided; not that it cannot be achieved, but rather that it should not be achieved. Even if all humanity settled on the same genuinely beautiful religious vision, it would be a poorer world for there being only this single species of religious beauty.

Accepting religious pluralism goes beyond tolerance, which may be sufficiently justified by the mere desire to avoid harmful or unpleasant conflict. It goes beyond open-mindedness, which may accept other views as partial or possible truths to be valued as contributors or potential contributors to the one grand truth. Accepting religious pluralism means accepting that there may be *fundamentally* different ways of interpreting reality, of valuing life (or not), of assigning meaning (or not) to existence, and of choosing whether to celebrate or bemoan the universe, and that these different ways may have equal "religious" validity. They all constitute True religion.

Pluralism of moral and political principles is harder to achieve, for ethical principles deal with how we are to live with and get along with one another. The coordination of our conduct is a natural interest of social animals, and to coordinate conduct we need common principles and rules. We may be able to tolerate differences of moral and political theory, but, inherent in the function of politics and morality, there are strong constraints on the degree of pluralism that we can practically accept in those realms. Most of us reject a pluralism of empirical truth because empirical knowledge must be vindicated by experience, must "pan out," must "work," in the sense of leading to successful outcomes, and the physical world seems to severely limit those beliefs that "work."[7] For analogous reasons, we are rightly uncomfortable with a pluralism of politics and morality,[8] for they too must work, and, although perhaps not as constraining as the nonhuman empirical world, the social world strongly suggests that some principles work and that others do not. Science and morality both have a strong, pragmatic dimension, and one aspect of that pragmatic dimension is the need to achieve consensus. We frequently need to agree on the facts and agree on the rules. Scientific and moral inquiry are processes that aim at getting that agreement. The accumulation of scientific evidence is meant to rationally mandate a belief. Moral argumentation, likewise, aims to ground rationally moral judgments and bind all who are rational.

Not so with aesthetic judgments. Although it may be true, as Kant maintained, that aesthetic judgments implicitly claim to be universally valid, there is no need intrinsic to the judgment to have others agree. There is no claim that rationality alone commands the judgment. I can effectively and unproblematically continue to believe that something is beautiful even if others fail to see its beauty and even if I cannot articulate all of the grounds for my judgment. This is how aesthetic truth differs from empirical (scientifically validated) and moral truth. As long as there are empirical or moral disagreements, we must work to reconcile them. But, contrasting aesthetic truths do not undermine each other and call for no reconciliation.

Tales of Freedom

For those who profess belief in the new God, the most aesthetically satisfying story that can be told about themselves and the universe is a tale, or some version of a tale, of universal homecoming. As individuals, as a community, as a species, we should think of ourselves as on a spiritual voyage, a journey to connect, or reconnect, either with all of being or with some ideal of human potential. No one is alone or must remain alone. Separateness is illusory; alienation can be overcome. There is a perspective from which being is glorious, and each of us can share fully in the glory. The happy homecoming may be guaranteed, but most new-God theology makes only its possibility guaranteed; its realization depends on our moral and spiritual choices and effort. In the telling of this story, God is the name of the home, God is the name of the impulses that drive the journey, and God is the name of the travelers.

A similar plot can be told in nontheistic terms, but it would be a different story, expressing different aesthetic values. A quest tale with everyone united in a "loving God" feels different than a historical narrative with everyone united in a "flourishing, supportive, all-inclusive, human community." The names that we give to characters and settings, motives and obstacles, and achievement and failures strongly flavor a story, and different names make a storyline attractive for different tastes.

Not only do "the facts" support both tellings of this "homecoming" plot, but they also allow for other plots altogether. Reality is rich in "facts," and a sensitively chosen selection can construct a plot that will reflect the sensibility of the chooser. There is a set of facts that will make a plot that supports a story of eternal antagonism, a set of facts for a tale of unending suffering, a set for greed or cruelty or vanity triumphant. There are, as well, sets for Kafkaesque or Beckettian tales of the absurd. We can also choose sets of facts that will not cohere into any sort of tale at all. What is done by free people depends on their creative abilities and aesthetic values. Presumably, after the messiah comes, the world will be inhabited by free people with abundant creativity and a wide range of tastes and therefore be filled with religious differences. In contrast to the Grand Inquisitor, an improving world will become ever more diverse in religious Truths.

I like the homecoming plot and am sensitive to the beauty of the story that tells it in religious language. It is, in many ways, a richer version than its secular analogue. The Godly telling of the homecoming, though, does not readily permit a switch to the telling of a radically different story. Secular language is more conducive to the creation of an anthology of multiple plots and antiplots. The atheist, in some frames of mind, can focus on the human capacity to grow in empathy, and in other moods dwell on the persistence of human callousness. A common secular vocabulary tells both stories. Of course, if one is willing to play fast and loose with "God" so that the term is emptied of all content, "God" will support any tale as well, or as poorly, as any undefined sound or mercurial concept. The aesthetic power of "God," however, rests on its association with some, however vaguely delineated, set of connotations. It is hard to give oneself wholly to a story in which God is good and then to one in which God is evil.[9] The religious sensibility for whom God is an enduring aesthetic value requires one God, however amorphous. Indeed, a nontheist is better positioned to use "God" as a fully variable trope because the nontheist's God can be nothing but transparently metaphorical, and the nontheist can pick or construct the God, or gods, that best serve a present expressive purpose. Such a God is being used as a decorative illustration of some aspect of reality, not a serious interpretation of it. It will serve a peripheral aesthetic purpose rather than be a central aesthetic value. Only the committed theist, the person who chooses consistently to understand reality as containing or manifesting divinity, the person of faith, experiences the beauty of God.

The major aesthetic advantage that nontheism has is the diversity of aesthetic visions that it can seriously entertain. The secularist can use the same vocabulary to tell tales with radically different flavors and morals. Although the theists' stories may have digressions of many different colors, in the end, the character of God will dominate the narrative, and the same God will always result in the same story. The theologians' God can only live in a happy romance (although Kaplan's is in more of a *bildungsroman* with a doubtful outcome). Each must judge for herself whether that potential breadth of aesthetic experiences in nontheistic *weltanschauungs* compensates for the loss of aesthetic depth that belief in God can provide. Granted, God stories provide a depth that comes in many models, but you get to choose only one.[10]

The Beauty of the Good

Keats, scrambling epistemology, metaphysics, and aesthetics, claimed that the only available and only needed knowledge was that truth was beauty and beauty truth. This does nicely as an abstract of a free person's religious life: Religious Truth is that which makes life meaningful, worth living, and purposive.[11] Such Truths are found by theists and atheists alike. When found, they give life itself aesthetic value; Truth is beauty. Such Truths, however, can only be known, they can only be recognized, they can only be *verified* by their aesthetic effects; beauty is Truth. Our grasp of the truths of nature and morals may always be tentative and fallible, but we have a self-validating grasp of the intrinsic value of that which we find beautiful, and we find ourselves unable to deny that an entire life experienced as beautiful would make our life worth living, would be the Truth that we seek in life. What more knowledge do we need than that? "That is all ye know on earth and all ye need to know."[12]

Keats's epigram is noticeable for the absence of goodness. Knowing what ought to be done is surely as crucial as knowing the Truth—knowing what is of ultimate personal value.[13] My Truth may be the knowledge required to make my life worth living, but to live well, to live a good life, I must also be concerned with what makes others' lives worth living.

In one important sense what makes their life worth living is the same that makes mine worth living: the finding of meaning, the realization of one's own Truth. Nevertheless, if the nature of religious Truth is that it is a freely chosen response to one's experience, I should not expect others' Truth to have the same content as does mine. Each free person judges for herself what gives her life meaning, and not all will make the same judgment. Goodness requires respect for others, not empathy. I can fail to appreciate the Truth of the other's vision, but to be good, I must act to enable her to find that Truth. My freedom is the foundation of Truth and beauty; others' freedom is the basis of goodness.[14]

What "moderns" have in common, atheists and theists alike, is neither Truth[15] nor beauty. What we share is our notion of goodness. We have goodness in common by virtue of our understanding that Truth and beauty are the fruit of freedom and that nature is the mother of freedom. Goodness asks us only to value equally everyone's freedom, but to do that we must understand the material basis of freedom. The modern rejection of supernaturalism is of the first moral moment, for it tells us how to support the growth of freedom. It tells us that freedom, and therefore the possibility of finding Truth, does not involve the shedding or transcendence of the heavy muck of nature, nor has it anything to do with escaping the rigid, inflexible mathematics of nature's laws. Freedom is achieved by arranging nature, including our own natures, so that our aesthetic responses to reality are not driven by a crude, unreflective fear, hunger, shame, or bodily exhaustion. Nature, in the course of natural history, has already arranged itself in the marvelous nervous system of human beings to achieve a godlike freedom. It remains for us to arrange our social lives to make further progress in realizing freedom so that each may come closer to Truth and beauty.

In that task, new-God believers and no-God believers are coworkers. Our theologians may sometimes lapse into supernaturalism to retain some of the attractions of the old God. Their work, though, should be primarily seen as attempts to find God, and even the joy of experiencing God, in a thoroughly disenchanted, factual world. Their naturalism should not be taken as a reluctant concession to secular thought, but rather as a deepening of religious understanding, an understanding that makes the essential work of religion this-worldly. For the freedom in which Truth is actualized is of this world. It is born of prosperity, good health, education, civil liberty, and social equality—the material circumstances, along with the human central nervous system, that constitute the natural setting of freedom, the arena of Truth's emergence.

Atheists, long known as "freethinkers," have always thought that whatever salvation there was to be had was to be had here. For me, a lover of happy endings, it is comforting to conclude that the seemingly largest of religious divides, that between those who believe in God and those who do not, not only can suggest a common moral program, but also a common social vision. It is a vision of free men and women finding what meanings they will in the common life that makes their freedom possible. That vision may never be fully realized, but all who work for it are doing God's work—or something like it.

REFERENCE MATTER

APPENDIX A
THE INEFFABLE

Many an issue is decided with the defining of terms. That is why there is something so obviously right and terribly wrong in logicians' attempts to begin debates with some definitions. Right, because without definitions we are talking at cross-purposes or perpetuating fallacies of equivocation. Wrong, because premature stipulation runs roughshod over the obscurities, ambivalences, and genuine disagreements that constitute the heart of most moral and metaphysical issues. So we should begin with definitions, not as cornerstones of a firm foundation that will fix the superstructure but rather as tentative architectural sketches that will suggest the contours of various possible buildings.

When it comes to "God," even the most tentative of working definitions is immediately sidetracked, for the first thing that some theologians are inclined to say about God is that nothing can be said about God. God is ineffable, that is, incapable of being defined, described, or expressed. God, they say, cannot be said. It takes little ingenuity to make hay with the paradoxes that flow from theologies of ineffability. Later in this appendix I will indulge in such haymaking. First, however, I want to examine the possible grounds for claiming the "absolute impossibility . . . of talking about God" (Lerner 1994, 37).

Incomprehensibility

One possible ground is incomprehensibility. Ineffability is claimed to be a consequence of incomprehensibility and they are, indeed, closely linked, but the ineffable should not be conflated with the incomprehensible. These are distinct ideas. Unlike the ineffable, the incomprehensible can be referred to, can be discussed, can be named. What we cannot do is understand it.

Understanding admits of degrees. While it is hard to say what would count as a full understanding of anything, it is not difficult to imagine that, of some things, human intelligence might be incapable of achieving a full understanding. Indeed, human intelligence might be incapable of achieving a *full* understanding of anything. Everything might be incomprehensible (for humans) if comprehensibility means complete understanding. This might be so because the complexity of things is beyond human grasping. Perhaps, if this is something different from complexity, the sheer volume of truths required for total understanding may outstrip our storage capacity. If we place the threshold of comprehensibility so high as to require complete understanding, we make only a modest claim in calling a thing incomprehensible. God may surpass our understanding, but if you ask too much of understanding, so does a fruit fly.

Incomprehensibility is, however, a remarkable attribute if we employ a low threshold of comprehensibility. If we claim that something is comprehensible whenever we are capable of knowing *any* truths about it, then the claim of *in*comprehensibility is a claim of total ignorance. Something is incomprehensible only if we can know nothing about it, but to know nothing about something is not even to know that it exists. Total ignorance requires no less. At that extreme, incomprehensibility does become a ground of ineffability, for if we cannot know that something exists, or cannot even know that it might exist, our ignorance of it would prevent us from speaking of it. Ineffability might be a consequence of extreme incomprehensibility.

Are we totally ignorant of God's possible existence? The question seems to answer itself. We might not be capable of knowing much about God, and all of our speculations about the divine nature might be wildly off base but, as we engage in a discussion of God's existence, there seems no way intelligibly to deny our awareness of God's possible existence.[1] This awareness, implicit in the activity of discussing God, amounts to knowledge, however minimal, of God.

Now perhaps such minimal knowledge, amounting to nothing more than knowledge of God's possible bare existence, rules out absolute incomprehensibility, but still leaves enough of God beyond our ken to merit the term "incomprehensible." Perhaps. However, that level of incomprehensibility does not make for ineffability. Being able to talk about

God does not require that we be able to talk about God accurately or in all of her dimensions.[2] "Largely incomprehensible" doesn't entail ineffability. If God is mostly incomprehensible, we will still be able to talk about her, even if most of what we say will be false, and the sum of what we say will be incomplete.

God's incomprehensibility is often explained as a function of how she must come to be understood. Suppose that knowledge of God is only to be had by acquaintance with God. One must have an experience of God to have any descriptive knowledge of God. There may be evidence, such as others' reports, which can provide knowledge of God's possible existence, but any further knowledge requires the experience of God herself. Although a blind man might believe that colors exist without the experience of seeing them, his knowledge will not be of the essence.[3] Therefore, we may get a qualified incomprehensibility and ineffability: God can be genuinely understood only by one who has personally experienced God. There is no way to describe the experience because (1) it is a simple, homogenous experience not composed of familiar parts, or (2) it is a complex experience and all of its ultimate atoms are unfamiliar simples, or (3) it is an experience composed of familiar elements that are arranged in utterly new types of relations. In any event, there is no understanding God without this experience, and there is no describing the experience in terms that are meaningful to those who have not had the experience. If God is an experience that is radically different from other experiences, then God, or the "God experience," although it can be labeled and named, must remain a name that carries no essential meaning for the inexperienced. To that extent, God is beyond language, ineffable.

We should note the extremity of the claim that to know God is to have met God. Few other things, if any, must be experienced to be understood. Indeed, most things are similar enough to other things that analogies, metaphors, and descriptions in terms of familiar elements convey a degree of understanding. This is true even for things radically foreign to one's experience. I have never experienced war, and it may very well be the major human experience that I least understand. Still, I would claim some minimal understanding. I have suffered pain, despair, and injury. I have been afraid, surprised, bored, tired, hot, cold, uncomfortable, confused, and dirty. I have been exhilarated by competition, challenges, and danger. I have been exuberant in triumph, worried over my own and others' safety, filled with rage and sadness, and mourned the death of friends. I do not doubt that most of these warlike experiences of mine were pallid compared to their real war equivalents. Since, however, I know in general what it is to have both the weak and intense versions of an experience, I have some ability to extrapolate to more intense samples of an experience, even if I am only familiar with its milder cases. Of course, there is a gestalt to war that no amount of extrapolating from nonwar experience may capture. Nevertheless, it may be possible to provide a similar gestalt to those who have never gone to war. The best war accounts try to do this. The libraries and museums that are filled with war literature and war art suggest that many who have been caught up in war feel that communicating a measure of their experience is possible.

Think, then, what it is to say that there is absolutely no understanding of God without the experience of God. It is to say that the God experience is completely unlike any other experience one has ever had.[4] All of the descriptions of God are not merely inadequate, they are false, misleading, and totally uninformative.[5] At best they are evocative for those who have experienced God, although it is unclear why even that should be the case. Why should a metaphor likening God and maternal love evoke God for one who has experienced both if God is *wholly unlike* maternal love? For the God-experienced, if God is radically unique, only naming her is needed, and for the God-inexperienced, neither naming her nor anything else is helpful.

God's incomprehensibility is sometimes attributed not to its uniqueness as an experience, but to its greatness as a concept. The idea of God is so big that we cannot expect our limited minds to apprehend it. The part cannot grasp the whole, the finite cannot contain the infinite, the inferior cannot judge the superior, the depths cannot survey the heights—variations on this theme are endless. It is a metaphor more than an argument, but it is a metaphor with considerable persuasive appeal. I believe that the psychology of the appeal is more moral than logical. It tells us not to get uppity and start presuming to understand, let alone judge, our betters. Indeed, the doctrine of ineffability, at least in the Western religious traditions, is best understood as flattery. "God, you are so much greater than our meager selves that our language, which is after all a human capacity, does not apply to you." Traditional prayers are full of praise and self-abasement. What is the outer limit of praise and self-abnegation? Silence.[6] The truly great things leave us speechless, and before the mightiest masters we dare not speak a word. God's magnificence and power should leave us speechless, and the advocates of ineffability take this quite literally (at least as doctrine, hardly ever as practice). It is as though they were saying, "God?—what can you say" or "How great is God ?—fuhgeduhboudit!"[7]

God's ineffability is most often asserted as an introduction to a discussion about God. This is usually accompanied by appropriate apologetics, for few such theologians are unaware of the obvious objections to the practice: "If you truly believe that God eludes language, why do you speak of God?" or, worse, "If God is beyond language, why should I listen to you speak of God?"

The answers from theologians of the ineffable vary, though few of the replies persistently hold in mind the conceded premise of the objections, namely, that God is absolutely ineffable. Michael Lerner declares God-talk an "absolute impossibility," and in the same sentence he blithely goes on to talk about God because "I've taken upon myself the task of talking about God." Before the paragraph is done, the "absolute impossibility" has been quite forgotten, and Lerner speaks of "vantage points . . . and . . . entry points" that make "divine energy" "accessible to the Jewish people" (Lerner 1994, 37). Sometimes, compulsion is the plea; those who have experienced God, goes a typical apology, "feel a compelling desire" to speak of the experience, knowing that language is "inevitably inadequate" (Lerner 2000, 32). The compulsion, however, is not treated as an irrational tic having no meaningful theological content, but rather as language that moves its hearers as does poetry and song. God is no longer ineffable, beyond language, but merely beyond the language of literal propositions.[8] That does not, however, get our writers to start sounding more like psalmists and less like scholastics. If this is poetry, it is poetry dressed in the robes of standard theology.

Poetry and Duality

Arthur Green's inclination toward ineffability rests on the impossibility of "speaking" God's unity in grammatically dualistic language to existentially dualistic, mundane consciousness. Because grammatically dualistic language is the only language that Green has, and existentially dualistic, mundane consciousness is the kind of consciousness that he must address, and because "hints of the ultimate Oneness of Being" have to be found hidden within the dualistic language that ordinary consciousness can hear and speak," he indulges in God-talk "in order to communicate religious insight" (Green 1992, 43–44). Still, our "deepest truth" remains "all is one," and dualistic language, a sop to "ordinary experience," cannot be expected to express this deep truth (1992, 17). Indeed, the deep truth may not even be compatible with sanity (1992, 27). All may be one, but we are two. Our twoness cannot say the one. Still, we will try.

The progression is common. It begins with a claim of absolute ineffability, but the need or desire to speak of God is invoked as a reason to indulge in God-talk despite the ineffability. Why should we not dismiss the ensuing discussion? How does the theologian of the ineffable martial on? Tacitly, the claim of ineffability is modified; it is not that God cannot be spoken of, it is only that God cannot be spoken of in ordinary language or, although we can speak of God, no amount of talk does full justice to God. In other words, the original claim of absolute ineffability is abandoned. Language, as poetry, hints, metaphors, pointers, and evocations does, it seems, have some power to speak of God. Perhaps even normal propositional talk, so long as we realize that it leaves out important features, tells us something useful of God. In sum, one response to the objections to continued God-talk in light of God's ineffability is to acknowledge the objections and then ignore them.

Paradoxical Enlightenment

A more philosophically respectable response to the objections claims that God-talk is not about God at all, but is meant, rather, as a demonstration of the inadequacy of such talk. The very failure of theology is offered as proof of God's ineffability. Sometimes, this strategy takes the form of theology as paradoxical riddles, riddles not meant to be solved, but instead meant to frustrate and exhaust. The frustration and exhaustion get the auditor to abandon attempts to understand God or find God in language. We are put through an exercise in futility meant to reveal the exercise's futility.[9]

An unsolvable riddle is a path to enlightenment rather than an obnoxious trick when its insolubility is due to a false assumption at the core of the riddle. Struggling with the riddle reveals the false assumption. Without the false assumption, the riddle disappears. It is not solved, it is dissolved.[10] The riddle cannot be stated without the false premise. Not being bothered by the riddle is an indication that one has ascended to a higher understanding. This is theology as Zen koans. Paradoxical theology as a spiritual discipline might be a justification of this practice, but it is not one employed by Western theologians of the ineffable. They are no Lewis Carrolls of theology writing nonsense in order to make good sense more vivid. They mean for their words to convey something of God. These are the writings of earnest preachers, not of Zen pranksters.

The real function of the ineffability doctrine, undoubtedly not consciously intended, is to relieve theologians of the responsibility to speak consistently of God. It is an all-purpose, theological reply to any objection: "Is my theology self-contradictory or incoherent? Well, what do you expect? I said at the outset that God is beyond language." Any verbal and conceptual inconsistencies in the theology are transferred to a pragmatic inconsistency between the theological content and the practice of theologizing. It saves the theologian some embarrassment, but at the cost of trivializing his theology.

Theologians would be better off without the ineffability dodge and the mystery-mongering that it encourages (e.g., Green 1992, 51). They have ingenious, interesting, and insightful things to say. Their topic is difficult and profound; that they do not have a fully satisfying account of their God is no shameful failure. Human knowledge progresses by confronting incoherencies of belief. Scientists who accept irreducible mystery as the "explanation" of theoretical problems have explained nothing and ceased to be scientists. Indeed, we sometimes say that they have become theologians, but that is not right. Priests, shamans, magicians, or poets are closer to the mark, but even these terms do not well characterize the scientist who accepts mystery. Such a scientist is one who is simply no longer engaged in intellectual inquiry in his field. The ornithologist who rests in mystery may remain a bird enthusiast and a bird propagandist, but he is no longer an ornithologist. So too with theologians: The theologian who rests in mystery may be a servant of God and a guide to God, but he is no longer an inquirer into the nature of God, no longer a theologian. He is a spiritual coach. It is a respectable change of role, and many theologians, including the ones that I have looked at most closely, frankly aspire to being spiritual guides as much as, if not more than, being theologians. Religious knowledge is not their primary goal. Rather, they want to have a religious effect. All well and good, but I wish to untangle their theology proper from their spiritual coaching. The former is ill-served by the doctrine of ineffability, even if it is a basic principle of the latter.

The doctrine of ineffability is also motivated by fear of hubris, but it is not needed. We can speak of and aspire to knowledge of God and still show appropriate humility before her. The claim that God is knowable and can be spoken of is far from the claim that God is known and truly spoken of. Let theologians be awed by the difficulty and profundity of their subject. Let them proclaim their sense of inadequacy for the task. Let them be constantly conscious, and keep their audience constantly conscious, of the highly fallible nature of all theological assertions. Let them argue that we are unlikely to ever fully understand God and that we have made small progress in the understanding thus far achieved. But, for God's sake, as long as they are talking of God, let them stop saying that nothing truthful can be said of God—it out-Cretans the Cretans.

If there is anything beyond language, no one has ever spoken of it or ever will speak of it. Nor is this, the previous, or the next sentence truly about it. No more verbal fretting on that matter. The God that we are concerned with can be, and has been, spoken of incessantly, not least by the theologians of ineffability. I have wanted to take this talk seriously.

APPENDIX B
THE UNTENABLE GOD

This book begins with the incredibility, for "moderns," of the old God. Having assumed that the old God is not, for many people, a live option, the book proceeds to compare belief in the new God with belief in no gods. For some, the comparison may leave neither option looking like it is responsive to their needs. Some "moderns" may find no gods too unnourishing to live by and the new God hardly distinguishable thin gruel. In our dissatisfaction with the choices, we may want to reexplore the possibility of belief in the old God. If belief in the old God is what we really need, perhaps we can overcome our modern skepticism and latch onto that substantive deity.

There may be all sorts of psychological devices for inducing belief in the old God, but a critical immersion in the arguments for its existence is not one of them. The literature arguing for and against the existence of the traditional Western God is ancient, ongoing, and immense. The vitality of the discussion in some circles precludes declaring universally accepted conclusive results. Nonetheless, I think that the state of the debate is about as conclusive as any genuine philosophical question can get: There is no *epistemic* justification for belief in the traditional Western God. This chapter will not attempt to fully establish that claim—a task that is repeatedly, thoroughly, and well done elsewhere (e.g., Martin 1990). However, readers of this book may find useful a short summary of some of the standard arguments for the old God, along with equally brief summary refutations. If no God or the new God feels like Hobson's choice, before being forced to it, reassurance may be wanted that there is no obscure, rationally grounded escape hatch.

The Cosmological Argument

A group of arguments termed "cosmological" try to infer God from the claim that before there can be anything, there must be first things (Aquinas 1272). Before there can be movement, there must be a first mover; before causes, a first cause; and most generally, before being, a first being. If something cannot emerge from nothing, and there is indubitably something now, there must have always been something. This something, this being that has always been, this "eternal being," is identified as God.

Accepting the premise that nothing of nothing comes,[1] we can still ask why the ground of being must be a single being, rather than an infinite series, each member of which had a beginning. Everyone has a mother, but there need be no Eve—just a never-ending lineage of mortal mothers. So why not with beings in general?

If the notion of an infinite series rankles, we can grant a form of primordial being without ascribing to it any of the other traits of the old God. Ignorant, blind matter could be the ground of being—without will, morals, or intelligence. Abstract mathematical objects may have generated the universe—without understanding, purposes, or preferences. The vibrating membranes of string theory may just always have been there. By themselves, all that the cosmological arguments rule out is that there was ever nothing (and that only on a premise which, although I find it intuitively appealing, is itself undefended——the "nothing from nothing" principle). Eternity does not divinity make.

The Ontological Argument

Unlike the cosmological argument, the ontological argument has had little popular appeal, but it has been a great favorite among philosophers (Plantinga 1965). Its various versions come down to this: One can conceive of a being that *must* exist, that is, one can imagine a being that has the property of "necessary existence." Existence would be the essence of such a being, just as being three-sided is the essence of a triangle. Triangles might not exist, but all triangles are three-sided. Three-sidedness is part of the very idea of a triangle. To conceive of a triangle properly is to conceive of it as having three sides. Similarly, one has not conceived of a necessary being properly if one conceives of it as not existing or even of possibly not existing. To conceive of a necessary being is to conceive of it as existing.

The trouble with the argument is that it is not clear that one *can* conceive of a necessary being. I can mouth the words "necessary being," but that I have any particular idea associated with them is doubtful. Hume denied that there is such an idea, asserting that anything that could be thought of as existing can also be thought of as not existing, and Kant seemed to be getting at much the same thing in his denial that "existence is a predicate" (Plantinga 1965).

There is a way of combining the cosmological argument and the ontological argument that gives us a stronger version than either alone. Suppose there are no necessary beings. Then all beings are contingent, that is, although they exist, they very well might not have. We then may ask, since their nature does not preclude non-existence, why they do in fact exist. If our explanation of their existence refers to other contingent beings, the question of these other contingent beings' existence rises in turn. Indeed, unless we posit a necessary being, all of being becomes contingent, and the question of why there is something rather than nothing becomes unanswerable. Existence is a brute, inexplicable fact. It is not simply that we do not know why there is being, it is that there truly is no reason for being. If you are attached to Leibniz's principle of sufficient reason—the claim that everything has a reason that fully explains it—ultimate and total contingency is unpalatable. Hence, a fully explainable, thoroughly rational universe must contain necessary being. This reasoning does not provide a concept of necessary being, nor even prove that there is a coherent concept of necessary being to be had, but it does provide some basis for believing that there might be necessary being and depict an *epistemic* reason for *wanting* it.

Even if you are persuaded that there must be that which cannot not be, it is still a long way from there to the traditional Western God. That being that cannot help be might be anything. Perhaps there is an argument that proves that the necessary being is nothing less than the totality of being, that is, the universe. That still leaves us far from the old God, for this totality, while necessarily existing, need not be a knowing being, a powerful being, or a good being.

The Argument from Design

Some arguments have such strong intuitive appeals that even decisive rebuttals fail to drive them from the field. The argument from design—the argument that it is not just this world's existence, but rather its well-wrought appearance, that proves the existence of the old God—I consider the prime example of a fallacious intuition's persistence in the face of devastating criticism. Perhaps this fallacious support for theism persists because we are hard-wired to seek anthropomorphic explanations—the evolutionary endowment to highly socialized, self-reflective animals. Our recognition of other minds and all the benefits that that recognition confers may require a natural assumption to seek intentionality behind regular effects. The scientific revolution rested, at least in part, on our ability to overcome this ingrained bias. Still, the bias remains a natural attitude, so frequently useful, that only its demonstrated disutility, and not its theoretical futility, tends to alter it, but as a rational justification for belief in God, it is indeed futile.

The world is certainly full of complex patterns, intricate dynamic relations that sustain elaborate forms, regularities that give absolute obedience to the most rigid laws, and all in all manifests an order that makes our lives and our purposes possible. If chaos is the natural state requiring no explanation, if a simple, blind, and goal-less regularity would suggest minimal need for explanation, then this highly structured world of ours is the epitome of that which demands elaborate explanation. True, ignorant armies do clash by night, but we are still rightly impressed by the massive amount of well-sighted intelligence at work in the day.

Proponents of the argument from design argue that a world that exhibits so much apparent design is reasonably believed to have a designer. There must be, they say, a mind behind all this method. The alternative, that primal being blindly fell into this complex and useful condition, they find too improbable for reason to accept.

How improbable is it that this orderly world resulted from initially purposeless developments? Before tackling that question, we should note that positing a designer begs rather than answers the question of whence comes order and apparent design into being. "God brings order to the world, God's mind designs creation" is the "best explanation" that the argument from design would have us infer, but how did God become orderly, how did God's mind become so finely designed that it could design our world? Design and order are *posited* by the argument from design rather than explained by it. The problem of design's existence is kicked upstairs to God, but it is left as the same problem. Of course, it is possible to say that order is inherent to mind, that the intelligent, purposeful nature of God is simply an essential and eternal feature of God. We might, however, just as well say that order is inherent in the world, that the intelligent, purposeful nature of unconscious being is simply an essential and eternal feature of it. Neither claim explains the genesis of order and purpose. Both deny the premise, essential to the argument from design, that chaos is the default condition, the state of being needing no explanation.[2] The conclusion of the argument from design is that God, hardly a chaotic jumble, is a state of being needing no explanation, but if you are going to assume order and purpose, there is no rational advantage to assuming it in God than in the godless world. You might as well be left with a mysterious world as with a mysterious God.[3]

Now it may be countered that all that is meant by "God" in the argument from design is that the world is originally grounded in intelligence, that is, ordered purpose, and that the argument does not intend to establish a transcendent God. An immanent God will do as well. The key point is that intelligence must be assumed as eternal. It is not that God explains original intelligence, it is that nothing can explain intelligence's origins, that intelligence must be assumed; in that assumption we assume God.

I think we do have plausible explanations for the world's order, intelligence, and purposes without resorting to positing eternal mind, whether immanent or transcendent. Even if we did not, even if we had to assume some mind inherent in being, this is a far cry from the old God. The original intelligence need not be invested in one being nor the original purposes in one will. Gods do as well here as God. The intelligence may be yoked to temporary and limited power rather than traditional omnipotence. Moreover, values embodied in purposes can be malevolent as well as benevolent. Hume famously showed (1762) how on the evidence of the world, if we choose to see conscious design in it (a choice Hume finds resistible), we ought to infer a group of morally and technically imperfect designers. The old, perfect God is hardly the best explanation for this world's seemingly imperfect design.

Need we start with mind, or even much order, at all? Given enough chances, the most improbable of events become probable, almost certain. In the fullness of time, all possible patterns will likely emerge and, if there are any simple regularities inherent in being, some of those patterns will have the features necessary to sustain themselves. Nothing possible is improbable if you keep at it long enough.

For those who want to limit our chances to the time available since the big bang,[4] and therefore keep some extreme, long-shot developments (humans, for example) in the highly improbable category, Darwin has described how the circumstances of living beings can accelerate and sustain the appearance of purposeful form, bringing forth designerless "design" and finely honed purposes faster than random, molecular, musical chairs would lead us to suspect. Perhaps dynamics analogous to evolutionary pressures accelerates the emergence of stable forms in nonliving beings too.

The logic of chance and evolution as master explanations of the emergence of order have faced renewed challenges by neo-arguments from design relying on the so-called "anthropic" principle (Barrow and Tipler 1986). It is claimed that the numerical values that we find in nature's most basic regularities are just those needed to make life, or perhaps even our universe of organized matter, possible. Any other values would not do. Now, because the values could have been anything at all, the fact that we got precisely the values that we need to be who we are looks like a stroke of incredible luck. Too incredible, say the neo-designers. They have somehow calculated the odds. Very small. More likely, we had someone put in the fix. The "anthropic principle" is the "fix was in" hypothesis, which requires a fixer: God.

The argument contains multiple confusions. First, we have not, nor could we have, any background information on the formation of the totality of being. It is therefore a little absurd to talk about the odds of the universe (the totality of being) being what it is. We do not know how many universes are possible. Maybe two, and we exist because a coin toss went our way. My metaphysical intuitions (unfounded, but whose are not?) tend toward believing that there was only one possible universe (a Pythagorean faith), and so our existence was a necessity, involving no chance at all. The neo-design argument assumes that an infinite number of universes were possible, making our universe the longest of long-shots.

However, let us accept the premise that an infinite number, or at least a very large number, of universes were possible. Does the realization of our one-in-a-zillion universe point to God? Yes, say the neo-designers, for it is too gullible to believe that we lucked into just the Planck Constant that we needed to create temperate planets, let alone baseball and Van Gogh.

Similar reasoning makes believers out of many lottery winners and plane crash survivors. You pray that you will win the lottery. The odds are 1 in 100,000,000 against you. You win. Either God answered your prays or a fantastically unlikely event occurred. Neither is true. From an objective point of view, a very predictable event occurred. *Someone* won the lottery. Only the winners' egocentric perspective makes them think that something in need of special explanation occurred. Likewise, someone or other is likely to survive a plane crash that proves fatal for most passengers. The particular passenger's survival required myriad circumstances to fall just the way that they did. Any tiny change would have doomed him (and saved someone else). His survival strikes him as a miracle. It does not look so miraculous to the families of those who did not survive.

If many universes are possible, but only one is actual, we are in the survivor universe. We won the lottery. If those other, unrealized universes had perspectives, they would be unimpressed. True, most of them *we* would have found uninteresting; indeed, most of them probably would not have perspectives even if they were realized, and so would not have found themselves interesting. What of that? Their existence would still have been miraculously against all odds.

Furthermore, there is no reason to believe that there is not quite a large number of other possible universes that could have evolved perspectives. Maybe, although a subset of all the possible universes, the set of possible universes with intelligent, reflective perspectives is infinite, and any of its members' actualization would have inclined its inhabitants to see a divine hand in their existence. It is hard to shake egocentric reasoning.

The actualization of a particular, perspectiveless universe would be just as unlikely as the actualization of any other possible universe, including our own. Just because we would find the patterns created by an unending whirl of expanding, superheated particles uninteresting and uninspiring does not make its actualization any less of a long-shot than was ours. A long shot was bound to come in if only one universe of a large number of possible ones was to be actualized. That we were the long-shot naturally moves us, but there is nothing to suggest that it was not a natural outcome of a game of chance.

There is also the possibility that every possible universe[5] is realized, and therefore the existence of ours, rather than being miraculous, is a consequence of its being possible. If every possible lottery winner wins, our winning requires no explanation beyond being a possibility. In the actualization lottery—the lottery to go from the possible to the real—we do not know how many winners there are. The results are not published. All we know is that we won. *We* are, by definition, only in our universe (although lots of close look-alikes may be in similar universes). In those many other universes, we are not around to lament our absence and curse the long odds that prevented, or made unlikely, our being there. Those other universes either have indifferent, unreflective beings, or intelligent beings celebrating their miraculous existence against all odds, or very intelligent beings who make no inferences about providence unsupported by sound reasoning.

Other Arguments: Miracles, Mysticals, and Morals

If belief in miracles is required to buttress belief in God, we have already abandoned modern rationality and might as well frankly make our theism solely a matter of faith. A miracle is a violation of the laws of nature, and laws of nature are generalizations from exceptionless, verifiable past experience. Inductive rationality begins with the rejection of the miraculous, with the supposition that nature is law-like. We can be mistaken about what the laws are, but to deny that there are exceptionless laws (perhaps only statistical laws in some cases) is to abandon the canons of inductive rationality. The weight of evidence is *a priori* always against belief in the miraculous.

People lie, people misperceive, people misinterpret, people deceive themselves, people misremember, people influence each others' reports, people go insane, people in groups become collectively delusional. Odd circumstances give rise to unusual events, hidden natural factors go unobserved, charlatans are endlessly clever at creating illusions, coincidences are bound to happen sometimes. All of these phenomena are available to explain the apparently miraculous and any are *more probable* than a lapse of a law of nature or rather, more rationally acceptable, as the laws of nature give us the very context for judging probabilities. Certain experiences may make belief in miracles psychologically irresistible, but never logically justifiable.

Mystical experiences, too, can make belief in God psychologically irresistible, and while not as logically untenable as a basis for theism as belief in miracles, mystical experience is hardly a sturdy epistemic foundation for belief. Even if it could be shown that mystical experiences are sufficiently similar to each other to suggest a common cause (a controversial showing in its own right), it requires a leap of logic to conclude that the common cause is a nonpsychological factor that is reliably revealed or inferred from the content of the experiences. It is one thing to argue that God is the best name for the mystical experience itself (see chapter 6 for a discussion of this approach), but it is quite another to claim that God is the cause of the experience. Experiences do not reveal their causes in their content. We suffer pain without learning a thing about neurology; we can enjoy music without any knowledge of harmony and listen to it on the radio with no awareness of broadcasting.

The subject of an experience has no privileged perch when it comes to discovering its cause. The content of an experience may provide a clue to its cause, and the subject does have special (although not incorrigible) access to content. However, the clues in content can be misleading, and only objective investigation linking experience to object can establish a causal connection. Moreover, no objective investigation has led from mystical experience to God. Unless God is observed outside of the mystical experience, no such connection can be established. At best, God is an unobserved, theoretical entity meant to explain mystical experience. However, unlike the more successful theoretical entities, the God posit does not do a great job in helping to predict or control the phenomena that it is meant to explain. Even though, as it turned out, Scrooge's experience of Marley's ghost did have more grave than gravy about it, Scrooge was rational to hypothesize various causal possibilities. God as the causal explanation of mystical experiences is no better than many other hypotheses—ranging from psychosis and hypnosis to naturally broadened consciousness and extraterrestrial communications.

Moreover, if the commonalties of mystical experience are taken to point to a divine cause, they hardly point at the old God. If anything, there is much more of a pantheistic feel to the typical description of a mystical experience. Hindus account for their mystical experience by Brahma, the ultimate Being constituting all being. Buddhists' experience of Nirvana is explained as a consequence of contact with absolute nothingness at the core of all existence, and many a Christian, Sufi, and Cabalistic mystical experience is described as absorption into, or communion with, all of being.[6] If any remotely divine thing is suggested by mystical experience, it is much closer to the theologians' new God than to the traditional Western God.

I discuss in chapter 6 why belief in God is not needed in order to live a moral life. This appendix has the overlapping but simpler task of showing that the existence of morality is not evidence of the existence of the old God. The only reason to think that it might be would be an inability to imagine morality as a natural product of the human condition. If morality were naturally *in*explicable, its existence would give supernaturalism an epistemic toehold. We have too many, however, rather than too few, naturalistic explanations of morality; some are rooted in rational egoism, some in inbred, evolutionarily adaptive sentiments, some in theories of kin selection, some in social psychology. The details are controversial, and there is much empirical research and conceptual analysis yet to be done. Progress, though, is good, and we hardly need resort to God to explain our ability to live by rules, have concern and sympathy for others, and be motivated by universal principles.

Those then are the major arguments purporting to show that God exists. There are two categories of arguments, which although related to arguments for God's existence, are importantly different in kind, and those categories of arguments will not be dealt with in this appendix. One category tries to show that we ought to believe in God, whether or not God exists. To a large extent that is the subject of this entire book. These arguments are not epistemic justifications of belief, but rather pragmatic ones.[7] The pragmatic consequences of the old-, new-, and no-God beliefs are the subject of chapters 4 through 10. To a certain extent, it is the attractive effects of belief in the old God described in those chapters that motivate this appendix. "Boy, belief in that old God looks good; are we sure that we moderns do not have good evidence justifying such belief? Does our loyalty to knowledge of objective reality really leave us only with the new- and no-God options?" This appendix reminds us that, alas, that is the case, and so the new God/no God decision, although not perhaps the choice that we want, is the choice that we have and is therefore worth a book.

We will also leave unexamined the kind of argument that tries to give positive reasons for showing that there is no old God. So, for example, the "problem of evil" names an argument that attempts to persuade us that the traditional God is incompatible with our world's suffering and wickedness. However, moderns need not hear those arguments. We are already unable to believe in the old God. This appendix was meant to show that there is no rationally respectable way to overcome that inability. If the problem of evil argument succeeds in disproving the old God, it is just piling on. If it fails to disprove the old God's existence, it still provides no positive, rational grounds for belief in that comforting deity. At best, a solution to "the problem of evil" tells us that reason does not rule out a path to the old God, but it does nothing to create that path.

In conclusion, our modern prejudices against old-God belief, perhaps much to our chagrin, survive epistemological critique. For "moderns," it is the new God or no God.

APPENDIX C
THEORIES OF TRUTH
AND CREDIBILITY

This is a book of reflections on a certain type of belief, and so, as truth is the first virtue of belief, the book unavoidably raises a number of questions regarding truth. Among the more prominent questions on which the book takes implicit positions are: What is truth? How is truth recognized? Is it valuable? Why is it valuable? Is there only one kind of truth? Are there incompatible truths? What is or ought to be the relationship between truth and belief? Do or should some types of belief have different relationships to the truth than other types of belief?—in other words, views on most of epistemology, lots of ontology, and the lion's share of philosophy of language. Such views are often tacitly assumed in the preceding chapters. I have not argued for these views nor will I in this appendix, but readers might find explicit statements and explanation of them helpful.

The theory of truth that I believe most closely resembles unreflective common conceptions of truth is usually termed the "correspondence theory of truth."[1] On this view, reality *is* a certain way, and truth consists of the accurate representation of the way that reality is. Granted, there are great difficulties in understanding how one thing represents another at all, let alone how it can represent it accurately or inaccurately. Basically, the theory holds that a proposition (or a belief, that is, a mental entity with propositional content) is true if there is some fact to which the proposition "corresponds." The nature of this correspondence is variously explained as resemblance (in one way or another), causation, or

141

association. The nature of the "facts" to which the proposition corresponds is also variously described. However they are characterized, some relationship makes the proposition a representative, a stand-in, for the fact. The existence of the fact does not depend on the existence of the proposition, and it is the existence of the fact, along with the proposition having the right kind of relationship to the fact, that makes the proposition true.

The major competitor to the correspondence theory of truth is called the "coherence theory of truth." In the coherence theory, the beliefs and propositions that are true are not made true by a relationship that they have to reality, but rather that their truth is a function of the relationship that they have with each other. Truth is a matter of cohering well with the total set of items already accepted as true.[2] Truth is like a club defined by its members. Being true means that you are clubbable, and what makes you clubbable is simply that you are compatible with the other members of the club.

The coherence theory seems to imply a relativism of truth.[3] All you need to be true is to get along well in the club that you are in; the club itself does not have to meet any standards, at least none set by reality, to be truth-conferring. Presumably, there are a number of coherent clubs with different members, and hence different and incompatible sets of truths.

Whatever its merits as a theory of truth, the coherence theory is rather persuasive as a component of any theory of credibility. Credibility is conferred, in large part, by context. A belief is more easily permitted to remain in the house of our beliefs if it gets along well with the other residents. We are loath to welcome in a belief if its acceptance entails evicting many others, especially if those others include long-cherished housemates at the very center of domestic life. If certain conceptions of God are immediately incredible to moderns, it is because of the other things that they believe. Cohering with other beliefs may not be the sole criterion of credibility, it may not even be necessary, but it is surely the determining factor in most cases. When it comes to figuring out what ought to be believed, what ought to be *taken to be* true, what we already take to be true, looms large.

Coherence is not an all-or-nothing affair. A belief can more or less cohere with a set of beliefs, the degree being a function not only of the total number of other beliefs in the set with which it coheres, but also of the status of the members with which it coheres. Some members may have a more valued, central place in the set. W. V. O. Quine has described a belief system as a "web of belief" and discussed how believability is a matter of position in the web (1953, 1960, 1978). The firmness of belief is determined by the centrality of its web connections. In the same way that some nodes are more important than others to the integrity of a spider's web, some beliefs are more important to the integrity of a system of belief and therefore are more firmly established.

A pure coherence theory that employed this web imagery would have us picture a web unattached to and unaffected by an extra-web reality. A belief's truth would be shaped by nothing outside of the web, but Quine's web of belief rubbed up against reality in the form of stimuli to the senses. Perceptions, presumably partly caused by extra-web reality, influenced the web at the margins. Although influential, for Quine, the extra-web reality never definitively determines the truth of any given belief—it merely might cause a reconfiguration of the web. Our beliefs react to what we perceive, but as a systematic collective, not as individuals. Furthermore, although the web of belief must take reality into account in determining truth, the nature of the accounting is *not* a matter of representing. For Quine, it is some kind of compatibility with experience. However, if representing an experience does not make a belief or proposition compatible with the experience, what does?

This question brings us to a third theory of truth, the pragmatic theory. The pragmatic theory claims that a belief or proposition is true if it is useful, or in some versions, if it will ultimately prove more useful than any competing belief. Presumably, the sorts of experiences that a belief tends to give rise to, the capacity of a belief to manipulate and control experiences in accordance with will and desire, and the power of a belief to create the world that we want to live in is the measure of its truth. This is a relativism of truth *if* we think that different beings would ultimately find different beliefs most useful.

Theories that analyze truth solely in terms of usefulness leave no space for a distinction between a belief's truth and its usefulness. To be useful *is* to be true. The correspondence theory, in contrast, allows for such distinction. A belief may be useless and true or useful and false. Nonetheless, although keeping them conceptually separate, the correspondence theory of truth explains why truth and utility often go together. Beliefs guide action, and actions' success is best explained by how well they are guided by beliefs that reflect reality. A true belief fosters realistic adjustments that help to attain goals. False beliefs might luckily suggest the same adjustments, or better ones, than do true ones. There might even be cases where false beliefs heuristically succeed better than true ones (a possibility discussed in chapters 5, 6, and 7). Yet surely, in the long run, and usually in the short one, it is most useful to know what is really going on, if, that is, anything is really going on.

Hence, both the pragmatic theory of truth and the correspondence theory, in different ways, tie usefulness and truth together. Only a pure coherence theory leaves usefulness unconnected to truth because truth is neither defined by usefulness (à la the pragmatic theory) nor is truth connected to any extra-belief reality, a connection that would explain its usefulness (à la the correspondence theory). In pure coherence theory, true beliefs are a reliable guide to nothing other than to other beliefs in the given belief system. The system itself need meet no standards of usefulness or indeed any standards beyond internal consistency. It is not simply resistant to reality-imposed revisions, it is immune to them. This sort of theory of truth is only plausible if one believes that there is no reality, at least none with any features, apart from the belief system. I reject such a radical relativism.[4]

The theory of truth that most informs the reflections of this book is a hybrid drawn from the epistemological views of Susan Haack (1993). Haack offers the crossword puzzle as a model for understanding knowledge, belief, and truth. True beliefs, like correct answers to a crossword puzzle, must fit together. Failure to cohere with other beliefs is sufficient to make a belief false, just as failure to fit in with other crossword answers makes a crossword answer incorrect, but the coherence of a belief set is insufficient for truth. Just as crossword answers must fit together *while simultaneously* answering the clues of the puzzle, beliefs, if they are to be true, must fit together *and* account for our experiences. Experience, the way that reality is thought to impinge on us, are the clues to which a true belief set must answer. Answering to experiences is the correspondence aspect of truth.[5]

The crossword image helps to elucidate the distinction that I make in chapter 10 between truth and Truth. Although they are different, the difference is a matter of degree. "T(t)ruth" is not being used equivocally. What makes something true, in either sense of T(t)ruth, is that it is a correct answer in a crossword puzzle, but it is a complex, multilayered puzzle, with different types of answer spaces, connected to the puzzle in different ways and demanding different of types of answers. An empirical truth is an answer in a region of the puzzle that must respond to many exacting clues. A moral or political truth has fewer clues to satisfy than do empirical truths, but, in order to work in the puzzle, moral and political answers must cohere directly with answers, indeed, with spaces in the puzzle, that other puzzlers provide. In the moral realm, we are solving a puzzle that we are also creating with others. Finally, there are spaces in the puzzle whose answers, while still constrained by needing to cohere with other answers in the puzzle, including the empirical and ethical answers, are so situated as to be relatively tolerant of a wide range of answers. Not any, but many answers will fit. These are the spaces in the puzzle whose answers give meaning, purpose, and beauty to the whole game.

There may be more than one set of answers that constitute a solution to the empirical spaces of the puzzle, but possibly not. In any event, we have yet to find even a single, full solution to the empirical sections of the puzzle. Indeed, we have yet to find all of the clues, let alone getting all of the answers to fit together. We can understand scientific experiments as trying to generate clues in order to test whether particular beliefs can serve as answers in the final solution to the puzzle, the solution that will "work" when all of the clues and all of the other answers are filled in. Science tends to assume that two logically incompatible beliefs will not both be allowed by reality, that is, only one answer will respond to all of the clues and fit in with the other answers that also respond to all of the clues. However, that may not be so; there are puzzles with multiple good solutions, and although empirical reality, the reality that stimulates the senses, seems unlikely to allow for multiple, equally good solutions, it cannot be ruled out.

Getting agreement and thereby coherence to the ethical questions is also difficult. There may be many apparently possible solutions to ethical regions of the puzzle, but in practice, we have yet to find a single, *stable*, ethical solution. The "clues" in the ethical regions are, in part, the moral intuitions of others as well as one's own. There is a sense in which the right solution can only be certified as such when it is universally acknowledged to be right. There may be multiple, logically coherent, universal moral consensuses that fit in perfectly with the empirically adequate answers to the puzzle, but, so far, even a single such consensus eludes us. A good ethical answer must build toward that consensus.[6] That is a strong constraint on one's freedom to fill in the moral blanks with anything that strikes your fancy. It is enough to hope for a single set of ethical truths, and we will be lucky to approach it, let alone find it.

The solutions to the areas of the puzzle that deal with the meaning and purpose of life, while partially determined by the other regions of the puzzle, are probably infinite. The connections to ethics and physics exclude some "meaning and purpose" answers, but there is no end to the number that they permit. These are the religious Truths, which are in some ways not only the most important but also the least constrained parts of the puzzle. How one completes this part of the puzzle, as I have argued in chapters 9 and 10, is largely a matter of taste.

I have described what makes a belief "true," and is it the same thing, in general, that makes a belief in God True: After every possible experience is taken into account, after all actual, stable moral intuitions are figured in, if one can coherently include a belief in God into one's set of beliefs so that it makes the set of beliefs as aesthetically satisfying for you as possible, then that is a true a set of beliefs, and one's belief in God is True (where the capitalized "T" simply indicates that it is a truth far removed from, and therefore less constrained by, the empirical and moral truths). I call this ontological pluralism rather than ontological relativism to underline that not any God belief is true, only those that fit in the puzzle and respond to someone's deepest aesthetic inclinations (but I have speculated that there are an infinite number of those).

This appendix began with the claim that truth is the first virtue of belief, but it is not the only virtue of belief. Usefulness in belief is also virtuous, and a true but completely useless belief, though it would have the "first" virtue, would be of seriously diminished value. By making them definitionally equivalent, the pragmatic theory of truth rules out the possibility of useless true beliefs, or more to our purpose, it disallows ultimately useful false beliefs. The correspondence theory, as we have seen, explains why, in general, being true makes a belief useful. True beliefs are like accurate maps, and accurate maps are typically the most useful ones. In the correspondence theory, however, including the Haackian-inspired variant, which contains a strong correspondence dimension, usefulness does not *necessarily* adhere only to true beliefs, for in this view there is a distinction between truth and usefulness. Although the theory suggests that truth and utility run in tandem, at times they may not. Indeed, there may be kinds of situations where they may not correlate at all. False beliefs can be useful. This is especially so when the benefits in view are psychological.[7] If our primary interest is in how to feel about the world, rather than in how to successfully manipulate the world, the usefulness of the relevant beliefs may not coincide with their truth. So there is some reason to judge the value of belief in God separately from judging the truth of the belief. Those judgments are considered in chapters 4 through 7.

Useful false beliefs may be important, but we still want to know which beliefs are true. So, given the above account of truth, is the statement (and corresponding beliefs), "God exists," true?

Until the crossword puzzle is complete, which it probably never will be, we cannot say with certainty. There is a falliblist epistemology at work here, but the tentative conclusion must be that the statement, "the old God exists," is false. The old-God answers conflict too much with what looks like pretty promising empirical (and I would add, but somewhat more contentiously, ethical) parts of the puzzle. A foundational premise of this book is that new-God believers and atheists agree on "the facts," and one conclusion of my reflections is that new- and no-God believers are converging on the same moral answers. At this point, it seems to me that either new- or no-God answers might be part of complete solutions to the puzzle. These would be overlapping but different solutions. There might be more than one final set of complete true beliefs, and the new God might be in some and not in others. If we judge ontological commitments by the Quinean criterion of that which we must posit in our best language (Quine 1953), then, if we have equally good languages employed by diverse speakers, we will have diverse ontologies. It is what I have termed "ontological pluralism." I am skeptical that this ontological pluralism will survive in the empirical realm, but it might. I expect it to survive in the aesthetic and religious realms, but it might not.

If ontological pluralism in religion does survive to be part of a complete, final, true set of beliefs, would the claim "the new God exists" be "objectively" true? The answer, of course, depends on what is meant by "objectivity." If it means that the new God must be included in *any* complete, final, true set of beliefs, then no, the existence of the new God is not objective truth. I take "two and two equals four," "an atomic bomb was dropped on Hiroshima on August 6, 1945," and "humans evolved from other forms of life" to be objective in this sense of objectivity because I believe that such statements will be part of any complete, final, true set of beliefs. If, however, objective truth includes all things that exist in any *valid* perspective (that is, all things that exist in a complete, coherent set of beliefs that answers all of the clues), then the existence of the new God might well turn out to be an objective truth. Objectivity is not, in Thomas Nagel's phrase, "the view from nowhere" (1986), but it is reasonably thought of as the view from everywhere. So the question comes down to whether objective existence requires that something be seen from everywhere or only that it be seen from at least one perspective that is as good as any other perspective. The new God will not be seen in every epistemically acceptable perspective, she will be seen in some. At least that is the way things look to me now. I must leave it for others to characterize this perspective, which sees no God in the world, but sees that others, with no worse vision, see her.

NOTES

Notes to the Preface

1. What constitutes modernist belief? I do not assert that the acceptance of science and the rejection of magic are either necessary or sufficient to merit the labels "rational" or "modern" in general, but in my usage, they are the central criteria of modernist belief. If you are modern, there is a family of methods, principles, and attitudes that generate propositions, and theories that command belief or, better yet, communities of like education and mutual respect that profess loyalty to these methods, principles, and attitudes are the ones that we invest with the authority to command belief. What is meant by either "science" or "magic" is highly contested, but there is an everyday rough consensus regarding their meanings. Perhaps the consensus concerning science and magic is a fake agreement, a façade built of myriad equivocations in which, for instance, people mean different things when they say that something is "scientifically validated." There is something to this, but I do not think that it is the main story. Although we may be unable to agree on their analyses, there is widespread agreement on their instances; we know science and magic when we see them. There are methods and doctrines at the border, on which "our" opinions are divided, but the core exemplars are not at issue. So what constitutes the family of science? The family includes close observation, careful measurement, generalizability, quantification, controlled experimentation, predictive power, testability, logical argument, openness to criticism, fallibility, intersubjectivity, and repeatability—the hallmarks of science. There is a rival family, which includes the direct control of nature through symbolic manipulation, the direct breaking of natural regularities through the force of will alone, and the employment of powers that are essentially mysterious—the magic clan. Propositions that are the progeny of this latter family are dismissed by moderns out-of-hand. If you are not strongly inclined to befriend the first family and snub the second, and to treat the dominant belief

systems they have engendered accordingly, then the god(s) of our fathers may be live options for you. However, if you concede science and repudiate magic, you are modern. For moderns, the old gods will not do; there must be a new God or none at all. This book is a comparative evaluation of those two options—new God or no God—the modernist options.

2. That is, if there are any truth merits outside of an idea's personal and social implications. The pragmatic theory of truth, somewhat simplified, claims that a true belief is simply the one that it is best to believe. See appendix C for a fuller discussion of the pragmatic theory of truth.

3. I fear it because I do not want to take a debunking posture. What would we think of the editors who replied to the young girl's inquiry regarding the existence of Santa Claus with the resounding, "Yes Virginia, there is a Santa," and then went on to explain how Santa was the spirit of generosity, hope, charity, good cheer, etc., if, instead they had said, "No Virginia, there is no Santa, although he is a convenient personification of a number of admirable qualities that we should emulate and reflect on"? We would think the editors plodding, literal-minded dullards, with unpoetic souls and unplayful hearts. The editors, however, were not attempting philosophy of religion in an analytical mode, which has a different aesthetic.

Notes to Chapter 1

1. It should be noted that Lerner's, Green's, and especially Kaplan's influence have extended well beyond the Jewish Renewal or Reconstructionist movements with which they are identified.

2. Arthur Goldhammer points out (personal communication) that, on the contrary, religious thought often has made the desire for truth irreligious. Neither the eater of the fruit from the tree of knowledge nor Faust is viewed as the model of piety.

3. Patrick Buchanan, an unabashed advocate for the old God and his cultural milieu, certainly fears that it does. He writes (*Boston Herald*, November 15, 2004, 27) that "Christianity," by which he means traditional, old-God Christianity, is "in retreat," with churches "emptying out" throughout Europe. He goes on to argue that America is not "far . . . behind Europe in entering this brave new world."

4. Only for some. Arthur Goldhammer points out to me (personal communication) that for many, especially in religious matters, it has *not* been difficult to maintain dissonant beliefs; the Catholic Church, founded on a faith that idealized poverty, humility, and cheek-turning, was long a fabulously wealthy institution, with prelates termed "princes of the church" who launched and fought many a war. Catholics were (and are) hardly alone in their ability to separate theory and practice.

5. Harold Kushner, a popular, liberal, Jewish writer, says book-loads about God while hedging on the question of God's human mind independent reality (Shermer 2000, 259). Kushner is acceptable because of the general acceptance of new-God theology.

Notes to Chapter 2

1. God has received many descriptions; a central initial question must be, "What makes any of them a description of God?" I am not asking, or at least I am trying not to ask, "What makes a description a good or accurate description of God?" Presumably, an accurate description of God would require that there be a God and that the description would, more rather than less, "capture" or "match" or "correspond" to God or at least cohere well with other beliefs that we held related to God (see appendix C on the nature of "truth" for a fuller discussion). However, there is something very misleading about calling all descriptions that do not correspond to God or cohere at all with our other theological beliefs "bad descriptions" of God. Most such descriptions are not describing God at all. A good description of George W. Bush or the planet Neptune or the Quadratic formula are best thought of not as poorly done descriptions of God, but rather as *not* describing God. What is at play here is the intention of the describer. Something is properly called a bad description of God only if it is intended as a description of God. Intending to describe God is a necessary condition for describing God poorly. It is trickier and, indeed, to a large extent, the burden of this book is to lay out a necessary condition for a good description of God, in part because the concept of God is not easily separable from her description. In any event, our theologians explicitly claim to be talking about God, so we have the intention present that allows us to hold them responsible for their descriptions of the deity.

2. Some philosophers would question whether it is a proper concept at all. They worry that "being" or worse, "Being," improperly treats existence as a property that can define a set. In their view, it is a confused and confusing reification. I do not share this worry, although I admit some concerns regarding the proper characterization of the set "Being" as that which contains all "beings." Is it simply the set with a completely unrestricted membership? That seems wrong, since we want to exclude nonbeings from it. What, though, is the name of the set that excludes nothing? Possible Beings? Does that set exclude impossible beings? Must all sets have a boundary that allows for the possibility of exclusion? Interesting philosophical treatments of the problem are found in Plato's *Sophist* (c. 390 BCE), Hegel's *Logic* (1830), and Meinong's philosophical papers (Chisholm 1967).

3. Those functions are discussed, along with how well the theologians' God performs them, in chapters 4, 5, 6, and 7.

4. A Hegelian might argue, in support of Green and counter to Maimonides (1190), that an organism is more of a unity, more "one" than an undifferentiated being. The latter can be divided without loss of quality, but not so the former.

5. Should I contract an incurable, aggressive cancer, then perhaps my heart is better off being immediately transplanted to an otherwise healthy cardiac patient. I, of course, would be better off keeping my heart, which will allow me to live another year before I am felled by the cancer. My heart, however, will only weaken if it remains in my chest as the cancer spreads, and then my heart will rot in the grave if it gets buried along with the remainder of my remains. From the heart's point of view, immediate transplantation following the fatal diagnosis is the way to go. The absurdity of the preceding discussion comes from granting the heart a point of view and an accompanying well-being, attributes that most of us do not think that the stand-alone heart has. In the "universe is to individual as organ is to organism" analogy, the conceptually independent interests of the universe's members create the great disanalogy that casts doubt on all of the supposed implications of the organic conception of the universe. Unlike my heart, I have interests that might be different from the interests of the whole, not to mention different from the interests of other parts. For instance, it is conceivable that I would be better off if I and all my contemporaries and the next ten generations of humans led happy lives, even if it led to the destruction of the universe in a thousand years. The parts of mundane organisms do not have interests separable from the organism. Richard Dawkins (1976) treats genes as having interests, but only as a heuristic device. They can best be understood as behaving selfishly, but Dawkins is at pains to emphasize that he does not think of them as having motives, desires, or conscious goals. They simply act as if they had the goal of being fruitful and multiplying, The parts of the organic universe (us, for example), however, appear to have nonuniversal interests. True, the appearance may be an illusion—that, after all, is the claim of our theologians and mystics everywhere—but it begs the question to argue that the universe is an organism of which we are all parts, and that therefore our interests coincide with those of the universe. The suppressed, question-begging premise is that all the parts of any possible organism find their good, insofar as they have any, in serving the organism. This is not self-evident.

Notes to Chapter 3

1. Perhaps this is what Kaplan means about being part of something "super personal" (1985, 86).

2. The theologians' vagueness on this matter is quite understandable when we note that under some characterizations, human self-consciousness, a realized state, is the process, or part of the process, that makes universal self-consciousness possible. When we add to the mix the fact that consciousness of any sort is best

seen as a dynamic, complex process, we might find it hard to fault the theologians for conflating self-consciousness, the creating of self-consciousness, and the conditions for the creation of self-consciousness in their description of God.

3. See for example Lerner (1994, 420). Actually, Lerner says that progressive social action is spiritual, but as he identifies "Spirit" with God (2000, 32), it amounts to the same thing.

4. (Kaplan 1985, 223). Kaplan is being intentionally amorphous. He will not fully define "salvation" because the human good is forever evolving (1985, 81). Lerner gives a nod in that direction too (1994, 409).

5. See for example, Nietzsche (1887) and Feuerbach (1841).

6. This, of course, assumes that propositions have truth-values beyond the propositions' usefulness—an assumption that many schools of philosophy would deny (see appendix C)—and Kaplan comes close to such pragmatist schools of thought. Kaplan denies that the "God idea" value lies in any cognitive content that it might have, rather than as "the difference the belief makes in human conduct and striving" (1985, 33). Belief in God is a "reaction of the entire organism to life" (Kaplan 1934, 330).

7. One possible argument against the possibility of universal mind would argue that "minds" are necessarily social products, and universal mind, as a singleton, is incoherent. Conversely, if not social, mind still needs an external environment, the "not myself," and therefore cannot be composed of the totality of being. Ironically, mystics often employ this type of reasoning to explain why God, the whole of being, has to fracture into a multiplicity, but the reasoning seems to me to undermine the very possibility of the self-conscious universe.

8. Lerner (1994, 181) makes God into an impersonal energy source. See also Green's rejection of God as a "thou" (1992, 5). That God is in no way a person is a strong theme in all of Kaplan's work.

Notes to Chapter 4

1. In appendix B, I argue that there are no extant persuasive arguments for the existence of anything like the traditional God but, for the most part, I just assume that the traditional God is not a viable option for "moderns."

2. Politicians and social theorists have long seen common religious belief as a promoter and sustainer of social harmony. It took centuries of wars to begin to replace common belief with mutual tolerance as the basis of social order; the struggle is ongoing. Mutual tolerance is only necessary because common belief is no longer obtainable at acceptable cost.

3. Those immersed in a secular milieu pay a price for *observing* such traditions.

4. See chapter 4 of my *Respecting the Wicked Child* (Silver 1998) for further discussion of meaning and alienation.

5. I do not mean to imply that fear and self-interested hedonism might not be motives that contribute to the creation of good character. Indeed, in the next chapter, I will argue that they can. Here, I argue only that *once built*, good character should no longer rely on them as the motive of morality.

Notes to Chapter 5

1. Admittedly, only a minority of our contemporaries fully inhabit the modern world, but as I argued in chapter 1, it is a significant and perhaps growing minority.

2. See appendix C for a discussion of the relationship between a belief's usefulness and its truth.

3. Appendix A discusses God's "ineffability," the theologians' justification for their refusal to be held accountable for their descriptions of God, and in chapters 2 and 3, where we attempted to understand the nature of the new God, we discovered some of the consequences of that freedom from verbal responsibility: varying, vague, and at times inconsistent conceptions of God. No settled conception of God, when attributed to one of the theologians, is likely to capture the theologians' variously described God. Moreover, due to no slackness of the theologians, but rather due to the rhetorical convenience that I find in lumping them together, a single conception attributed to all three theologians will not describe a God that any of them would fully recognize as his God. In sum, it is incomplete at best and inaccurate at worst and certainly unfair to saddle the theologians with a single conception of God, but I will begin by doing just that. For before judging the usefulness of a belief in God, we need to say, with at least some precision, what the nature is of the God being judged.

4. This conception of God is silent on whether it is one feature, a collection of features, or all of the world's features collectively, that are (or is) responsible for these goods and potential goods. Whichever set is responsible, be it a singleton or the set of all sets, that set is God. The conception is also silent on the nature and location of the divine structure(s). They may inhere in human minds, human bodies, or the biosphere. Alternatively, the God-structure may permeate all of reality. The conception does require an immanent God—God is not distinct from nature—but which part, or parts, of nature is or are God, or indeed, whether it is nature taken in its entirety that is God, is left open by the conception. The theologians have many things to say on what of nature is God, often inclining toward pantheistic and holistic views, but I foist no such commitment on them with this baseline conception. Here, God is simply a special structure in being, and although that special structure may not be specifiable short of describing every aspect of being, it may, on the other hand, be a very particular and even rare part of nature.

5. For a related discussion of progressive politics as essentially optimistic politics, see *Respecting the Wicked Child* (Silver 1998), chapter 4.

6. The philosophers of science discuss such matters as whether every genuine explanation gives predictive powers and whether the thing explained must be deducible from the explanatory premises.

7. In a note to the preface, I discussed what that form is: basically, we want an explanation that fits well with established scientific findings, is quantifiable, testable, etc. (see 149–50).

8. Unsurprisingly, Kaplan is most free of this reluctance to give up God as a kind of explanation.

9. See the work of Brian Skyrms (1996), Richard Dawkins (1976), Daniel Dennett (1995, 2003), Robert Wright (1994), Robert Frank (1988), and George Ainsle (2001) for some of the best examples of this work. Darwinians across the disciplines have been prominent in the attempt to provide a naturalistic explanation of the "higher" human capacities, but in principle, scientific explanations of these phenomena need not be restricted to a Darwinian paradigm.

10. Never having had a mystical experience, I am at a disadvantage here. It *is* the case that mystics have the unshakable conviction that attaching the name "God" to their experience of the universe as a unified Being infused with "spirit" does go a good way toward explaining that experience—i.e., telling themselves that they experienced God appears to explain the experience *to them*. While, as I argue in the text, I do not see how the God label advances understanding, perhaps some deference ought to be given to the authority of those with firsthand knowledge of the experience in need of explanation.

11. Nietzsche (1886) thought that we humans would be beyond morality once that we realized that *we* create morality.

12. Kathleen Sands (personal communication) thinks that a tendency for the universe to incline toward the good is the minimal requirement for theism, and therefore the baseline "God" simply fails to qualify as God, new or otherwise.

13. What is the evidence that helps it go down? It is becoming almost a commonplace to note that the self is a social construction. We are socialized into a sense of self. Different cultures may do it somewhat differently and may create different selves. Society makes us into separate beings. These are widely accepted, plausible claims, but they do not entail that the resulting selves are arbitrary and unnatural fictions. Social processes are also part of nature, and the socialization that molds nature into individuals works with material realities and relationships—skeletal, neurological, nutritional—that surely, guided by selective pressure, foster the creation of a range of certain types of selves. One might say that selves and self-interest are natural features on the landscape of being, no less real than any undifferentiated, unindividualized being whence they emerged and in which they may eventually be submerged. I do not here argue that a stringent monism might not capture a deep truth about reality. I only argue that this monism is not based on self-evident truths that it would be irrational to

deny. All may be one, or best understood as one, but that view is not a dictate of science or common sense. It may be compatible with both, but it is currently demanded by neither. So monism must be classified as an act of faith. If we have intellectual limits on how much faith we have to spend, we should count acceptance of monism as a debit. Organicity also goes in the debit column. Granted, everything might affect anything and everything else. The proverbial flutter of the butterfly wing might explode a distant galaxy, but this is far short of the claim that every part of being is a role player in a system whose homeostasis depends on each part's performance. Organic relations are more than occupancy of a common causal space, but the baseline God needs no more than that. So long as the possible causal connections inherent in the universe permit the rise of good things, the baseline conception is satisfied. To conclude that the causal connections that allow for good things constitute organic relations is a further expenditure of faith and an additional tax on our credulity.

14. The lyrics of this popular ditty ("Santa Claus is Coming to Town") continues, "so be good for goodness' sake." Catchy, but a logical solecism. In logic, the song should have continued "so be good for the sake of the electronic equipment, dolls, sports gear, and other gifts that you hope to get but will only get if the omniscient and just Santa judges you worthy of receiving." If you were good for goodness' sake, the all-seeing Santa would be irrelevant as a motivator of your virtue.

15. Arguments for a happiness/morality connection often depend on question-begging definitions of "true happiness" to become persuasive. If we define "true happiness" in a way that conceptually distinguishes it from "moral," so that there are no logical ties between the two, it is doubtful that a good case can be made causally connecting immorality and unhappiness, a good enough case, that is, to make belief in the connection a motive for morality. I have argued that there is a link between happiness and morality (Silver 1980) and remain persuaded of the link, although I do not think that my or any other arguments that I know are fully persuasive.

16. Admittedly, this judgment is based on the personality types that I find lovable; Jehovah and Jesus have certainly been love objects of many people.

17. Perhaps that is because there are simply a lot more believers than nonbelievers, so even if belief were irrelevant to morality, we might expect to find more moral heroes among believers.

18. I dilate on the relevance of my dislike of roller coasters in chapter 9.

19. For those unfamiliar with some of the members of my personal catalogue of heroes and villains, here is a gloss on some of those mentioned above. Janusz Korshak was a Polish-Jewish writer and educator who stayed with the orphans that he was charged with as they were taken to the Nazi death Camps. Judah Magnes, an American rabbi, helped to found the Joint Distribution Committee to aid Jewish refugees from pogroms and was an early fighter for Jewish and Arab equality and coexistence in Palestine. Mother Teresa worked with the

dying indigent of Calcutta. The Lamed Vovniks are anonymous, righteous men for whom, according to Jewish folklore, the world is maintained. The following are on the other side of the ledger. The BJP are Hindu fanatics who have slaughtered Muslims in India and destroyed mosques. Zealots were ancient Jewish fanatics who murdered political opponents, Jews as well as Romans. Kahanists are a Jewish political grouping who are antidemocratic in principle and are de facto racists who seek theocracy in Israel and are quick to resort to violence.

20. Although, as we have seen in chapter 1, it might make one acceptable in America, where the details of theology are either of little interest or are little understood.

Notes to Chapter 6

1. I presume that a goal is eternal life, but that our mortality dooms us. Of course, there is no reason that eternal life be one of our goals or that any of our most important goals be unachievable in a temporally limited lifetime. The notion that our individual goals are doomed, if not tied to our mortality, might have to rest on a Buddhist-type psychology of human desire, which reveals desire, as a system, to be unsatisfiable. However, if we are unconvinced by that psychology, we might plausibly argue that rather than being doomed, individual goals have a greater likelihood of success than does God's much more formidable desires.

2. Basically, the argument is that if the sole goal of the universe is continued existence, organicity does not seem to further it. The collection of all beings will carry on whether or not it is organically related, or for that matter whether or not it contains the possibility of goodness. Being of one sort or another is immortal. (Some physicists now talk of the possibility of all being having popped into being from nothing, a "vacuum fluctuation," although the only sense that I can make out of this is that our world emerges at random from the realm of all possible worlds, which realm is not nothing. At worst, actual being may disappear into the realm of possible being.) If I most want immortality, and I identify myself with all and any being, I can rest easy, but the baseline God, i.e., the possibility of goodness, did not create my ease. My comfort comes from the identification with being *per se*. Organicity does not add to my ease either, except insofar as organicity may have enabled my identification with all being. The identification, however, is of questionable value since it creates only value-free endurance, eternal life as everlasting "whatever."

3. Thomas Nagel (1986) speaks of a view from nowhere as being the ideal of objectivity, but I think that the view from everywhere better captures a plausible epistemological stance that we can equate with "truth" (see appendix C). Moreover, seeing from everywhere at once is, to me, marginally less mystifying than seeing from nowhere.

4. For instance, how would such souls, which, *ex hypothesi*, have no distinguishing psychological traits or spatial-temporal location, be individuated?

5. Ryle (1949) meant the phrase not only to be a criticism of the separable Cartesian self, but also of the view that aspects of the psyche were composed of nonphysical mental stuff. One can reject the "soul" view without rejecting all forms of mind-body dualism.

6. This is basically Derek Parfit's (1984) closest-continuer idea of the self.

7. I believe that what is often mistaken for purely retributive feelings is the desire to teach criminals the wrongness of their actions combined with the belief that the only way to truly drive the lesson home is to have them suffer the harm they did or some equivalent. Such views may be extensionally equivalent to retributivism, but it has a different, and to my mind, more understandable logic.

8. Must the suffering be a *necessary* means to the good end in order to be justifiable? Could suffering, which is a means to a good, but neither the sole means nor the least painful means, still be justified? I do not think so. If suffering is unjustifiable whenever it serves no purpose, i.e., is wasted, any unnecessary suffering is unjustifiable. It is excessive and wasteful. There was no point to the surplus suffering. Of course, under real conditions, it is often impossible to identify the absolutely most efficient (in terms of minimal suffering) means to an end, and so any not grossly wasteful suffering that is turned to goodness is redeemed by that goodness. Of course, in all cases where the negative value of the suffering is greater than the positive value of the end (and who knows how to measure such things precisely?), the suffering is automatically wasteful and unjustifiable. It should also be noted that I am using justifiable in a restricted sense, meaning "given a plausible rationale that one can reasonably find acceptable." I do not mean to imply that the imposition of the suffering for the sake of the end would necessarily be just.

9. In *Respecting the Wicked Child* (1998), I have extensive discussions on making life meaningful.

10. I must reiterate my doubts that we can have such meaning without purposes. "Making sense" means "understandable," which means "intellectually acceptable," which in cases with a moral dimension may mean "morally acceptable."

11. Here, I am using explanation not to refer to scientific-style theoretical explanations of repeatable empirical events, but something more along the line of a historical explanation or a literary interpretation of a particular event. Yet as metaphysics, it will be the kind of history and criticism that have the feel of necessity.

12. If a semantic explanation is to be metaphysical, we must be dealing with Idealist metaphysics, but such are the only kind of metaphysics that can give us ultimate "why" explanations. Materialist metaphysics are doomed to resting with a perplexed shrug at the being of some inexplicable brute fact.

13. The claim here is that comprehended misfortune is easier to bear than mysterious troubles. This may be denied by those who believe that random

misfortune—bad luck—is easier to accept than the misfortune that is the outcome of a lawlike natural process. I see no way of arbitrating between these
differing psychologies. This just might be a matter of taste, and I am merely
elaborating above on my dislike of mystery, a taste that I will say more of in
chapter 9.

14. Another possibility for "God's" consoling power is that it is the willful
assertion of meaning in the face of manifest absurdity. Faith is the nonrationally
grounded insistence that the world is meaningful because only that attitude
makes life bearable. This is a common religious existentialist's response to absurdity. (Atheist existentialists choose to embrace the absurdity and either see it as
liberating or just grin and bear it.) The theologians do not develop this approach
much, although Green toys with it when he states, "we do not deny absurdity,
we reject it, we *defy* it." This, though, is a temporary pose for Green, not a
deeply held position, for he quickly goes on to state that although we know that
absurdity "represent[s] a truth . . . we know a deeper truth as well" (1992,
156–57). In other words, on the most fundamental level for Green, the universe
is not absurd and giving it meaning is not a mere act of will, but rather a recognition of the deepest truth, an act of knowing. Indeed, Green states (1992, 33–35)
that imagining God helps us to "catch" or "reflect" the divine light. It does not
generate it.

15. I am not sure how that image is supposed to work. I guess it is meant to
make the audience less intimidating, but I think that one might well find a room
full of naked people quite intimidating and unsteadying. I do not think that the
image would diminish my nervous excitement.

16. Kaplan (1934, 397) wants us to judge our "God-Idea" not by its cognitive content, but rather solely by the conduct that it generates.

Notes to Chapter 7

1. Art Goldhammer (personal communication), asks "why not direct . . .
feelings of unearned wealth politically rather than theologically," and reminds
me that John Rawls and Michael Sandel have argued that the community merits
gratitude as the source of much of our unearned good fortune. Why not make
the state or community—unmysterious, perfectly secular entities—the recipients
of our gratitude? Certainly, the polis, as Socrates famously argued, is the source
of many "blessings," and we ought to be, as good little kibbutzniks and ancient
Greeks were, taught to attribute those goods to the source from whence they
really came. In America, the social nature and origins of many goods are ob-
scured, and dissipating this obfuscation would surely be moral and political progress. An equal distribution of socially created goods is one of the marks of a just
society, but before that can happen, they must be recognized as social goods. So
let us thank our just institutions, not God. Rawls has argued that justice even

requires that society equalize all undeserved goods, regardless of their origins, so long as that can be done without diminishing liberty. So again, we would be able to thank just institutions, not God, for enhancing our well-being.

The foregoing is true as far as it goes, but some undeserved goods are simply immune to a morally acceptable egalitarian distribution or to any human-planned distribution at all. Technological and policy advances may allow us to distribute that which was previously undistributable, but it is unlikely that we will ever be able to eliminate fortune as a major factor in happiness. There will always be the equivalent of being in the right place at the right time, or more commonly, not being in the wrong place at the wrong time, that will spell the difference between spectacular success and outright failure, between continued well-being and catastrophe. Life is sometimes a game of inches.

2. Lerner tries to finesse the question of whom to thank by implying that we can, with the same effect, thank God or the universe (2000, 288).

3. Another difficulty in coherently conceiving of individual good fortune is that it seems to require not only a self, but also a substantive self that is separate from one's characteristics, in other words, it requires a soul (see chapter 6). What do we tend to be thankful for when giving prayerful thanks? Most often for the things that are constitutive of our empirical selves: our health, our temperament, our talents, our family, our friends, our community, our education, our occupation. If I say I am lucky to be MS, I seem to imply that there is an "I" separable from MS, an I who might have ended up in less fortunate circumstances, but if I simply *am* the MS circumstances, it is unclear that I can be considered fortunate for being what I am. The circumstances may have been otherwise, but then I simply would not have existed. Perhaps, if there are no Cartesian selves, the only thing that we can coherently regret or celebrate is our very being, the fact that these happy circumstances exist. However, we would not be celebrating that I am they, as though that were an additional lucky fact, one of which I am the beneficiary. The best that we can do for making sense of individual good luck without resort to a soul is to conceive of the individual as a community of circumstances and features; the community's membership can change and insofar as it gets good new members, the community, as a collective, is fortunate. Mostly, I suspect, that when we are contemplating our fortunes, we think of our *desire set* as our self, and are asking how well that set is being satisfied. We rarely consider ourselves lucky or unlucky in the desires that we have, except as a theoretical concession to social norms and moral correctness.

4. Kaplan (1936, 399), in arguing for the retention of "God," quotes with approval John Powrys's assertion that only that term has sufficiently rich connotations to do the work that we need done.

5. Neither, however, does any language that has terms with distinct meanings and referents.

6. Although I suspect that most readers will intuitively agree that it is a bad mistake to confuse experiences with their objects, the danger of the confusion is

not simply analyzed. I believe that the difficulty has something to do with keeping open the possibility that beliefs can be false, i.e., that there is space for error to creep in between the world and our experience of the world. Of course, certain kinds of idealism want to deny that there is any world beyond our experience of the world. Snow is none other than our experience of snow; to speak of the former is to speak of the latter. If, though, that is the case, none of our experiences of snow can mislead us about the nature of snow, for it has no existence outside our experiences. Some may grant an extra-experiential existence for snow, but argue that an experience of snow is always veridical insofar as it is an experience of *snow*. An identical experience, caused by brain stimulation for example, is an apparent experience of snow, not an experience of snow. Moreover, any experiences that falsely portray snow are, at least in part, not caused by snow and are therefore not experiences of snow. These analysts take the expression, "the experience of snow," to embody its own success and think that we must use the expression, "the experience that appears to be of snow," to refer to failures. The problem here is that all of the synchronic features of the experience of snow and the experience of what appears to be snow can be identical, the experiences only distinguished by their historical origins. I think it troubling to require different terms to speak of items with identical forms and content merely because of their parentage. It may sometimes be justified, but it smells of ontological racism. Simpler, I think, to distinguish snow from our experience of snow and admit that the latter is paradigmatically and usually, but not always, caused by the former. Even if we do want to insist that the latter, strictly speaking, is always caused by the former, we will do well to have separate terms for each, if for no other reason than that we can intelligibly have this epistemological discussion.

7. Compare Kaplan's argument (1936, 397–99), where he argues for a historical development of the "god-idea," which reverses the idealistic direction and has God mature from a notion of an objective being to a collection of human attributes and functions.

8. The imagery here may be specifically Christian, but it is descriptive of much Jewish mysticism too, which fetishizes the Torah as word, letter, and object and conflates God and the name of God as much as any tradition possibly can. Some Jews refer to God exclusively as *HaShem,* "the name."

9. Green does not consistently take this strong position. For him, imagining God helps us to "catch" or "reflect" the divine light, it does not generate it (Green 1992, 33–35). Like Kaplan, Green does want to root the divine in the human, but his formulations, more than Kaplan's, are vague regarding ontological priority. The "lines between the divine and human are less than rigid," Green tells us (1992, 124). Even Kaplan is not immune to this ambivalence. Kaplan attempts to transcend a "humanistic interpretation of life" by appealing to the emotional experience of "cosmic" urges (Kaplan 1985, 78). For all the naturalist, rational, and moral appeal of making us God's maker, even our theologians cannot fully give up the ghost.

10. Curses, addressed to God, are problematic, whether another person or God himself is being cursed. We may not want to consider "dear God, please damn my neighbor" or "God, I hate you and may your projects come to ruin" as prayers, but that aside, when you talk to God, it counts as prayer

11. Something like petition and thanksgiving can take forms that turn God into a grammatical third person: "We hereby thank God . . ." or "May God grant us . . ." are functionally pretty close to direct petition and thanksgiving, but they are made possible by the implicit invocation of God as a grammatical second person. It is possible to praise, adore, and contemplate something that you cannot address, but it makes no sense to thank something or plead with something, however indirect the verbal approach, unless it were also possible to address your gratitude or plea directly to that entity being thanked or pleaded with.

12. Some philosophers would argue that consciousness does not amount to anything more than that which is appropriate for others to treat as though it had beliefs, desires, intentions, etc. See Dennet (1987).

13. Only the value of prayer-produced resignation to our fate seems to survive, indeed to flourish, when God, the symbol of Being or of human personality, is misinterpreted as the symbol of that mysterious master personality, the God of our fathers, for that old God's will is as indomitable as the universe's reality and a plausible symbol of it. Resignation is the one value producible by reverential prayer, and it is one that the theologians do not value.

14. I suggested above that it is hard to limit the context in which "God" is an emotion/action guiding image.

15. Our discussion has suggested two generalizations regarding prayer: (1) If prayer is valuable it is because it changes the one who prays and (2) prayer must be (at least implicitly) directed to a person. Martin Buber (1958) has famously connected these claims. For Buber, God is the "eternal Thou," that Being whom we treat always and entirely as a person, and who thereby most fully and reliably affords us opportunity to be the "I" of an "I-Thou" relationship and escape the "I" of an "I-It" relationship. Buber contends that these are very different "I"'s, and although the "I" of the "I-It" is intrinsic to the human condition and has its proper place, it is inferior in human value to the "I" of the "I-Thou." The "I" of an "I-Thou" is vulnerable, for it is an "I" in relationship with a free, unpredictable being, a relationship from which nothing of the "I" is held back, but it is the only "I" that lives in the present, the only "I" that is completely alive to the world.

In prayer, we talk to God and therefore create the dialogical relationship from which the "I" of the "I–Thou" emerges most perfectly. Prayer is valuable because that is where I forge my most alive, authentically human self, the self that is in relationship to another self. Clearly, this "I" of the "I–Thou," this dialogic self, has a life outside of its relationship to God. Traditional theologians may believe that in any genuine spiritual encounter, whether with art, nature, or another human, it is ultimately God, or a creature of God, that we encounter. Even traditionalists, however, concede that not all speaking and listening is prayer. Our question must be whether the speaking that we do to God in prayer and the "I" that emerges from that relationship cannot be had in more mundane dialogues, whether the "I" of the "I–Thou" really does need "God," an "eternal Thou," to become fully realized. Buber seems to think that it does because invariably even our relationships to other humans become "I–It" relations and are prevented from a permanent lapse into "I–It"ness by our notion of the ever-present potential to take the "I–Thou" stance.

16. Of course, I defined prayer as talk, implicitly or explicitly, directed toward God, and therefore talk to humans is, ipso facto, not prayer. Although, in examining whether talk to humans can be functionally equivalent to prayer and to what extent there can be this equivalence, it is useful to talk about "praying" to humans.

Notes to Chapter 8

1. Moreover, if we conceive of the organic universe as a self-conscious being and call it God, it is God understood by analogy to the human person.

2. A collection of essays, *Objections to Humanism* (Blackham 1963), consists mostly of objections to *secularism*.

3. While this "in effect worship" might involve ritual practices and certainly opens the door to such practices (e.g., "Temples of Reason"), they are not necessary to make an attitude "in effect worship." Rather, it is the acknowledgment and reverence for humanity, along with its demand that our lives be mostly guided by the love of humanity, that gives humanism a worshipful attitude toward humanity. Are not acknowledgment, reverence, and devotion the essence of God worship?

4. Halberthal and Margalit (1992, 246) consider the position that human elements in worship might make nonidolatrous worship an impossibility.

5. However, it is also questionable whether we want to call it a humanism unless we want to apply that term to any view that significantly values humanity. By that measure, few sane outlooks would *not* be a humanism. Most comprehensive philosophies place a fairly high value on human being. Catholicism certainly does, but I would not call it a "humanism." To use that term in a usefully precise way, we ought to reserve it for views that in some way make human welfare the highest value and/or human judgment the determinant of all value.

6. Even if they are not "essential" functions, the discussions of chapters 4 through 7 suggest that they are very useful functions.

7. Self-conscious, organized humanisms often engage in such practices. For the rituals, think of the Ethical Culture Society, the Society for Humanistic Judaism, strains of Unitarian-Universalism, and Comtean Positivism. For the

declarations and manifestos, visit the websites of the various humanistic associations, e.g., the American Humanist Association, the British Humanist Association, and the Council for Secular Humanism.

8. There are exceptions. Certainly, there have been hedonist humanists who made any human pleasures, including the animal pleasures of a full belly and simple sex, the be-all and end-all of their value systems. Even among humanist hedonists, however, it was the "higher pleasures," pleasures whose attainment engaged our uniquely developed intelligence, that were most prized.

9. Some philosophers (e,g., Nussbaum 1986) claim that sometimes there are no ways to make rational, ethical decisions. Such dilemmas constitute moral tragedy.

10. A pluralism of values should not be confused with a tolerance of different value systems. It is one thing to be tolerant of many different philosophies of life, and even to want to see many value systems flourish and to approve of a marketplace of ideologies. That attitude is compatible with the belief that a single philosophy of life, humanism, is the true one, and the belief that in that true philosophy a single value, human freedom, or a single identifiable set of values, those conducive to human well-being, reigns supreme.

11. The run-of-the-mill street humanist will deny any aspiration to fulfill the functions that religion fulfills, but with that denial, she devalues her humanism, making it not a comprehensive philosophy of ultimate value, a guide to leading life well, but rather just a vague, wavering inclination. I have nothing to say against vague, wavering inclinations, I just do not want to call them "humanism." Being without a comprehensive philosophy is an alternative to theism, but it is not an alternative *philosophy*. Whether we "need" a comprehensive philosophy is debatable; that many find having one extremely tempting strikes me as fairly evident. Later in this chapter, I will discuss how something more than wavering inclinations, but less than a fully settled *weltanschauung*, might do as an alternative to both humanism and theism.

12. It is a standard observation that moral development involves an ever-widening circle of moral concern. Egoism is a lower moral level than a concern that extends to the entire tribe, and tribalism lower than one that encompasses all of humanity. If, however, we take humanity to be functionally equivalent to God, we might well put a full stop to possible further moral development.

13. We can dismiss nihilism, an obvious, but not very appealing, possibility. A flight to no values hardly seems a viable escape from idolatrous values.

14. So the charge of idolatry is avoided, but because the new God is too vague to be shown positively to be worthy of worship, the charge of vacuity remains on the table.

Notes to Chapter 9

1. Although there is a strain of religious criticism of Marx that accuses him of denying human freedom, the more understanding religious critiques justly focus in on Marx's enthusiastic humanism.

2. There is much more to be said, and that has been said, concerning Marx's views on alienation. However, although a simplification, this synopsis is not a distortion and will serve for my purposes.

3. Utopian speculation is always a danger as an immediate and specific guide to practical action and sometimes a danger to theoretical insight. I believe, though, that if it is used as a heuristic, utopian speculation is indispensable to fundamental social philosophy, of which I deem theology a branch.

4. It may seem surprising that I characterize mysticism as a religion of those tending to be relatively at home in the world. Most brands of mysticism are attempts to transcend the world and appear escapist *par excellence*. Classical Indian religions, Hinduism and Buddhism, the most mystical of mainstream religions, aim at blotting out personal identity and liberation from this miserable illusion that is the phenomenal world of human existence. Mysticism at first glance does not seem to be the religion of those reconciled to the world. There are two points to be noted here. First, the empirical point that mysticism has not historically been a mass phenomenon. On a popular level, old-style gods dominate the Buddhist and Hindu masses. The Brahmin and elite monks are more properly mystical than lower-caste Tamils or peasant Tibetans. The popular Sabbateans of the seventeenth century may have dressed their magical messianism in mystical garbs, but they were hardly Isaac Luria Kabbalists. The second point is more psychological conjecture than empirical observation; the "suffering" that the mystic seeks refuge from is not primarily social alienation. It is, on the one hand, a *weltschmerz* and existential angst that are too luxurious for the working class, and on the other, not an escape from anything at all, but rather the pursuit of the highest conceivable good, a pursuit motivated by an ennui with the already attained this-worldly goods.

5. Mind you, all this talk of unalienated labor is a matter of degree.

6. Perhaps this is because Nietzsche thought that the power required for freedom is necessarily limited in a world where power must be obtained by overpowering others. Perhaps he also believed that the psychological material for freedom is naturally rare and cannot be socially created.

7. Epistemological values, though, can be viewed as a subset of aesthetic values, for they rely upon normative judgments, so that even the epistemological division between old-God believers and "moderns" may be characterized as a matter of taste.

8. That "moderns" are correct to judge that the old God is without any rational support is argued in appendix B.

9. The nature and existence of God(s) is the oldest subject of theoretical dispute, so reducing theology to a matter of taste, the oldest subject said to be *not* worth disputing, involves a certain irony, but ironical overtones should not deter lines of investigation. Most complex psychological phenomena have equally complex and multiple origins and implications. The tastes for theism and atheism are surely complex, and any generalization about them is bound to be

quite irrelevant to many particular cases, and even where relevant, radically incomplete. This is true of generalizations about any aesthetic preference, not just generalizations of aesthetic preferences that are religious in nature. No doubt some people like rock 'n' roll for its calming effect, and some people will be new-God devotees because they derive pleasure from discomforting traditionally religious (or militantly atheistic) parents. However, these are surely atypical causes: Few love rock 'n' roll as a sedative, and few worship the new God to displease their elders. There are more explanatory analyses of both rock 'n' roll's pleasures and liberal religious taste to be had. The unavoidable existence of counterexamples do not render the analysis of a taste useless. Even partially valid generalizations shed some light and therefore create some enlightenment.

10. This slogan must be interpreted in a nonstandard way to capture the theologians' stance. It is not merely that there is, or should be, universal, reciprocal solidarity, but also that the fortune and identity of each individual is not really separate from the "all."

11. I should say that I am using "beauty" as the most general term to describe aesthetic value, rather than as referring to a particular form of aesthetic value. In the literature, it gets both uses. I use "aesthetic value" to refer to all values that are not moral. I will not defend the claim here (in part because I am not confident that upon more extended reflection it is defensible), but I take values to be moral if they are derived from the ideal of equality. Some moral values are obviously derived from that ideal; others, kindness, for example, less obviously so, but I think it likely that a case could be made that a moral value such as kindness is rooted in a recognition of equality. Not that we are only kind to those whom we view as equal in all respects, but rather we are kind to those whom we view as equal in some relevant respect. Nothing that I say in the text turns on this. One can use whatever plausible view of moral value one wishes and still understand that by aesthetic value I am simply referring to moral values' complement, i.e., the entire world of values that are not moral values.

12. It shares much of the essential aesthetic of the old theology. The new theologians want to retain that old-God beauty while jettisoning the old theology's epistemology.

13. I am not claiming that dramatic narrative is dominant in all of religion's aesthetic modes. Obviously, nonnarrative music, art, architecture, and movement are prominent components of religious aesthetic experience, but in our talk *about God*, dramatic narrative aesthetics are dominant. I am much more at ease with religious poetry, music, and art than I am with prayer and theology.

14. Toba Spitzer (personal communication) wonders if I have not mischaracterized the aesthetic divide between no-God believers and new-God believers. She suggests that it is not so much a difference of *taste* as it is a difference of perceptiveness; nonbelievers' understanding of God is analogous to "tone-deaf" people's understanding of music: They are simply missing something. This analogy takes the difference entirely out of the realm of the purely aesthetic and

makes the divide one over the facts. Tone-deaf people, if they insisted that differ-ent pitches were the same because they perceived no difference, would simply be wrong about the nature of reality, like blind people claiming that light does not exist. This is pretty much the position of the old-God believers; atheists, according to old-God believers, are simply religiously blind and fail to see the factual reality of God.

However, Spitzer's analogy can be recast to raise a sharper challenge to my analysis. Suppose that there were those, call them "music skeptics," who failed to see why some others insisted that they heard "music." The music skeptics heard all of the qualities of all of the sounds that constitute music; they perceived the pitch, duration, timbre, rhythmic patterns, harmonic relations, etc., and could correctly answer any questions regarding the sounds that others called "music." No objective sound quality or relationship was unperceived by the music skeptics. Furthermore, music skeptics understood how others, "music be-lievers," responded to the sounds. They understood how various sound patterns induced in music believers feelings of joy, tension, excitement, sadness, fear, and a host of other, including more specific, emotions. They could even say which particular sound patterns tended to induce which emotions in others. Moreover, they understood that having these sound-induced feelings frequently was very pleasurable and highly valued by the music believers, but they themselves felt neither emotion nor pleasure when hearing what others called "music." What could music lovers say to such people? They certainly would not admit, nor should they admit, that they, the music believers, might be mistaken in calling the sound patterns "music" and valuing them as such. Their experience of the sounds *as music* is to them an undeniable, self-evident truth, one that they could speak of with confidence to fellow music believers. Furthermore, although there would be no identifiable cognitive deficit that the music skeptics suffered from, no fact that they were missing, it would be reasonable of the music believers to judge that the skeptics were missing something, something that was, in some important way, really *there*.

This seems to be a gestalt issue—a matter of being able to see certain facts *as* God, just as the music believers can hear certain sound patterns as music. Such seeing and hearing may not be a decision or choice motivated by taste, but simply a perception, a perception not of new elements or objective relationships, but of *how* the facts can be seen or heard.

Now, even if the music analogy were apt, we would still want an account of why those of normal intelligence, psychology, and hearing did not respond to music, and likewise, why some could not get the God gestalt.

However, I do not think the analogy apt; atheists can have refined metaphysi-cal gestalts that are different from those of the theists. Atheists can hear a music of the spheres—with all the same notes heard by the rational theists—it just does not sound like God to them. Perhaps it sounds like the music of indifferent, inexorable entropy. Atheists are not tone-deaf. They just hear in the universe an ungodly tune. That they cannot, or will not, hear a God song may be a flaw, but no more of a flaw than the theists' inability or unwillingness to hear the songs of ultimate contingency, hopeless doom, or utter meaninglessness.

Notes to Chapter 10

1. It is certainly the special province of that part of religion that is theology. Although theology, rather than religion in general, has been the subject of this book, in this chapter I am using the term "religion" to refer to more than explicit theological beliefs, but less than all of the practices, rituals, and customs that are typically part of religion. Here, "religion" refers to one's ideological stance to reality and human life. So conceived, all people are religious, in the same way that all are physical and psychological. It is not something that humans have a choice about. It is a mode of our being. Religion in this sense is the attitude that one takes to life and experience. It is the fundamental motive (insofar as such matters are governed by fundamental motives) for getting out of bed in the morning or for staying in bed. Seeing the world despairingly as a confused, meaningless clash of atoms is as religious as seeing it joyfully as a pre-ordained unfolding of God's plan. Experiencing one's life as a lonely series of painful threats is as religious as experiencing it as a welcome invitation to join a delightful play. Only the scientific stance of the objective observer approaches the non-religious, but that is an impossible role for humans to sustain. Humans are agents, and agents have attitudes. Even the scientist as a practitioner of science implicitly makes value claims and has goals. With religion, we find at least proto-theology. Certain conceptualizations tend to be implicit or underlie certain attitudes. Hence, something like theology is at the core of religion, but religion, an attitude, is more than the theological thought that it may express. Furthermore, not all people are conscious of their attitude toward the world nor of an accompanying theology, so not all are conscious of their "religion" in this sense.

2. Henceforth, whenever I capitalize the word "Truth," I am always referring to the religious Truth, which, in accordance with the note above, means the Truth of an attitude, a stance that one takes toward life and experience. More on various senses of "truth" in appendix C.

3. Perhaps, to underline this agreement on the facts, and because we normally take a difference of belief to point at some factual disagreement, we should be calling them new-God and no-God *professors* rather than believers.

4. See appendix C for a discussion of the notion that the truth is a single, value-neutral description of reality.

5. Whether that entails that religion, conceived properly, should be understood as making no ontological claims, is discussed in appendix C.

6. Hence, on my view, those old-time religions, the ones that cleave to the old God, are neither true nor True.

7. We can understand scientific experiments as trying to distinguish between beliefs that work and do not work, and as assuming that two logically incompatible beliefs will not both be allowed by reality, i.e., one will be shown not to work, to be falsified. See appendix C.

8. I should not be taken here as suggesting that we should do anything other than welcome and encourage a diversity of political and moral opinions. I do say, however, that we: (1) for many purposes must impose some views as operative and (2) should not rest content with ongoing moral/political disagreement. We should not squelch it, but we should forever strive for a rational reconciliation. We welcome diversity in these areas as a necessary condition in the search for truth, and we accept the permanence of diversity because we believe that we will always remain fallible. We can, and probably forever will, live with moral and empirical disagreements, and even were we infallible, we might allow diversity knowing that much harm can and has been done by *imposing* a consensus.

9. Although it is compatible with their factual *description* of the world, it is difficult to imagine the theologians fitting God as a character into the following story. "Out of the blind dynamics of an eternal, initially unconscious universe emerge forms constructed to replicate their kind, which in turn evolve some forms that are aware of themselves and the universe and think of themselves as separate from the universe. More than anything else, this awareness is filled with suffering. The instances of happy consciousness created in the universe through good fortune, generosity, kindness, understanding, love, pleasure, and courage, although glorious when considered by themselves, are actually paltry in both quantity and intensity when compared to the wretched awareness that portions of the universe become through poverty, greed, cruelty, ignorance, hatred, pain, and fear. Although some few instances of awareness in the universe achieve unspeakable joy through the contemplation of the source of their being and look upon their reabsorption into the universal flux with equanimity, for most instances of awareness, the knowledge that they are temporary configurations is a horror that adds to the already overwhelming surfeit of suffering. While the efforts of the self-conscious elements of the universe might turn this miserable picture around, there is little reason to believe that it will. More likely, the excess of suffering will continue and perhaps increase, until, what is almost bound to happen in any event, the conditions for self-conscious configurations cease and the universe returns to blind, unknowing, ever-changing patterns. After eons without any awareness, consciousness will likely return for another round of mostly suffering." A nonbeliever can tell that story as an absurdist comedy or perhaps as defiant, though doomed, heroic Sisyphean tragedy or even as a "we are going for the win despite the odds" inspirational romance. The faithful, by seeing God in the story, have trouble with these more downbeat genres.

10. Which is not to say that believers cannot think that there are many descriptions of God, but true believers must think that all of the descriptions amount to the same thing. My claim here is that while there are lots of theistic

religious stances, sincere believers, unless they go through a conversion experience, must occupy only one of them. An individual atheist has more "religious"
flexibility available.

11. By speaking of an individual's religious Truth as something freely chosen,
I do not mean to deny that these choices are historically and psychologically
conditioned. That Jews will tend to find Jewish versions of Truth, and Buddhists
Buddhist versions, is not, *caterius paribus*, in the least evidence that the choices
are not free. It just tells us that free choices are not random or arbitrary, but
rather flow from who we are, which always is a unique blend that includes lots
of commonly shared ingredients.

12. Nietzsche despised equating truth and beauty (1886). If he meant, as I
believe he did, that the true descriptions of the world are not necessarily beautiful, and may even be ugly, then he was surely correct. However, I think it in
harmony with Nietzsche's spirit to identify beauty with the sort of interpretive
Truth that I speak of above.

13. For consequentialists of a certain stripe, by describing ultimate value,
Keats does include moral goodness because such goodness amounts to nothing
more than action that maximizes value. However, unless you agree that a view
of value is all that is required for moral theory, you will find Keats's verse an
incomplete philosophy.

14. Of course, the dialectic is more complicated than that; one may find that
goodness is the most beautiful thing there is, i.e., that the meaning of one's own
life is most fulfilled in helping others to find the meaning of their lives. Truth,
beauty, and goodness can easily get wrapped into mutually referring definitions/
understandings where it becomes impossible to say which concept has priority.

15. Of course, we do share small *t* scientific truths.

Notes to Appendix A

1. One way that has been suggested resorts to the claim that "existence" has
a unique meaning when applied to God. God's existence is wholly unlike the
existence of other beings. We equivocate when we say that God and other things
exist, for nothing exists in any way like God. The argument goes that because
we do not understand God's existence, our assertion that God might exist does
not represent any knowledge of God, thereby preserving her total incomprehensibility. However, that raises the question of whether we are asserting anything
at all when we use words whose meanings are unknown to us. We return to this
question when we discuss the *via negativa*.

2. Of course, a question does arise whether talk can become so inaccurate
that it is unclear what is the subject of the conversation. Some hold that reference
by "rigid designators" allows us to speak of things of which we only know the

name, but if "sense determines reference," then sufficient ignorance of a subject makes for impossible reference. See Frege (1892) and Kripke (1978).

3. Dennet (1987), and functionalist philosophers of mind in general, would deny that some private experience, some "qualia," provides any incommunicable understanding. He argues that understanding, knowledge, experience, and the like are all ensembles of information that can be carried in a variety of formats.

4. This raises the interesting problem of whether one can understand or even have such a *sui generis* experience. Many a cognitive scientist would claim that all new experiences are, one way or another, extensions of previous experiences. If this were true, we would require something like innate experiences or a faculty that allowed for first experiences to get the chain of experiences started. Perhaps there is a religious faculty that enables one to experience God even though God is unlike any other experience that one ever had. Of course, there may be a weaker claim that the unique may be comprehensible, but indescribable (and therefore inexpressible) because description necessarily involves categorization, and the unique fits into no categories. I see no reason why, however, a set with one member cannot be named and said. It is a further question how informative a mere name is, but uniqueness does not make a thing unnamable or inexpressible.

5. Such thoughts lead to Maimonidian "negative" theologies; we can only truly say what God is not (the "*via negativa*"). Pursued aggressively enough, this negative definition can imply significant knowledge of God while saving a kind of ineffability. Our knowledge is implicit; we understand the logical space that is left for God to occupy, but there can be no explicit delineation of the logical space that God actually does occupy.

6. Note Frank Kermode's take on Cordelia's silence. Kermode (2000).

7. Art Goldhammer (personal communication) speculates that rather than (or in addition to) elevating the status of God, the invocation of ineffability asserts the superiority and power of those with knowledge of God. Goldhammer imagines them saying, "You who muck about in the lower sphere of logic cannot ascend to the heights on which we God-talkers romp freely . . . [and] . . . if you don't know what I'm talking about when I say 'ineffable,' then don't dare contradict me, for obviously you don't grasp the ground of my thinking." This is never the tone of Green, Kaplan, or Lerner, but I do think that Goldhammer has captured part of the typical psychology behind invoking ineffability.

8. This is Edward Kaplan's explanation of Abraham Joshua Heschel's volubility in the face of God's ineffability. He argues that Heschel denounced "literal mindedness" regarding "ultimate issues" (Kaplan 1996, 47) and rejected silence concerning God because it would "annul the community of verbal communion and all religious literature" (49). In general, Edward Kaplan characterizes Heschel's work as a theological poetics.

9. The theologians might, but for the most part do not, attempt a more positive epistemological justification of paradox. Paradox may emerge when two

compelling lines of inquiry give inconsistent results. While this may indicate that at least one and perhaps both results are somehow wrong, the paradox may represent more of the truth than any alternative formulation currently available. The ultimate truth may have to be consistent, but that does not mean that our best interim results will be. Therefore, a refusal to abandon inconsistent claims may be a refusal to give up our best current description of the truth, even though we know that it cannot be the truth. Green (1992, 63) at times appears to be taking this approach. I have no quarrel with this contingent tolerance of paradox motivated by epistemological modesty and loyalty to one's experience of the facts, although awareness of our fallibility should not become an embrace of mystery and an excuse to rest in paradox. Paradox should be a spur to further inquiry and seen as evidence that a theology is not fully adequate and has something seriously wrong.

10. Wittgenstein (1953) thought that a related approach worked best for most philosophical problems.

Notes to Appendix B

1. Alan Guth (1997) appears to challenge "the nothing from nothing" principle, but his starting "nothing" seems to encompass basic laws of nature and the possibility of quantum fluctuations. The absence of matter and energy may suffice to qualify as nothing in the physicists' lexicon, but the philosophically inclined require an even sparser nothing.

2. Outside of any metaphysical commitments, one can take ordered intelligence as the default position with equal justification. Chaos, as the default state needing no explanation, only follows from a materialist, non-teleological, mechanistic approach that is fundamental to the scientific worldview. Scott Shalkowski (1989) argues that atheism and (old-God) theism are equally rational because there are no good arguments for either. I disagree with Shalkowski that there are no good arguments for atheism; I find the argument from evil against God persuasive. Still even if it is not, even if Shalkowski is right that arguments against God's existence are no better than arguments for his existence, Shalkowski's case is still problematic for "moderns" because it rests on viewing chaos and ordered intelligence as equally rational initial assumptions. Perhaps so. Maybe one can as well start explanations as an idealist as one can as a materialist. The modern scientific enterprise, though, is based on materialist assumptions. As I take "moderns" as committed to that enterprise, idealism is not as acceptable a default position to moderns as is materialism.

3. Most of the best replies to the argument from design are found in Hume (1762).

4. I do not know why we should. There may only be about 14 billion years' worth of time to play with, but why limit the game-space to time? Our big bang may have been the one "successful" start to a multitude of attempted beginnings.

5. Here, I have switched my typical use of the term "the universe" from "the totality of being" to "an enclosed realm of being."

6. Aldous Huxley's *The Perennial Philosophy* (1944) is an excellent compendium of cross-cultural descriptions of mystical experiences.

7. Once again, it is worth pointing out that some philosophers would deny the distinction between epistemic and pragmatic justifications, arguing that the former reduces to the latter.

Notes to Appendix C

1. Like every "theory" of truth that I discuss in this appendix, the "correspondence theory" denotes a family of theories, some members of which are significantly different from others. A full discussion of theories of truth would need to distinguish these major variations.

2. Just as it is a problem to account for the nature of "correspondence" in the correspondence theory, it is difficult to give an unproblematic account of the cohering in coherence theory.

3. Unless there is only one coherent set of propositions, which seems to be the view of such rationalists as Spinoza, Leibniz, and Hegel. Davidson (1974), because he rejects the very idea of a conceptual scheme, also rejects the relativistic claim that we can have competing rationalities.

4. Again, in certain kinds of idealisms the coherence theory implies no relativism because there is no reality outside of the sole coherent system of ideas.

5. The crossword imagery is a bit misleading here. In a crossword puzzle, the relationship between correct answers and the clues are relationships between linguistic entities as much as are relationships among the answers themselves, whereas with beliefs and experiences, we are positing relationships between a belief or proposition and a reality, which is neither. However, this is a problem for all correspondence theories, and so it is unsurprising that, as a hybrid of the coherence and correspondence theories, the crossword puzzle image retains the difficulty of elucidating the "corresponding" process. It also does nothing to explain "cohering," for it is not suggested that our beliefs cohere as do answers in a crossword puzzle. The crossword image is merely meant to show how coherence and correspondence, whatever they are, must work together to produce truth.

6. In the "ethical regions" of the puzzle, I am incorporating the kind of social acceptance theory of truth that Richard Rorty appears to endorse (1979), but in a limited way, for the correct socially acceptable answers are constrained by more than social acceptance.

7. If belief in God gets you into heaven or gets supernatural forces to intervene in the world on your behalf, *only if there really is a God*, then those uses of the belief *do* depend on its truth. Belief in God, however, might get you into

heaven without there being a God, and although such a belief cannot get a nonexistent God to intervene in the world on your behalf, belief in God may get the world to react to your desires in positive ways, even if there is no God. Hence, even these nonpsychological uses of theism are not strictly dependent on its truth. The psychological uses of belief are even more truth-independent. Moreover, and further removing the justification of new-God belief from truth claims, perhaps credibility, i.e., acceptability of belief, is not a holistic affair. Do people genuinely seek coherence with other beliefs before accepting a belief? Maybe a declaration of belief, especially "belief in" something, is nothing more than a declaration of acceptance of *that* belief and locally related ones, and people feel under no obligation to connect those local beliefs with other beliefs, let alone with an extra-belief reality. "Belief in" may be an assertion of acceptance of some propositions while disclaiming any obligation to justify the propositions through the justificatory procedures demanded by coherence or correspondence views. Coherence and correspondence are for "believe that" propositions. For new-God believers, "God" may be the all-purpose, pseudo-ground for important, but isolated and ungrounded beliefs.

REFERENCES

Ainsle, G. 2001. *Breakdown of Will.* New York: Cambridge University Press.

Aquinas, T. (1272) 1945. *Summa Theologica.* New York: Random House.

Ayer, A. 1936. *Language, Truth, and Logic.* New York: Dover.

Barrow, J., and F. Tipler. 1986. *The Anthropic Principle.* Oxford: Oxford University Press.

Bentham, J. (1789) 1973. *Introduction to the Principles of Morals and Legislation.* New York: Anchor.

Blackham, H. 1963. *Objections to Humanism.* Westport, Conn.: Greenwood Press.

Buber, M. 1958. *I and Thou.* New York: Scribners.

Chisholm, R. 1967. "Meinong." In *The Encyclopedia of Philosophy,* edited by P. Edwards. New York: Macmillan.

Cobb, J., and D. Griffin. 1976. *Process Theology.* Philadelphia: Westminster Press.

Cohen, A. 1973. *Everyman's Talmud.* New York: Schocken.

Darwin, C. (1859) 1958. *The Origin of Species.* New York: Mentor Books.

Davidson, D. (1974) 2006. The Essential Davidson. Oxford: Oxford University Press.

Dawkins, R. 1976. *The Selfish Gene.* Oxford: Oxford University Press.

DeBerry, T. 1969. *The Buddhist Tradition.* New York: Vintage.

Dennett, D. 1984. *Elbow Room: The Varieties of Free Will Worth Wanting.* Cambridge: MIT Press.

———. 1987. *The Intentional Stance.* Cambridge: MIT Press.

———. 1991. *Consciousness Explained.* Boston: Little Brown.

———. 1995. *Darwin's Dangerous Idea.* New York: Simon and Schuster.

———. 2003. *Freedom Evolves.* New York: Penguin.

Dostoyevsky, F. (1871) 1953. *The Devils.* London: Penguin.

———. (1881) 1970. *The Brothers Karamazov.* New York: Bantam.

Drabble, M. 1998. *The Oxford Companion to English Literature.* New York: Oxford University Press.

REFERENCES

Easwaran, E. 1987. *The Upanishads: A Translation for the Modern Reader.* Tomales, Calif.: Nilgiri Press.

Feuerbach, L. (1841) 1989. *The Essence of Christianity.* Amherst, N.Y.: Prometheus.

Frank, R. 1988. *Passions Within Reason.* New York: Norton.

Frege, G. (1892) 1984. "On Sense and Reference." In *Collected Papers in Mathematics, Logic, and Philosophy,* edited by B. McGuiness. New York: Blackwell.

Gevirtz, G. 1995. *Partners With God.* West Orange, N.J.: Behrman House.

Gould, S. 2001. *Rock of Ages: Religion in the Fullness of Life.* New York: Ballantine.

Green, A. 1992. *Seek My Face, Speak My Name.* London: Aronson Press.

————. 2000. *These Are the Words.* Woodstock, Vermont: Jewish Lights.

Guth, A. 1997. *The Inflationary Universe.* Reading, Mass.: Addison-Wesley.

Halberthal, M. and A. Margalit. 1992. *Idolartry.* Cambridge: Hebrew University Press.

Haack, S. 1993. *Evidence and Inquiry.* Cambridge: Blackwell.

Hegel, G. (1807) 1977. *Phenomenology of Spirit.* Oxford: Oxford University Press.

————. (1830) 1975. *Logic.* Oxford: Oxford University Press.

Hobbes, T. (1651) 1962. *Leviathan.* New York: Collier.

Hume, D. (1739) 1973. *Treatise on Human Nature.* Oxford: Oxford University Press.

————. (1762) 1980. *Three Dialogues Concerning Natural Religion.* Indianapolis: Hackett.

Huxley, A. 1944. *The Perennial Philosophy.* New York: Harper.

James, W. (1902) 1958. *The Varieties of Religious Experience.* New York: Mentor.

Kant, I. (1790) 1972. *The Critique of Judgment.* New York: Hafner.

Kaplan, E. 1996. *Holiness in Words: Abraham Joshua Heschel's Poetics of Piety.* Albany: State Universtiy of New York Press.

Kaplan, M. 1934. *Judaism as Civilization.* New York: Schocken.

————. 1936. *The Meaning of God in Modern Jewish Religion.* New York: Schocken.

————. 1956. *Questions Jews Ask.* New York: Schocken.

————. 1958. *Judaism Without Supernaturalism.* New York: Schocken.

————. 1985. *Dynamic Judaism.* Edited by Mel Scult and Emanuel Goldsmith. New York: Schocken.

Kermode, F. 2000. *Shakespeare's Language.* New York: FSG.

Kupperman, J. 1999. *Values . . . And What Follows.* Oxford: Oxford University Press.

Kushner, H. 1981. *When Bad Things Happen to Good People.* New York: Schocken.

Kripke, S. 1978. "Identity and Necessity." In *Naming Necessity and Natural Kinds,* edited by S. Schwartz. Ithaca: Cornell University Press.

Lerner, M. 1994. *Jewish Renewal.* New York: Putnam.

REFERENCES

———. 2000. *Spirit Matters*. Charlottesville, Va.: Hampton Roads.

Maimonides, M. (1190) 1963. *Guide to the Perplexed*. Chicago: University of Chicago Press.

Martin, M. 1990. *Atheism*. Philadelphia: Temple University Press.

Marx, K. (1844) 1977. *The Economic and Philosophical Manuscripts*. In *Karl Marx: Selected Writings*, edited by D. McLellan. Oxford: Oxford University Press.

———. (1845) 1977. *Theses on Feuerbach*. In *Karl Marx: Selected Writings*, edited by D. McLellan. Oxford: Oxford University Press.

———. (1847) 1977. *The German Ideology*. In *Karl Marx: Selected Writings*, edited by D. McLellan. Oxford: Oxford University Press.

———. (1851) 1977. *The Eighteenth of Brumaire*. In *Karl Marx: Selected Writings*, edited by D. McLellan. Oxford: Oxford University Press.

Mehta, V. 1965. *The New Theologians*. New York: Harper and Row.

MacIntyre, A. 1967. "Pantheism." In the *Encyclopedia of Philosophy*, edited by P. Edwards. New York: Macmillan.

Nagel, T. 1986. *The View From Nowhere*. New York: Oxford University Press.

Nietzsche, F. (1882) 1973. *The Gay Science*. New York: Vintage.

———. (1886) 1968. *Beyond Good and Evil*. In *Basic Writings of Nietzsche*. New York: Modern Library.

———. (1887) 1968. *The Genealogy of Morals*. In *Basic Writings of Nietzsche*. New York: Modern Library.

Nussbaum, M. 1986. *The Fragility of Goodness*. Cambridge: Cambridge University Press.

Parfit, D. 1984. *Reasons and Persons*. Oxford: Oxford University Press.

Plantinga, A. 1965. *The Ontological Argument*. New York: Doubleday.

Plato (c. 390 B.C.E.) 1961. *Collected Dialogues*. Edited by E. Hamilton and H. Cairns. Princeton: Princeton University Press.

Quine, W. V. O. 1953. *From a Logical Point of View*. Cambridge: Harvard University Press.

———. 1960. *Word and Object*. Cambridge: MIT Press.

———. 1978. *The Web of Belief*. Cambridge: Harvard University Press.

Radhakrishnan, S. 1953. *The Principle Upanishads*. New York: Harper and Row.

Richardson, W. 2002. *Science and the Spiritual Quest*. Berkeley: University of California Press.

Rorty, R. 1979. *Philosophy and the Mirror of Nature*. Princeton: Princeton University Press.

Russell, B. 1946. "Good and Bad." In *Polemic1*. Cambridge: Cambridge University Press.

Ryle, G. 1949. *The Concept of Mind*. New York: Harper and Row.

Shalkowski, S. 1989. "Atheological Apologetics," *American Philosophical Quarterly* 5, no. 26: 1.

Shermer, M. 2000. *How We Believe*. New York: W. H. Freeman.

Shilling, S. 1967. *God in the Age of Atheism*. New York: Abingdon Press.

REFERENCES

Silver, M. 1980. "Self-Concept and Self-Interest." Ph.D. diss., University of Connecticut.

———. 1998. *Respecting the Wicked Child.* Amherst: University of Massachusetts Press.

Skyrms, B. 1996. *Evolution of the Social Contract.* New York: Cambridge University Press.

Spinoza, B. (1677) 1960. *Ethics.* New York: Doubleday.

Tickle, P. 1997. *God Talk.* New York: Crossroads Press.

Vanhoozer, K., ed. 2003. *Postmodern Theology.* Cambridge: Cambridge University Press.

Weinberg, S. 1993. *Dreams of a Final Theory.* London: Radius.

Wine, S. 1995. *Judaism Beyond God.* Hoboken, N.J.: Ktav.

Wittgenstein, L. 1953. *Philosophical Investigations.* New York: Macmillan.

Wright, R. 1994. *The Moral Animal.* New York: Pantheon.

INDEX